Secrets of Becoming

Negotiating Whitehead, Deleuze, and Butler

Edited by

Roland Faber and Andrea M. Stephenson

Fordham University Press

New York   2011

Copyright © 2011 Fordham University Press

All rights reserved. No part of this publication may be reproduced, stored in a retrieval system, or transmitted in any form or by any means—electronic, mechanical, photocopy, recording, or any other—except for brief quotations in printed reviews, without the prior permission of the publisher.

Fordham University Press has no responsibility for the persistence or accuracy of URLs for external or third-party Internet websites referred to in this publication and does not guarantee that any content on such websites is, or will remain, accurate or appropriate.

Fordham University Press also publishes its books in a variety of electronic formats. Some content that appears in print may not be available in electronic books.

Library of Congress Cataloging-in-Publication Data

International Whitehead Conference (6th : 2006 : Universität Salzburg)
Secrets of becoming : negotiating Whitehead, Deleuze, and Butler / edited by Roland Faber and Andrea M. Stephenson.—1st ed.
  p. cm.
The essays from the conference have been substantially rev. and new material has been added.
Includes bibliographical references (p.).
ISBN 978-0-8232-3208-6 (cloth : alk. paper)
ISBN 978-0-8232-3209-3 (pbk. : alk. paper)
ISBN 978-0-8232-3210-9 (ebook)
1. Whitehead, Alfred North, 1861–1947—Congresses. 2. Deleuze, Gilles, 1925–1995—Congresses. 3. Butler, Judith, 1956—Congresses 4. Becoming (Philosophy)—Congresses. I. Faber, Roland, 1960– II. Stephenson, Andrea M. III. Title.
B1674.W354I57 2006b
192—dc22
2010026350

Printed in the United States of America
13 12 11 5 4 3 2 1
First edition

CONTENTS

List of Abbreviations — vii
Foreword
   ANDREA M. STEPHENSON — xi

Introduction: Negotiating Becoming
   ROLAND FABER — 1

Part One   NEGOTIATING EVENTS AND MULTIPLICITIES

1. Whitehead, Post-Structuralism, and Realism
   KEITH ROBINSON — 53
2. Nomad Thought: Deleuze, Whitehead, and the Adventure of Thinking
   JEFF BELL — 70
3. Transcendental Empiricism in Deleuze and Whitehead
   STEVEN SHAVIRO — 82
4. Can We Be Wolves? Intersections between Deleuze's *Difference and Repetition* and Butler's Performativity
   ANDREA M. STEPHENSON — 92

Part Two   NEGOTIATING BODIES AND SOCIETIES

5. Butler and Whitehead on the (Social) Body
   MICHAEL HALEWOOD — 107
6. Conflict
   ISABELLA PALIN — 127
7. Becoming through Multiplicity: Staying in the Middle of Whitehead's and Deleuze-Guattari's Philosophies of Life
   LUKE B. HIGGINS — 142

Part Three   NEGOTIATING IMMANENCE AND DIVINITY

8. Surrationality and Chaosmos: For a More Deleuzian Whitehead (with a Butlerian Intervention)
   ROLAND FABER — 157

9. Divine Possibilities: Becoming an Order without Law
   ALAN R. VAN WYK   178
10. "God Is a Lobster": Whitehead's Receptacle
    Meets the Deleuzian Sieve
    SIGRIDUR GUDMARSDOTTIR   191
11. Uninteresting Truth? Tedium and Event in Postmodernity
    CATHERINE KELLER   201

Notes   215
Bibliography   265
List of Contributors   275

ABBREVIATIONS

AC   Judith Butler. *Antigone's Claim: Kinship between Life and Death.* New York: Columbia University Press, 2000.

AI   Alfred North Whitehead. *Adventures of Ideas.* New York: Free Press, 1967.

AO   Gilles Deleuze and Felix Guattari. *Anti-Oedipus: Capitalism and Schizophrenia.* Minneapolis: University of Minnesota Press, 1983.

BC   Armour, Ellen and St. Ville, Susan, eds. *Bodily Citations: Religion and Judith Butler.* New York: Columbia University Press, 2006.

BTM   Judith Butler. *Bodies that Matter: On the Discursive Limits of "Sex."* New York: Routledge, 1993.

C1   Gilles Deleuze. *Cinema 1: The Movement-Image.* Minneapolis: University of Minnesota Press, 1986.

CC   Judith Butler. "Critique, Coercion, and Sacred Life in Benjamin's 'Critique of Violence.'" In *Political Theologies: Public Religions in a Post-Secular World*, edited by Hent de Vries and Lawrence E. Sullivan, 201–19. New York: Fordham University Press, 2006.

CN   Alfred North Whitehead. *The Concept of Nature: The Tarner Lectures Delivered in Trinity College November 1919.* Cambridge: Cambridge University Press, 1964.

CV   Gilles Deleuze. "Cours Vincennes—St Denis: l évènement, Whitehead—10/03/1987." www.webdeleuze.com/php/texte.php?cle=140&groupe=Leibniz&langue=1.

D   Gilles Deleuze and Claire Parnet. *Dialogues.* London: Athlone, 1987.

DI   Gilles Deleuze. *Desert Islands and Other Texts 1953–1974.* Paris: Semiotext(e), 2004.

DR   Gilles Deleuze. *Difference and Repetition.* New York: Routledge, 1994.

E   Gilles Deleuze. *Essays: Critical and Clinical.* Minneapolis: University of Minnesota Press, 1997.

EP	Gilles Deleuze. *Expressionism in Philosophy: Spinoza*. New York: Zone Books, 1990.
ES	Judith Butler. *Excitable Speech: A Politics of the Performative*. New York: Routledge, 1997.
FR	Alfred North Whitehead. *The Function of Reason*. Boston: Beacon Press, 1958.
GA	Judith Butler. *Giving an Account of Oneself*. New York: Fordham University Press, 2005.
GT	Judith Butler. *Gender Trouble: Feminism and the Subversion of Identity*. New York: Routledge, 1999.
IM	Gilles Deleuze. "Immanence—A Life." In Deleuze, *Pure Immanence: Essays on A Life*, 25–33. New York: Zone Books, 2005.
Imm.	Alfred North Whitehead. "Immortality." In *Essays in Science and Philosophy*, 77–96. New York: Greenwood Press, 1968.
K	Gilles Deleuze and Felix Guattari. *Kafka: Pour une littérature mineure*. Paris: Les Editions de Minuit, 1975.
LS	Gilles Deleuze. *The Logic of Sense*. New York: Columbia University Press, 1990.
M	Gilles Deleuze. "Mediators." In *Incorporations*, edited by Jonathan Crary and Sanford Kwinter, 280–94. New York: Zone Books, 1992.
MG	Alfred North Whitehead. "Mathematics and the Good." In *Essays in Science and Philosophy*, 97–113. New York: Greenwood Press, 1968.
MT	Alfred North Whitehead. *Modes of Thought*. New York: Free Press, 1968.
N	Gilles Deleuze. *Negotiations, 1972–1990*. New York: Columbia University Press, 1990.
NP	Gilles Deleuze, *Nietzsche and Philosophy*. New York: Columbia University Press, 1983.
NT	Gilles Deleuze. "Nomad Thought." In *New Nietzsche: Contemporary Styles of Interpretation*, edited by David B. Allison, 142–49. Cambridge, Mass.: MIT Press, 1977.
P	Gilles Deleuze. *Pourparlers (1972–1990)*. Paris: Les Editions de Minuit, 1990.
PL	Judith Butler. *Precarious Life: The Power of Mourning and Violence*. London: Verso, 2006.
PLP	Judith Butler. *The Psychic Life of Power: Theories in Subjection*. Stanford, Calif.: Stanford University Press, 1997.

Abbreviations

PNK   Alfred North Whitehead. *An Enquiry Concerning the Principles of Natural Knowledge*. New York: Dover, 1982.

PR   Alfred North Whitehead. *Process and Reality: An Essay in Cosmology*. Corrected edition, edited by D. R. Griffin and D. W. Sherburne. New York: Free Press, 1978.

RM   Alfred North Whitehead. *Religion in the Making*. New York: Fordham University Press, 1996.

S   Alfred North Whitehead. *Symbolism: Its Meaning and Effect*. New York: Fordham University Press, 1985.

SMW   Alfred North Whitehead. *Science and the Modern World: Lowell Lectures, 1925*. New York: Free Press, 1967.

SP   Gilles Deleuze. *Spinoza: Practical Philosophy*. San Francisco: City Lights Books, 1988.

TF   Gilles Deleuze. *The Fold: Leibniz and the Baroque*. Minneapolis: University of Minnesota Press, 1992.

TP   Gilles Deleuze and Felix Guattari. *A Thousand Plateaus: Capitalism and Schizophrenia*. Minneapolis: University of Minnesota Press, 1987.

UG   Judith Butler. *Undoing Gender*. New York: Routledge, 2004.

WP   Gilles Deleuze and Felix Guattari. *What Is Philosophy?* New York: Columbia University Press, 1994.

WS   Judith Butler and Gayatri Chakravorty Spivak. *Who Sings the Nation-State? Language, Politics, Belonging*. New York: Seagull, 2007.

FOREWORD

Andrea M. Stephenson

Foreword—the word that comes before the word. There is always something that can be said before, something that comes before, something that might be said to be the beginning. However, there is also something that can be said before the before, something that comes before the before. A foreword really is one small part of the before; it is one interpretation of the before. Science can account for the beginning of Creation to a certain point. Then, even the scientists have to say that there is something that happened prior to the known beginning—a before that cannot be said, a before that cannot even be thought.

Every piece of art, every life, every thought, every article, every book is an adventure—an adventure that has no beginning and no end because everything that exists already is formed by other things and already is implicated in the formation of something else, something new, something novel. To chart the adventure of any single thing is a complicated, perhaps even impossible, task. We could start with "in the beginning," but, as Deleuze and Guattari remind us in *A Thousand Plateaus: Capitalism and Schizophrenia*, the beginning is never really the beginning but the middle (81). Recognizing the impossibility of this position, we must choose a starting point if we are to start.

While the conversation between process and post-structuralist thought began in individual philosophical and theological work, the Third International Whitehead Conference in 1998 in Claremont, California, gathered the very few voices at that time that were attempting to consider process and post-structuralist thought to begin a collective exploration of the convergences between these two modes of thought. The result was *Process and Difference: Between Cosmological and Poststructuralist Postmodernisms*, edited by Catherine Keller and Anne Daniell. *Secrets of Becoming: Negotiating Whitehead, Deleuze, and Butler* attempts to further this exciting and important conversation.

This book's journey specifically "began" at the Sixth International Whitehead Conference held in Salzburg, Austria, in 2006. The conference was designed to explore the resonances of Whitehead's thought in various fields of study in contemporary scholarship, including philosophy, religion, and science. Many of the chapters presented in this book were part of the conference discussion on Whitehead and post-structuralist philosophy. This is a conversation that has, until recently, been considered ridiculous. After all, process philosophy, which traditionally has been linked to Whitehead's philosophical work, has been characterized as a cosmology or metaphysics that creates a system by which to understand the whole of life. Post-structuralism, on the other hand, has been seen as an attempt to deconstruct systems. Process philosophy and post-structuralism seem to some to represent ways of thinking that are too dissimilar and diverse to be placed together in any serious conversation. However, other thinkers, the authors of these chapters among them, have found that process thought and post-structuralism can be partners on the dance floor of contemporary philosophy and theology—sometimes tangoing quite closely and sometimes taking up different partners before coming together again. Some of these chapters will be better understood if we remember that Whitehead's philosophy is not synonymous with process philosophy; rather, process philosophy has been built upon Whitehead's speculative metaphysics, which can be read, understood, and interpreted through other lenses, including the post-structuralist lens.

While the impetus for the development of this book may be said to begin with the conference, each chapter represents a small part of its author's journey into the realm of Whitehead and post-structuralism. As such, the conference—the beginning—really is the middle once again. The professional interests of these authors include theology, philosophy, gender studies, sociology, and English. They are students and professors from various countries, including Iceland, England, Belgium, and the United States. The chapters are as multifaceted and varied as the authors, and yet there are threads that connect them. In particular, these chapters explore the interconnections, parallels, and disconnections between Alfred North Whitehead, Gilles Deleuze, and Judith Butler. The chapters that constitute this book represent an array of diverse paths that journey through nomadic lands of undulating plains, surprising plateaus, and infinite flights of thought. Perhaps we could say that such diversity is vital for an exploration of the intersections between Whitehead, Deleuze, and Butler because openness to diverse voices and novel ways of addressing the universe and its variety may be one of the major commonalities between these thinkers.

Our nomadic foray into this wilderness of rhizomatic connections "begins" with Roland Faber's "Introduction: Negotiating Becoming." This introduction is a substantial explanation of the major interconnections between Whitehead, Deleuze, and Butler. It seeks not only to give the reader important background information on each of the thinkers and their major themes but also to impart the fact that conversations such as the one between process and post-structuralism are legitimate and vitally important for the renewal of novelty in philosophy and theology, as well as many connected fields such as social sciences, cultural studies, and religious studies. "Introduction: Negotiating Becoming" delves into the way in which "becoming" is a dominant theme for Whitehead, Deleuze, and Butler. It demonstrates the way in which, as Deleuze explained, every philosopher's thought enfolds and is enfolded by other thoughts from other times, cultures, and people, and it illuminates the way in which, as Whitehead proposed, every thought is a process or an adventure, while acknowledging that, as Butler reminds us, all our thoughts and the symbols used to express them are determined to some degree by our social location.

Following this introduction, the book is divided into three sections: "Negotiating Events and Multiplicities," "Negotiating Bodies and Societies," and "Negotiating Immanence and Divinity." While the chapters are divided into these sections, each appearing as its own separate plateau, the divisions actually are fluid, as will be seen in the remainder of this foreword; chapters connect with one another and forge new paths between one section and the next. The first section, "Negotiating Events and Multiplicities," enfolds four chapters: "Whitehead, Post-Structuralism, and Realism" by Keith Robinson, "Nomad Thought: Deleuze, Whitehead, and the Adventure of Thinking" by Jeff Bell, "Transcendental Empiricism in Deleuze and Whitehead" by Steven Shaviro, and "Can We Be Wolves? Intersections between Deleuze's Difference and Repetition and Butler's Performativity" by Andrea M. Stephenson.

"Whitehead, Post-Structuralism, and Realism" attempts to locate Whitehead within post-structuralism. Robinson first outlines two different trajectories within post-structuralism—transcendent and immanent. The transcendent trajectory is exemplified by Derrida, while the immanent trajectory is demonstrated by Deleuze. For Robinson, Whitehead's philosophy shares enough similarities with the immanent trajectory to be called post-structuralist. To begin his exploration of these connections,

Robinson traces the concepts of ideas and reality from Kant, through Heidegger and Nietzsche, to Deleuze. With this background in place, the chapter then ventures to examine the way in which Whitehead transformed Kant's idealism into a type of nonessentialist realism (which he also calls pluralist or process realism). Robinson's journey through ideas and realism leads him to view Whitehead's philosophy as a renewal of metaphysics within the folds of an immanent post-structuralism.

While Robinson's chapter leads us up and down, inside and outside the world of events and reality, Jeff Bell's moves the nomadic journey into the realm of creativity and aesthetics. Specifically, he considers the themes of creative, or nomadic, thought, adventures of thought, and the chaosmos in relation to aesthetics in his chapter "Nomad Thought: Deleuze, Whitehead, and the Adventure of Thinking." This chapter explores Deleuze's creative, or nomadic, thought in relation to Whitehead's notion of adventure and Butler's concept of gender as culturally constituted. In relation to Butler, Bell notes that the fact that gender is constituted rather than pre-given means that identity is nomadic rather than fixed. Both Deleuze and Butler wish to maintain multiplicity, and Bell finds a strong connection between this concept of multiplicity and Whitehead's wish to retain multiplicities. In this vein, the philosophers posit a world that is a chaosmos. This chaosmos is created and maintained by nomadic thought—thought that does not think of multiplicities as unities or as a singular multiplicity. While these thinkers disagree on how this chaosmos is capable of existing without total destruction (Whitehead posits a God while Deleuze posits the synthesis of events and thought into a self, and Butler posits what Bell refers to as a "nomadic singularity"), this nomadic thought and chaosmos are highly important. Finally, this chapter explores the implications of nomadic thinking (or creative thinking) and adventures of thought for ethics and aesthetics.

"Transcendental Empiricism in Deleuze and Whitehead" by Steven Shaviro seeks to explore the transformation of Kant's transcendental idealism—in which Ideas exist in thought as juridical (determining legitimate uses of reason) and problematic (bringing up the questions "What can I know?" "What ought I to do?" "What may I hope?")—into transcendental empiricism in the works of Deleuze and Whitehead. While Kant could be said to come before Whitehead and Whitehead to come before Deleuze, each is implicated in the becoming of the others. Rather than Ideas remaining, as they do in Kant, in the thought, Whitehead and Deleuze embrace experience and becoming rather than static being. In considering Deleuze and Kant, this chapter emphasizes Deleuze's "virtual" in relation to Kant's transcendental Ideas. After examining the way in which the virtual transforms Kant's notion of Ideas, the chapter explores Whitehead's eternal objects in their similarity to Deleuze's virtual, thus leading to a consideration of eternal objects and Kant's Ideas. The chapter explains that philosophers now are asking different questions as we increasingly are confronted with the changeableness of the world around us and the desire to create new and different futures for ourselves. As we ask these questions, it is important to remember where philosophy has been in order to see where it can go, as Deleuze and Whitehead did with Kant's transcendental idealism.

The final chapter of "Negotiating Events and Multiplicities," "Can We Be Wolves? Intersections between Deleuze's Difference and Repetition and Butler's Performativity" by Andrea M. Stephenson, serves as a bridge between "Negotiating Events and Multiplicities" and "Negotiating Bodies and Societies," and delves into the intersections in the thought of Deleuze and Butler. (While the connection to Whitehead is not explicitly made in this chapter, the themes of novelty and creativity abound in such a way that the rhizomatic connections between the three thinkers are always lurking under the surface.) Stephenson frames her chapter through the image of the wolf-pack found in Deleuze and Guattari's *A Thousand Plateaus*, beginning and ending with the question "Can we be wolves?" which she develops as a question of how to live responsibly within the chaos of multiplicities. She explores these questions with respect to the categories of difference, repetition, and nonidentity in relation to the notions of multiplicity and performativity. Through an examination of these themes and the ways in which they intersect in the work of Deleuze and Butler, this chapter presents the reader with a glimpse of some of the possible social implications of these post-structuralist concepts, leading appropriately into the second section of the book, "Negotiating Bodies and Societies."

Following (or continuing, or interrupting) Stephenson's chapter, the book journeys from the more abstract realm of events, aesthetics, and ideas to consider the concrete playground of these more abstract notions—the physical world and the actual bodies that populate it. This brings us to the next intersection in our journey (though it could have been the first or the last, the introduction or the postscript, or somewhere else in-between)—"Negotiating Bodies and Societies."

This section deals with the issue of physicality in philosophy in the chapters by Michael Halewood, Isabella Palin, and Luke B. Higgins. The physical body, whether it be the body of the earth, of nonhuman creatures, or of humans, traditionally has been neglected or, worse, denigrated within philosophy and theology. Recently, concerns for the environment and the just treatment of all creatures have inspired thinkers in philosophy and theology to consider the place of the physical within these fields which, following the dualism inherent in Descartes, have been focused largely on the nonphysical. The chapters in this section delve into the depths of Whiteheadian process thought, Deleuzian nomadic thought, and Butlerian feminist thought to find novel ways of opening a space for corporeality within philosophy and theology.

Michael Halewood's chapter, "Butler and Whitehead on the (Social) Body," seeks to explore the results of the bifurcation of nature in which the body is dismissed as an illusion of language structures. His chapter first ventures through Butler's work on materiality and the body, including her emphasis on the fact that matter is important and should not be essentialized in philosophy. While Butler's work is a step forward in erasing the separation between the natural and the social body, Halewood argues that Whitehead's notion of "body as process" and his extension of the social beyond the human realm might "extend Butler's account and strengthen her critique." Halewood provides a robust discussion of Whitehead's approach to the body—an approach that, temporally, comes before Butler's but, for Halewood, can and should be used to illuminate, transform, and inform her body philosophy. For Halewood, Whitehead's descriptions of actual entities, eternal objects, and becoming could enable us to examine the material body without relegating it to static philosophical categories. This chapter places Whitehead in conversation with Butler in an effort to develop a theory concerning the body in which the body is recognized in both its materiality and its sociality.

Because we are all physical creatures living in close quarters with a variety of other people and other creatures, we must consider the way in which we live together. This is the major theme of the chapter by Isabella Palin. "Conflict" explores ethical pluralism, peace, and conflict. Palin illuminates an "alternative rationale for action in situations of 'conflict'" via the work of Whitehead, Butler, and Deleuze. She explores conflict through the framework of a preference not to choose violence either by submitting or by conquering. In other words, it has to do with becoming, in that becoming has to do with the way in which we *choose* to view and live in the world. "Conflict" seeks to examine our ethical life through Whitehead, Butler, and Deleuze in such a way as to lead toward a society of peace in which conflict has to do with construction rather than with violence and in which nonviolence is no longer equated with loss of power.

When we think of bodies and societies, we often think of our own human bodies and the way in which we live among other humans. However, Luke B. Higgins strives to remind us that bodies and societies include every living thing on the earth, and even the earth itself. He seeks to find a path toward ecological justice within Whitehead's and Deleuze's thought in his chapter, "Becoming through Multiplicity: Staying in the Middle of Whitehead's and Deleuze-Guattari's Philosophies of Life," which outlines the theme of multiplicity in Whitehead and Deleuze and Guattari. Higgins writes about Deleuze and Guattari using the construction "Deleuze-Guattari" in an attempt to highlight the rhizomatic nature of their joint works in which it is impossible to differentiate between Deleuze's thought and writing and Guattari's. Rather than develop a philosophy of a system in which everything is neatly organized into a hierarchical unity, Whitehead and Deleuze-Guattari propose that we remain within multiplicities. Higgins explores Deleuze's concepts of rhizomes, becoming, and the Body without Organs along with Whitehead's notions of multiplicities, novelty, and societies. By pointing out that both philosophers emphasize creativity and multiplicity, Higgins indicates that their thoughts are vital for enabling us to see ourselves within the multiplicity in such a way that we can recognize the interrelated complexities of the world in which we live, and that creative solutions can be found for the changing and challenging ecological situations in which we find ourselves.

The chapters in "Negotiating Bodies and Societies" encourage us to take a look at our concrete existence without divorcing it from the life of our minds. They help us to see the rhizomatic connections between mind and body, between individual and society, between human and nonhuman, and so on. Flowing out of (or into) the discussion of values and how we live in our world, we find ourselves connecting with another branch of the ever-changing stream of thought in Whitehead, Deleuze, and Butler: immanence, divinity, God.

In "Negotiating Immanence and Divinity," Roland Faber, Alan Van Wyk, Sigridur Gudmarsdottir, and Catherine Keller dance around, with, and through the question (which seems to be a perpetual question in post-structuralism) of whether we can talk about God, transcendence and immanence, and the Divine in today's world and, if we can talk about them, how we can talk about them. We seem to be wandering in a strange space now where the earlier religious and theological beliefs, while still held tightly by some, are being challenged and even dismissed by others as our understanding of the world and our place in it is changing through science and social theory. These authors agree that post-structuralism is not as anti-divine as many have contended and that the notion of immanence, which Deleuze uses in his argument against the idea of God, may be a viable way of looking at the Divine. By reading post-structuralists, such as Butler and Deleuze, through the lens of Whitehead's process thought, they present us with a new vision of the Divine as a part of the process of becoming, which helps us to negotiate truth, and takes part in the immanent physical world.

Roland Faber's chapter "Surrationality and Chaosmos: For a More Deleuzian Whitehead (with a Butlerian Intervention)" emphasizes, in connection with many of the chapters that have preceded it, the notion of multiplicities in Whitehead and Deleuze. Faber explores in depth, and in conjunction with Butler, the idea that identity is not singular. Just like these chapters or this book, identity is made up of parts—it is always changing, it is never unified and static. Faber designates Whitehead as a surrationalist—one who sees that the possibility of logic and rationality existing at all in a world of chaos is a wonder. Like Deleuze, Whitehead loves the multiplicities, chaos, and *khora* of surrationality rather than the unity and singular logic of rationality. While Butler sees the Law as the enemy of surrationality and does not see a way out of this rational, hierarchical, oppressive situation, Deleuze and Whitehead envision something beyond the Law—the *khora*. Exploring the notions of chaosmos (in Deleuze and Whitehead), performability (in Butler), and *khora* (in Deleuze, Whitehead, and Butler), Faber makes connections between the surrationality of these thinkers while also pointing to the differences that exist between them—in particular, the difference that exists between Whitehead and Deleuze in relation to the Divine.

Alan Van Wyk's chapter, "Divine Possibilities: Becoming an Order without Law," further explores the question of law and if/how an order can exist if the law is ruptured. Beginning with Butler's recent work on political theory, in which she puts forth the notion of the divine law as that which "ruptures" temporal law, this chapter discovers an affinity between this idea of being freed from the law and Whitehead's call for a "secularization of God" in which we might be able to discover a "secularized political theology." By exploring these themes, Van Wyk's chapter comes to the conclusion that two possible politics are put forth, both of which subvert traditional notions of law and order—a "politics of perpetual critique" via Butler and "a politics of peace" via Whitehead.

While Faber's chapter at the start of this section highlights the differences in the treatment of the Divine in Whitehead and Deleuze, Sigridur Gudmarsdottir proposes to find a way of speaking of God—at a time when

Foreword   *xix*

ontology has fallen out of favor—by using the notion of the *khora* found in Whitehead and Deleuze. In other words, if Being cannot be called God, can we talk of God at all? Her chapter, "'God Is a Lobster': Whitehead's Receptacle Meets the Deleuzian Sieve," takes a look at Faber's desire for a de-ontologization of God, as he describes it in his article "De-Ontologizing God: Levinas, Deleuze, and Whitehead" in *Process and Difference: Between Cosmological and Poststructuralist Postmodernisms*, such that God can be separated from connotations of Being, the absolute, and the transcendent. Gudmarsdottir then explores the concept of Plato's *khora* within Whitehead and Deleuze as a path toward talking about God without ontology. She posits that the possibility of an open, creative, chaotic *khoric* space could allow us to speak of God as Deleuze's lobster God—a God that inhabits the abyss, that creates out of chaos, and that could symbolize the creative chaosmos proposed by both Whitehead and Deleuze.

Catherine Keller brings together once again Whitehead, Butler, and Deleuze as she introduces us to the chaos of truth-claims in today's world of absolutism and relativism. Her chapter, "Uninteresting Truth? Tedium and Event in Postmodernity," examines the notion of truth in process thought and post-structuralism, focusing on the work of Whitehead, Deleuze and Guattari, Foucault and Butler, and Caputo and Derrida. Beginning with the notion of "truthiness"—truth of the heart—she then highlights the dilemma of living in a world in which truth is seen as either absolute Truth or as an illusion of power and language. In this chapter she seeks to discern the possible effects on our ability to make truth-claims of post-structuralist transformations of process thought. Post-structuralism has made us wary of truth talk and has been linked to the death of God in philosophy. Yet, in conversation with Whitehead and Caputo, Keller points the way toward a truth process.

Just as the foreword is not the beginning, the last section is not the end of the conversation. The folds, paths, streams, plateaus, and plains of thought considered in this book are merely fragments of the rhizomatic connections that exist and are being discovered between process and post-structuralist thought. It is our hope that the images, intersections, and disconnections in these chapters will serve to inspire further reflections, questions, and even disagreements as philosophy and theology continue to be enriched and renewed by these complex and interrelated thinkers. In teasing out points of connection within Whitehead, Deleuze, and Butler, these chapters give me hope. Not only do they provide me with a framework by which to understand the rich diversity within process and post-structuralist thought, but they also offer paths to find value in life in the midst of a world of skepticism and nihilism, to speak a message of liberation even when it seems the oppressive forces are too strong, to believe in something Divine in spite of the "death of God." It is only through these types of creative conversations that we can open new doors for communication and understanding as we attempt to live together and plumb the depths of human existence.

Secrets of Becoming

INTRODUCTION

Negotiating Becoming

Roland Faber

Only becomings are secrets; the secret has a becoming.

GILLES DELEUZE AND FELIX GUATTARI,
A Thousand Plateaus: Capitalism and Schizophrenia

Secrets of Becoming places into conversation modes of thought traditionally held apart. Whitehead's "philosophy of organism" (later transformed into what became known as *process thought*), Deleuze's "philosophy of difference" (also known as *nomadic thought*), and Judith Butler's "philosophy of gender" (normally identified as part of *feminist philosophy*) exhibit great diversity among themselves—too much for many to undertake the risk of envisioning an interesting conversation. The grand divergence in the questions with which these philosophies are interested, as well as the widely different fields of discourse in which these questions are situated, create the hiatus: metaphysics and gender theory, cosmology and cultural theory, religion and democracy, mathematics and psychoanalysis—Why should one try to bridge or connect them? And yet, isn't this strange "togetherness" of the multiple questions, divergent disciplines, and deep problems they raise precisely what might make their thoughts *negotiable* with one another?

Some thinkers—and this collection is witness to this fact—have found surprisingly genuine crossings and intersections between process, nomadic, and feminist thought, which they believe to be important enough to justify such a conversation, or even demand it. There is, in Deleuze's work, this odd affinity to remote philosophies, among them

Whitehead; there is this overlapping and mutually critical review of process and post-structuralist thought with feminist philosophy (e.g., with Irigaray, Kristeva, and in particular, with Deleuze). And besides an essential acquaintance with Nietzsche, a critical appreciation of Foucault and Derrida lingers in the background of most post-structuralist theories. The more one investigates the rhizomatic motions of these modes of thought (and practice), the more a landscape opens up in which these philosophies appear as inhabitants of a gathering, diffusively named post-structuralist—in a much wider field of populations, often referred to as postmodern—thought.

At first look, however, one will see immediately rifts in this landscape, fairly clearly dividing one field from the others. Moreover, philosophical geologists, or geophilosophers,[1] could question whether or not a valid map was being drawn at all. Isn't it true that the Champs-Élysées is in Paris and not in London? In other words: What does Whitehead, the Victorian co-author of the *Principia Mathematica* and infamous proponent of metaphysics, have to do with post-structuralist thought? And what does a French Catholic rebel of the 1968 movement have to do with the American-Jewish heritage of the Ashkenazi, for that matter? However, in all of these possible misconnections, we should not forget that their *event* of togetherness is unpredictable by timeframe, ideological occupation, and philosophical orientation. If *timeframe* is the problem, we should not forget how Nietzsche becomes part of the event (although he was much too early in time).[2] If *ideological warping* is the problem, let's remember his misuse in fascist thought (although much later). If *philosophical outlook* is the problem, we should not forget Deleuze's new engagement in metaphysical modes of thinking (despite, and in embracing, Nietzsche). All unpredictable crossings! At a closer look, the landscape becomes even more complicated. While both Deleuze and Butler might be referred to as post-structuralist thinkers, they will not match each other in their modes of thought or in their practices. One might become distressed all the more by the fact that both, while referring to a common ancestor, Michel Foucault (one writing a book on him, the other exhibiting his thought as a vital basis throughout her whole work), would agree neither on the reasons for engaging his thought, nor even on *what* to agree on.

For geophilosophers, this amounts to something like three Berlins divided by two Berlin Walls! But aren't they also connected by these walls? If we leave the "tree" of a bird's eye view to look from below, from the perspective of a "rhizome," we might discover their weird connections: that there is the nonnegotiable fact that Whitehead, Deleuze, and Butler,

Introduction: Negotiating Becoming

with all divergences and antipathies, as well as all their sympathies and affinities, distrust a common mindset, and that they use their skills to deconstruct it. They detect *substantialism* as their archenemy and consider its total dismissal as the only "solution" to their (different) sets of questions. In an affirmative formulation, there is the surprising fact that Whitehead, Deleuze, and Butler understand their thought as being part of—or better, as being at the forefront of—a philosophy for which *Becoming* is eminent. Indeed, in the concept of "Becoming," they turn our understanding of the world upside down—with all the philosophical, scientific, aesthetic, and political consequences. "Becoming," however, does not play the role of a common denominator enabling us to abstract from their divergent texts, but has the very concerted function of creating an *active concept* of analysis, struggle, and operation.

In the course of this book, it is this emphasis on Becoming—its presuppositions, implications, and consequences—that interests us in the modes in which it appears to thoroughly permeate the philosophies of Whitehead, Deleuze, and Butler. Moreover—somehow like an experiment in quantum tunneling and non-locality—we will begin to observe the unsuspected co-vibrations of Becoming that, in its irregular channels, connects the divided sectors of process, nomadic, and feminist philosophy when these thinkers perform together "the event of becoming" as it transforms everything it touches. We listen to their negotiations while asking: How is it to be in the process of becoming; in the process of becoming—?

Metanoetics of Becoming

Maybe the best way to characterize the common field of becoming for Whitehead, Deleuze, and Butler is to understand their revolution in thought as based on (or at least initiated by) Nietzsche's call for *radical* becoming. The first essay, "Good and Evil, Good and Bad," in Nietzsche's *On the Genealogy of Morals* contains what could be understood as the Manifesto of Becoming:

> A quantum of force is just such a quantum of drive, will, action—indeed, it is nothing but these drives, willing, and actions in themselves—and it cannot appear as anything else except through the seduction of language (and the fundamental errors of reason petrified in it), which understands and misunderstands all action as conditioned by something which causes actions, by a "Subject." In fact, in just the same way as people separate lightning from its flash and take the latter as an action, as the effect of a

subject, which is called lightning, so popular morality separates strength from the manifestations of that strength, as if behind the strong person there is an indifferent substrate, which is free to manifest strength or not. But there is no such substrate; there is no "being" behind the doing, acting, becoming. "The doer" is merely invented after the fact—the act is everything. People basically duplicate the event: when they see lightning, well, that is an action of an action: they set up the same event first as the cause and then again as its effect.[3]

The "subject" is an abstraction post facto of the becoming of forces that happen to manifest themselves "together." There is no "substrate" behind this activity of gathering, only the illusion of an effect disguised as the cause of the activity it originates. Indeed, the revolution, the *metanoia*, that which seems to be the basis, ground, and cause, is, in fact, the effect of its own becoming. *Being is the effect of becoming!* Put in Whiteheadian terms, this metanoetics[4] of becoming is formalized in his *principle of process*:

> That *how* an actual entity *becomes* constitutes *what* that actual entity *is*; so that the two descriptions of an actual entity are not independent. Its "being" is constituted by its "becoming." This is the "principle of process."[5]

If being is *constituted* by becoming, it is never a substrate that underlies the process, but it is always only the *consequence* of the process of becoming. This *metanoia* in fact is revolutionary: Everything that can be said *besides* becoming can be said only *with* becoming or (being an ingredient) *in the process* of becoming! First, nothing is, in a strict sense, pre-given. Everything pre-given (matters of fact) has had its own becoming—there are neither "initial conditions" nor "first causes" from which to start. Second, being cannot be claimed to be the ground of all beings, except as it is the expression of this process of "being in becoming" itself, which is neither self nor substrate, neither subject nor object. The latter—the ontological ground—is expressed by Whitehead's "creativity" as the abstraction of activity "which is actual in virtue of its accidents" and "only then capable of characterization through its accidental embodiments"[6]—indicating the non-substantial activity of *becoming* itself, which is only actual *with* becoming. The former—the instance of becoming, which Whitehead terms "actual entity"—can only be abstracted by abstracting *from* becoming. This amounts to Whitehead's *ontological principle*, which says "that actual entities are the only *reasons*; so that to search for a *reason* is to search for one or more actual entities."[7] Referring to "reasons" is not referring to

Introduction: Negotiating Becoming

common grounds or higher realities or grounds or causes, but to becoming in its processes of becoming.

By conceptualizing becoming as "actual entities," two things happen: First, nothing that becomes, becomes forever, but it effectuates being. This "being," however, is becoming-past, a memory of becoming.

> In their becoming [becomings] are immediate and then vanish into the past. They are gone; they have perished; they are no more and have passed into not-being. Plato terms them things that are "always becoming and never really are."[8]

Second, in allowing for being to be the effect of becoming as its sedimentation, *something* can become. This "something," however, is nothing in itself, no substrate; it *is* only with new becoming *in* which it functions as its condition. Structures of becoming, therefore, are always in becoming but are also conditions of becoming in the sense that there is a paradoxical mutual rhythm between becoming and being. Yet, this is a *metanoetic* rhythm: not that of the being of a "subject" or "ground" or "cause" of a *What* that enfolds itself in a process of becoming, but that of a "superject" or "aim" or "effect" *attained* in the process of becoming and remaining *with* its renewal. The effect conversely "causes" ingredients of becoming to become the conditions (restrictions, structures, laws) for its renewal.

Deleuze's Nietzsche has discovered just that. In this rhythm, if there would be a being to be attained, it would have been reached already. Since time is infinite in both directions, past and future, "the present moment, as the passing moment, proves that it is not attained." Consequently, if the "infinity of the past time means that becoming cannot have started to become . . . it is not something that has become."[9] But *in* becoming, in the *instance* of a "present" becoming, every-*thing* is in co-existence of its *flux*, in the "state" of the solution of its sediments. Becoming is "incorporeal": it "is not mixed up with the state of affairs in which it is effectuated. It does not have spatiotemporal coordinates, only intensive ordinates." Deleuze's reconstruction of being "in becoming" emphasizes its elements as *"heterogeneous components traversed by a point of absolute survey at infinite speed"*[10] whereby the sedimentations of the states of affairs and their histories are in the flux of the moment of becoming. "Philosophy is [about] becoming, not history; it is the coexistence of plains, not the succession of systems."[11] It is (about) the intersection of multiplicities beyond their structural identity. This leaves us with his notion of the event of becoming.

In every event of becoming there are many heterogeneous, always simultaneous components, since each of them is a meanwhile, all within the meanwhile that makes them communicate through zones of indiscernability, of undecidability; they are variations, modulations, intermezzi, singularities, of a new infinite order. Each component of the event is *actualized or effectuated* in an instant, and the event in the time that passes between these instants, but nothing happens within *the virtuality* that has only meanwhiles as components and an event as composite becoming. Nothing happens here, but everything becomes, so that the event has the privilege of beginning again when time is past. Nothing happens, and yet everything changes, because becoming continues to pass through its components again and to restore the event that is actualized elsewhere, at a different moment.[12]

Being is *effectuated* in becoming and *per se* is only a multiplicity of components *in* becoming, permanently reconstructed in ever-new instants of becoming. Neither is there any Being as ground of Becoming nor is there any structure capturing this becoming-anew. As in Whitehead, structures dissolve into fluent components of instants of becoming. Hence, neither any "identity of a subject" nor any substrate underpins the process of reconstruction of structures in becoming, although, as in Whitehead, these structures are conditions of becoming. But, as in Whitehead, they are not causes (or principles, or grounds) that *activate* becoming but sediments that *are activated* and *are effected* by the very process of becoming they condition. No-thing "happens"—there is no substance that happens—but "in becoming" everything changes in the event of becoming-anew out of sediments that are always already effectuated by its effect.

As for Whitehead and Deleuze, the *metanoia* of becoming clears Butler's view of an *essentialism* that has haunted the genesis of philosophy and the Western worldview. With Nietzsche, she issues a reconstruction of structures of Being—which seem to be eternal Law and a Logos of permanence—generating a *genealogy* of their becoming in which their being-ground reveals their being-effect of repetition of power relations (which she adopts as "phallogocentrism"). For Butler, this genealogy of becoming has immediate implications for the body in becoming, body politics, and the culturally gendered understanding of the sexual difference.

Clearly this project does not propose to lay out within traditional philosophical terms an *ontology* of gender whereby the meaning of being a woman or a man is elucidated within the terms of phenomenology. The presumption here is that the "being" of gender is *an effect*, an object of a genealogical investigation that maps out the political parameters of its construction in the mode of ontology. To claim that gender is constructed is not to assert its illusoriness or artificiality, where those terms are understood to reside within a binary that counterposes the "real" and the "authentic" as oppositional. As a genealogy of gender ontology, this inquiry seeks to understand the discursive production of the plausibility of that binary relation and to suggest certain cultural configurations of gender to take the place of "the real" and consolidate and augment their hegemony through that felicitous self-naturalization.[13]

Again, as in Deleuze and Whitehead, being is the effect of becoming; genealogy is the deconstruction of the "naturalization" of being's plausible patterns that are created in order to secure their hegemony (by their becoming "natural"). The phallogocentric reconstruction of seemingly naturally gendered "reality" uncovers the cultural mechanisms by which power relations take their self-evident prevalence (and oppressive regulations) to become *the* being, the substrate, the natural essence of its (the beings) own becoming. Conversely, however, "one is not born, but rather *becomes* a woman"; as any naturalized notion, "*woman* itself is a term in process, a becoming, a constructing that cannot rightfully be said to originate or to end."[14] In Butler's metanoetics of becoming (and with Nietzsche), "gender is always a doing. Though not a doing of a subject who might be said to preexist the deed."[15] *Subjects* are not *identities* out of which they (besides other operations also) become, but are results of their own becoming. In the process of such becoming, however, what becomes, becomes *subjected* to the *structures* that become—calling these structures their *being*.[16]

With this heritage from Nietzsche, for all three of our thinkers, *ontology* has to be *genealogically deconstructed* as based on its own becoming, which is always prior to being; that means it has to be critically unmasked of its culturally, socially, politically imposed mechanisms that disguise their becoming as pre-given being, as a *nature* "(out) of which" becoming only seems to appear as a surface effect of deep essence. On the contrary, for all three thinkers, all "nature" is *naturalized*; all structures are *constructed*; all patterns are stable only by *repetition*; all powers are only *internalized subjections* to the very effects of their own production. If this view is rightly called "post-structuralist," all three of our thinkers (regardless of the divergences regarding time, space, and characters of their own philosophical development) are in a superposition by which their thought is expressed by "becoming." Insofar as this verb/infinitive changes *everything*, their thought is a *metanoetics* of becoming, shouting out loud: "All is Event!"

All Is Event!

In negotiating becoming, it soon becomes a question whether one legitimately may think of Whitehead as a "post-structuralist thinker" *at all*. Isn't Whitehead much more a hardcore *rationalist*? Isn't the post-structuralist impulse to deconstruct all of metaphysics a fairly obvious sign that Whitehead remains on the "other" side of the divide—the metaphysical antiquity—or even worse, remaining an undeconstructed (and easily deconstructible) rationalist of "pre-Kantian modes of thought"[17]? Moreover, the history of the reception of Whitehead seems to petrify this impression: Whitehead was defended *as* a metaphysician (in exactly the meaning of this tradition that post-structuralist thought was to deconstruct). When he was "used" to criticize *modernity*—thereby stylizing him as a "postmodern" thinker—the intention often was to reinstall lost modes of a non-materialist, post-scientific, and anti-Cartesian *holism*.[18] Whitehead was becoming a household name in "metaphysical literature" of an evolutionary spirituality of the cosmos,[19] a new form of spiritualism (or idealism), in the best case compared with Hegel's idealism of Absolute Spirit[20] (and buried in the pre-Marxian critique and reversal).[21] Whitehead was caught between continents and philosophies in Europe and America, in a sense, really becoming "the Other" of the philosophical landscape: neither a classical metaphysician nor a classical rationalist; neither a thorough empiricist nor a real pragmatist; neither an existentialist nor a phenomenologist; neither a Continental philosopher nor an analytic thinker.[22] In all of those circles, Whitehead's enthusiastic (although *also* "otherwise") reception in theology and religious thought—with ripples as far as Buddhist philosophy and Asian modes of thought—has hurt his reputation as a *thinker* one has to take seriously. His quarrel with Einstein's mathematics of General Relativity, which he seemingly (at least in the public debate) has lost, has not furthered any admiration in the scientific world; and the destruction of the grand opus of the *Principia Mathematica*—for which he, if at all, still is known to a wider audience—by Gödel's theorem definitely declared him part of *history* (of philosophy, of science) rather than part of ongoing discourses for which his *thinking* would arouse us today.

Within all of these dislocations of Whitehead, we find a steady stream of "process philosophy" relying on his "philosophy of organism,"[23] but engulfing his thought antithetically as "constructive postmodernism"—at odds with any undertaking to situate Whitehead in the post-structuralist movement (or, at least, as one of its forebearers). Moreover, in deep distrust of the Derridean "deconstruction" as a valuable description for Whitehead's thought, these forms of "constructive" process philosophy are understood as alternative paths of postmodernism besides/around post-structuralism.[24] Whitehead as a *constructive* postmodernist—together with Henri Bergson, William James, Charles Sanders Peirce, and Charles Hartshorne—is seen as a stronghold of resistance against the alleged "debilitating relativism" of *deconstructive* postmodernism and as a *holistic* alternative that does not dismiss truth through relativist readings but seeks a new form of postmodern *unity* of thought and reality—a new form of *metaphysics of the whole world* in terms of Whitehead's conceptualization. By mistrusting the nomadic multiplicities of deconstructive and post-structuralist thought, which can never be united into a non-fragmented whole, this tendency furthers the prejudice that Whitehead is part of a movement of neo-rationalism, not at all postmodern, but reviving modernity in terms of pre-materialistic modes of thought and neo-foundationalism. In the midst of this controversy, however, it is the fresh reading of a post-rationalistic Whitehead in the very first collection of articles collected as *Process and Difference*[25] that has pointed us to an alternative, post-structuralist understanding of Whitehead and especially a vital Deleuzian connection.

Indeed, it was Deleuze with his counter-reading of Whitehead who cut through the predicaments of these displacements of his philosophy.[26] Despite the fact that Deleuze did not honor Whitehead with a whole book (as he did others), Whitehead is present persistently in Deleuze's work, and today we know (and are, in fact, discovering) how deeply the formation of Deleuze's thought was influenced by Whitehead, aside from the more obvious and related "usual suspects": Spinoza, Leibniz, Bergson, and (less obvious, but nevertheless equally important "philosophical rivals") Nietzsche and Kant.[27] Obviously, against all odds, Deleuze, in the 1960s, when Whitehead was virtually removed from any philosophical discourses (where he remained for the next decades), thought of Whitehead's core metaphysical piece "*Process and Reality* [as] one of the greatest books of modern philosophy."[28] The reason for Deleuze's appreciation of Whitehead in *Difference and Repetition*—his very first major work written on his own behalf!—was not so obvious (to others) and remained rather silently present during his own journey. It was sparked by Whitehead's *radically different* "categories," i.e., his "list of empirico-ideal notions," which for Deleuze "are really open and which betray an empirical and pluralist sense of Idea."[29] This "conception of a differential Idea" in which "the nomadic distribution carried out by phantastical notions as opposed to sedentary distributions of the categories" reverses the whole "problem of [vertical] Being" into "the problem of the manner in which being is distributed among beings" in "univocity"[30]; that is, in Whitehead, as in Deleuze, becoming cannot be "represented" (or released) by vertical Being, but "happens" only as groundless *Event* of becoming.[31]

It is precisely *this* reading of Whitehead that Deleuze elaborates in the midst of his discussion of Leibniz. In this book on Leibniz, *The Fold*, the center chapter asks the question: "What is an Event?"[32] and the answer given is, surprisingly, not given via Leibniz but via Whitehead. More hidden, it appears in a Deleuzian lecture on Whitehead in a series of lectures in 1987 given at the University of Vincennes-St Denis in France—again on "the event" (*tout est événement?*).[33] While the former reinterprets the basic ingredients of Whitehead's account of the event—namely "prehension" and its related moments—by a more systematic layout of a Whiteheadian landscape of concepts, the latter enfolds "the event" in a (kind of) "creation story" that stretches back to the primordial point of the initiation of "the event" and enfolds the birth and evolution of a universe of *vibrating relations*. The starting point for these adventures in thinking *cosmology*, however, may surprise: It is the rigorous claim that "*All* is Event!" More surprisingly, Deleuze rediscovers that Whitehead's basic conviction—as is his own—is *not* based on a rationalistic metaphysics but is rooted in an *empiricist* approach. In asking the question, what we can find in our *experience*, it seeks the "conditions of real experience"[34]—that which Deleuze calls "transcendental empiricism"[35] and Whitehead captures in his "critique of pure feeling"[36] in which, in a radical reversal of Kant, his "transcendental aesthetics" come first.

To explicate the radical implications of *how*, in Whitehead, "*cette espèce de cri retentisse à nouveau: tout est événement!*" ("this sort of cry echoes anew: all is event!"), Deleuze, in his 1987 lecture, chooses an example from our mesocosmic (human) experience: the Giza pyramids.

> Toute chose, dira Whitehead, est passage de la nature. En anglais c'est "passage of nature," passage de nature. Corrigeons un peu pour retrouver Leibniz: toute chose est passage de Dieu. C'est strictement pareil. Toute chose est passage de nature. La grande pyramide est un événement, est

Introduction: Negotiating Becoming

> même un multiplicité infinie d'événements. En quoi consiste l'événement? A la lettre toute chose est une danse d'électrons, ou bien toute chose est une variation d'un champ électro-magnétique. Voilà que nous mettons un pieds très prudent dans la physique. Par exemple, l'événement qui est la vie de nature dans la grande pyramide, hier et aujourd'hui. Il faut peut-être pressentir qu'il n'y a pas une seule grande pyramide, mais qu'il y a peut-être deux grandes pyramides. C'est ce qu'il dit dans le texte. Mais n'allons pas trop vite . . . pour le moment c'est comme ça. Voilà. Il n'y a pas de choses, il n'y a que des événements, tout est évènement.[37]

Everything, said Whitehead, is the passage of nature. In English, it is the "passage of nature," *passage de nature*. Let's correct ourselves a little to connect with Leibniz again: Everything is a passage of God. It is strictly similar. Everything is a passage of nature. The Great Pyramid is an event, it is even a multiplicity of infinite events. Of what does the event consist? Everything, literally, is a dance of electrons, or, rather, everything is a variation of an electromagnetic field. Here let us dip our toes, carefully, into the physical. For example, the event which is the life of nature in the Great Pyramid, yesterday and today. Perhaps it is necessary to be aware that it is not the only great pyramid, but that there are perhaps two great pyramids. It is this which he spoke of in the text. But let's not go too quickly here . . . for the moment it is like that. Here it is. There are no things, there are only events, all is event.

Not very aloof from Whitehead's own example in *Concept of Nature*, namely Cleopatra's Needle in London, Deleuze, in his lecture, explores the eventfulness of *everything* as being the expression of Becoming (the "passage of nature"). It is precisely in the multiplicity of events that the event carries its patterns, and it is in the multiplicity of events that Deleuze, with Whitehead, states a *metanoetics* of the event: that there are no things with (private) attributes but only divergences and convergences of series of events. Here, the musical analogue is close to both philosophers: These series of events are *polyphone harmonies of vibrations*. Again, in line with Whitehead's *Concept of Nature*,[38] Deleuze envisions the story of creation of the universe "out of chaos" as "Chaosmos," as the dis/harmonic movement of vibrations[39]—from divergent "intersections, foldings, and limits."[40]

> Je commence à répondre en disant que ce premier stade repose sur une analyse de la vibration. Finalement au fond de l'événement il y a des vibrations. Au fond des événements actuels il y a des vibrations. Le premier stade c'était le "many," des vibrations n'importe comment, des vibrations aléatoires. Pour ceux qui connaissent Bergson, peut-être que vous vous

rappelez la splendide fin de Matière et Mémoire, le fond de la matière est vibration et vibration de vibrations. . . . Tout est vibration. Pourquoi la vibration met-elle déjà ce début d'ordre? . . . Voilà, une vibration qui se forme dans le "many," et dès ce moment là la diversité disjonctive commence à s'organiser en séries infinies sans limite. Il faut supposer que chaque vibration a des sous-multiples, a des harmoniques à l'infini, dans le pur cosmos. Le cosmos c'était le many, c'est à dire le chaos. C'était le chaos cosmos. . . . Deuxième stade de la genèse : les séries de caractères intrinsèques et extrinsèques, elles, convergent vers des limites. Cette fois-ci on a une idée de séries convergentes. . . . C'est beau. C'est d'une très très grande beauté.

I begin to respond by saying this first period rests on an analysis of vibration. Ultimately, underlying the event, there are vibrations. Underlying all actual events, there are vibrations. The first stage was the "many," the how of the vibrations is not important, the vibrations are random. For those who know Bergson, perhaps you remember the splendid conclusion of *Matter and Memory*, the foundation of the matter is vibration and the vibration of vibrations. . . . All is vibration. Why is vibration already at the beginning of order? . . . So, there is one vibration which itself forms from the "many," and in this moment the disjunctive diversity begins to organize itself in infinite series without limit. It must be supposed that each vibration has submultiples, has harmonics ad infinitum, in the pure cosmos. The cosmos is the many, that is to say, chaos. It is the chaos of the cosmos. . . . The second stage of the genesis: the series of intrinsic and extrinsic qualities converge toward the limits. This time there is an idea of convergent series . . . it is beautiful. It is a very great beauty.

With the cry "All is event!" Deleuze identifies Whitehead as one of the few philosophers—among them Nietzsche, Leibniz, Bergson, and himself—to understand the relationship between experience and reality as one that is conditioned in such a way so as to be able to account for *novelty*. To ask for "the event" is not to seek "how to attain eternity, but in what conditions does the objective world allow for a subjective production of novelty, that is, of creation"?[41] Three times—Deleuze says in his 1987 lecture—has the "cry for the event" been echoed through the history of philosophy: with the Stoics (which he has tackled in *The Logic of Sense*), with Leibniz (which he developed in *The Fold*), and with Whitehead. Where the Stoics, in order to introduce the event, relied on a materialism of surface-effects[42] and Leibniz remained caught in a pre-harmonization of the "compossible,"[43] Whitehead radically broke with the latter while structurally integrating the former. The Event is dis/cordant;[44] it happens in divergent and converging series of vibrations[45] where "bifurcations, divergences, incompossibilities, and discord belong to the same motley world."[46] By this dis/cordant harmonics of "polyphony"[47] the universe "rhythmically" becomes "in a great pleasure, a musical Joy of contrasting its vibrations . . . without knowing their harmonies . . . to produce something new."[48]

Performance (That Matters)

One of the important implications of this Chaosmos of vibrations is that literally nothing is excluded, and everything can and should be restated as a series of dis/harmonic vibrations: whether it be an "object" like the pyramid with its change through time, the perceiving relationship of a "subject" in it "perceiving event" with this object, or the experience of the "subject" itself in being its own "object" of perception. In all cases, the event of becoming is the process by which nothing that happens is, in its subjective/objective moments, a predicate of an underlying substrate; rather, that which becomes repeats and alters patterns, structures, or modes of existence in order to *become* what it seems to be from the outset, but only *is* by re-instantiating such patterns in new events—be it the pyramid, the perceiving Self, or the transcendental Self of Apperception. Indeed, *this* deconstruction of the pinnacle of modern philosophy and modern society—the Cartesian *ego cogito* in the form of the Kantian transcendental unity of the Self—is the "convergent vibration," i.e., the *event* in which (cosmologically for Whitehead and Deleuze and culturally and politically in Butler) the Self emerges as their "togetherness." While it would not be true to say that Whitehead and Deleuze have not used their common *metanoia* of becoming in the context of social theory and practice—as can be seen in Whitehead's *Symbolism* and *Adventures of Ideas* and Deleuze's two volumes of *Capitalism and Schizophrenia*—it is of all-encompassing importance in Butler's post-structuralist–feminist thought. But exactly *how* does, in Butler, the common *metanoia* of becoming become a category of political practice?

Butler's genealogy of gender ontology is, indeed, a deconstruction of a "metaphysics of substance, and how [it] does . . . inform thinking about the category of sex."[49] Without mentioning Whitehead once, it is clear from the outset that this deconstruction of substance thinking is exactly what Whitehead was introducing seventy years earlier and can be seen as an exciting application of his metanoetics of becoming to questions of the reconstruction not only of sex and gender, but of the metaphysics *as such* that gives rise to it. Butler's deconstructive move, however, is *not* to be understood as debilitating relativism (of which Derrida was wrongly accused) but is precisely, in Whitehead's sense, a genealogy of the becoming of the *construction* of substantialism.[50] Butler's reflection on this process reads like an adaptation of Whitehead's method of *exposing of the process of the construction* of being by becoming, of things by events, of persons by societies.

> In the first instance, humanist conceptions of the subject tend to assume a substantive person who is the bearer of various essential and nonessential attributes. A humanist feminist position might understand gender as an *attribute* of a person who is characterized essentially as a pregendered substance or "core," called a person, denoting a universal capacity for reason, moral deliberation, or language. The universal conception of the person, however, is displaced as a point of departure for a social theory of gender by those historical and anthropological positions that understand gender as a relation among socially constituted subjects in specifiable contexts. . . . As a shifting and contextual phenomenon, gender does not denote a substantive being, but a relative point of convergence among culturally and historically specific sets of relations.[51]

The individual, the person, the subject—they all are already *convergences* of specific sets of relations (or vibrations) and patterns of their contextual or environmental social setting. Substantial unity is, in fact, the effect of these convergent sets of patterns of repetition that, for reasons still to be named, generate the impression (or illusion) of a solid *substrate* of their own effects, thereby playing the role of "causes" of their own generation. Especially in her newer work, *Giving an Account of Oneself*, Butler addresses this social construction of the subject in precisely this way: namely, that the "substantiality" (normativity) of the effect (the subject) becomes possible only through the *exclusion* of the diversity and inconsistency of the social traits that "define" the norms of repetition (Law). It is never "one," and it is precisely not "one" in the sense that a subject can never gather itself into the "presence" of its own account without performing permutations of its constitutional multiplicity.[52]

In one of the earliest formulations of the analysis of this reversal of substantivism, Whitehead, in his *Concept of Nature*—which Deleuze adopts as the basis of his analysis of convergent sets of vibrating relations—makes an astonishing genealogical claim: that when "we speak of nature as a complex of related entities, the 'complex' is fact as an entity

Introduction: Negotiating Becoming

for thought, to whose bare individuality is ascribed the property of embracing in its complexity the natural entities."[53] While *in experience* the complex of related events in the flux of the "passage of nature"[54] is not hypostasized in any individuality, which is (silently) reversed into its own substrate, *in thought* a process of *abstraction* generates the "individuality" of a substantive entity and interprets the complex of relations as its property. While *in experience* the complex of relations is a set of "factors" in this inexhaustibly multifarious "fact" of nature that can never be substantialized, *in thought* it becomes an

> entity [that] has been separated from the factor which is the terminus of [experience]. It has become the substratum for that factor, and the factor has been degraded into an attribute of the entity. In this way a distinction has been imported into nature which is in truth no distinction at all. A natural entity is merely a factor of fact, considered in itself. Its disconnexion from the complex of fact is a mere abstraction. It is not the substratum of the factor, but the very factor itself as bared in thought. Thus, what is a mere procedure of mind . . . has been transmuted into a fundamental character of nature.[55]

This is an early formulation of Whitehead's "fallacy of misplaced concreteness"[56] that attacks substantialism as taking the *abstracted* unifications of patterns, characters, and forms to be the causes, reasons, principles, and grounds of the events, which, in their becoming, *generate* them in the first place. The "concrete," however, is not another substantive abstraction *underlying* the abstractions, but a "concrescence,"[57] a *becoming* (-concrete), a *converging* of vibrating sets of relations exhibiting social patterns. If we adopt Whitehead's conception of a "functional activity," i.e., of the becoming of sets of pattered vibrations by which "every actual thing is something by reason of its activity whereby its nature consists in its relevance to other things, and its individuality consists in its synthesis of other things so far as they are relevant to it,"[58] then for this social and environmental view of becoming there are no substances with properties, but only events with patterns.[59] The consequence is that

> With this conception of the world, in speaking of any actual individual, such as a human being, we must mean that man in one occasion of his experience. Such an occasion, or act, is complex and therefore capable of analysis into phases and other components. It is the most concrete actual entity, and the life of man from birth to death is a historic route of such occasions. These concrete moments are bound together into one society

by a partial identity of form, and by the peculiarly full summation of its predecessors which each moment of the life-history gathers into itself.[60]

It is precisely this *social reconstruction* of substantive claims to articulate the preconditions of becoming in which Butler is interested.[61] Where Whitehead attacks *thought*, which is only an effect of social feelings, as the medium of substantialization (and hence as the medium of a substantive reversal), Butler's subversive deconstruction unmasks the *ego cogito* as the final effect (or abstraction) of a logocentric, i.e., phallogocentric, process of patriarchal abstraction from the contextual sets of patterns.[62] And where Whitehead deconstructs society as "self-sustaining," whereby it is "its own reason,"[63] Butler deconstructs this "reason" as a (phallogocentric) rationalization of exclusions that constitute oppressive unifications of power.[64] "Personal identity," then, is "assured through stabilizing concepts" that guarantee the "gendered norms of cultural intelligibility by which persons are defined." Its critique is not so much based on a reconstruction of the "question of what internal feature of a person established the continuity or self-identity of the person through time," but to "what extent do regulatory practices of gender formation and division constitute identity."[65]

The problem of substantialism, in the early Butler, shifts from a more time-related, *diachronic* identity to a space-related, *synchronic* identity of social construction (although, as we will see, both cannot be abstracted from the other): *stabilization of identity is a social process of repetitive inheritance*—it is its *performance*.[66] In her later work, however, Butler explores precisely this *diachronic* construction of performance further by analyzing the *synchronic* construction as nothing but an *exclusory movement* of the diachronic multiplicity of the traits that feed into the present performance. And when the "narrative authority of the 'I' must give way to the perspective and temporality of the set of norms that contrast the singularity of my story,"[67] the "narrative 'I' effectively adds to the story every time it tries to speak."[68] The opaqueness of the present subject in its account of itself, that is, its inability to gather itself to a unit of presence, *is* its performance of the *shifting* rules it instantiates and negates at the same time.

For all three philosophers, the mark of "de-substantialization" is the dismissal of any *pre-formative unity*—be it as a substrate with *private properties*, be it as a subject with *natural identity*. Their pro/found (from *pro/fond*, "before the bottom," bottomless) non-essentialism interprets unity and identity always as a process of *their* becoming in which a multiplicity is unified but *never* gains static unity. The illusion of such unity arises from

Introduction: Negotiating Becoming

the socially stabilizing mechanism of structural integrity that *establishes* itself as the reason for the process of unification in *erasing* the *story* of its own becoming, its genealogy. All three philosophers may tell different stories of their generation or, at least, will tell it differently, but they agree on the deconstruction of the One (in which guise ever) as based on Multiplicity. The regulative power of this unity, in which it becomes seemingly primordial, substantial, causal, natural—in opposition to consequent, predicative, effective, and cultural—hides in the language of the "original" of which everything is a mere copy. Deleuze discusses a denaturalization of the original in his account of *simulacra*,[69] Whitehead in his rejection of the Platonic theory of the World-Soul,[70] and Butler in the refutation of "the *idea* of the natural and original."[71] For all three, the important insight is that the productive process of becoming is a process of re-instantiation of what is not given before or without this repetitive process. For Deleuze, there is no return of the Same but only "repetition in the eternal return [that] is the for-itself of the difference."[72] There is no *resemblance* between idea and instantiation but only instantiations of difference in repetition. Hence, for Butler, there is no "hetero-sexual original" so that the "gay is to the straight not as copy is to the original, but rather, as copy is to copy."[73]

In their deconstruction, categories and fixed differentiations, used to orientate or to exercise power, become fluent (again); they become what Deleuze with Whitehead names conditions of *real* experience and (transcendental) conditions of *novelty*, instead being fixed conditions of all possible experiences and, hence, (transcendental) conditions of the eternal. Most importantly, for Butler, all fixed differences, e.g., the heterosexual difference, are not "natural" (based on an original) as opposed to "cultural" (contingently conditioned) but always are *stabilizing naturalizations* of prescriptive processes of the erasure of becoming by (powers of) being. With this insight, the metanoetics of becoming turns into politically subversive and creative practice. Here, Whitehead's "historic route of occasions" with its inherited "generic character"[74]—naturalized as "substantial form"[75]—and Deleuze's repetitive differentiation become Butler's practice of a "parodic repetition of 'the original.'"[76] The naturalized form is subversively actualized in explicitly actualizing its inheritance as genealogical *performance* of its discontinuity. Where gender is

> the repeated stylization of the body, a set of repeated acts within a highly rigid regulatory frame that congeal over time to produce the appearance of substance, of a natural sort of being[, a] political genealogy of gender ontologies, if it is successful, will deconstruct the substantive appearance of

gender into its constitutive acts and locate and account for those acts within the compulsory frames set by the various forces that police the social appearance of gender.[77]

In order to "expose the contingent acts that create the appearance of a naturalistic necessity,"[78] Butler uses the acts of phallogocentric instantiation of substance and essence subversively against themselves: as performance of parody, masquerade, and drag.[79] Deconstructing substance as patterns of inheritance, as forms of repetitive becoming, is to understand the process of becoming *as* performance and the conscious *performing* of this performative character of becoming as subversive acts of practices of deconstruction.[80] Where "acts, gestures, and desires produce the effect of an internal core or substance," such "acts, gestures, enactments, generally construed, are *performative* in the sense that the essence or identity that they otherwise purport to express are *fabrications* manufactured and sustained."[81] In *"imitating gender,"* e.g., in drag, the imitation (simulacrum, copy of copies) *"implicitly reveals the imitative character of gender itself—as well as its contingency."*[82] Because they are *effects of contingency*, however, they can be actualized in reversing the intention of reifying (i.e., naturalizing) so that they reveal themselves as *"corporeal style,* an "act," as it were, that is both intentional and performative, where *"performative"* suggests a dramatic and contingent constitution of meaning."[83] The *"appearance of substance,"* then, "is precisely *that,* a constructed identity, a performative accomplishment" that allows for subversive dramatization in which gender transformation becomes possible because there is no "substantial ground of identity" but only "arbitrary relation between such acts." Performance implies "the possibility of a failure to repeat, a de-formation, or a parodic repetition that exposes the phantasmatic effect of abiding identity as a politically tenuous construction."[84]

Disintegration (Grand In/humanism 1)

Where Whitehead, Deleuze, and Butler meet in this way, i.e., in pro/found becoming, they perform a powerful critique of humanism.[85] Where Whitehead's "critique of abstractions" like the Same, the Subject, and (personal) Identity, Deleuze's affirmation of "Difference *in itself*"[86] prior to any resemblance of the Same, and Butler's performative deconstruction of (gendered) Identity intersect, instead of privileging human nature, experience, or status (in the cosmos, against nature), they seek the *becoming* of human being.[87] While Heidegger's *Dasein* is the "place" of the *Lichtung* of Being (and nowhere else), while phenomenology is the interpretation of human experiences, while existentialism understands itself as humanism, and while analytic philosophy presupposes the question of epistemology by privileging human existence, the three philosophers—and with them much of process, structuralist, and post-structuralist thought—have gone far beyond.[88] In a way, they reside in a new "open space" as it was de/fined (i.e., de/limited) by Nietzsche's "cry" that God is dead and, in consequence, that *humanitas qua humanitas* is dead.[89] The "cry of the event" seems to echo this dual death and to define a vanishing point for humanism.

Indeed, the post-structuralist's "death of the subject"[90] lingers in the thought of Deleuze and Butler or, as in Whitehead, is its consequence: Foucault's reconstructions of the genealogy of modern subjectivity as social constructs of power;[91] Lyotard's end of modern metadiscourses (or meta-story) that legitimizes the human priority;[92] Althusser's end of history as a process of human subjects[93] or Baudrillard's end of the illusion of "the end" itself as subjective remainder;[94] Derrida's end of a "metaphysics of presence," which always comes as metaphysics of (human) subjectivity, of mastery and control over Being,[95] or Žižek's end of ideology, which creates the subject it controls.[96] And in Derrida's account of Heidegger's letter to Jean Beaufret, "On Humanism," the appeal to humanism—as based on modern subjectivity—leads directly to racism, totalitarianism, Nazism, and fascism.[97]

If we follow the metanoetics of becoming of Butler, Deleuze, and Whitehead, we will find plenty of proof of such a *grand in/humanism*: the disruption of human sovereignty, the social construction of subjectivity, the implicit or explicit criticism of a "metaphysics of presence," the deconstruction of subjective independence, the subjective formation out of logocentric and phallocentric control, and the important political implication of resistance against any kind of totalitarianism. But this "in/humanism" has to be circumscribed carefully as a genealogical critique of the *natural integrity* of the (human) Subject.[98]

In Butler's attack on the natural integrity of the subject, it is the self-erasing process of the "naturalization" of cultural regulations she unravels under the self-perpetuating self-substantiations of the Subject. And it is because of the *performativity* of subjectivity that Butler disregards even that feminist account of political action that "has nevertheless assumed that there is a 'doer' behind the deed"[99] and, thereby, assumes a given (even natural) unity of the category of "woman" for such actions, generating the illusion of a politics that could be based on the abstraction of a unified "representation" of "women."[100] Such feminist accounts would still operate under the presumption of a humanism of the *ego cogito*, the sovereign subject with its independent Reason, which, in Butler's analysis, is just another name for the Phallus/Logos that reigns because of the *exclusion* of the female.

The mechanism, however, by which this disguised *givenness* of Being-a-Subject is implemented, is not easily overturned by the *knowledge* of its performativity and by strategically creating contextual-transformative *actions* that follow from unmasking its cultural contingency. In "following Foucault," Butler understands "power as forming the subject"[101] in such a way that there is never a power-free state or an utopian "'before,' 'outside,' or 'beyond.'"[102] In revising the danger of an "occasional voluntarism" of her "view of performativity"[103] in her early *Gender Trouble*, she later—e.g., in *The Psychic Life of Power*—recognizes even more that the performative power of transformation is not self-styled in ever-new "self-inventions" of gender. On the contrary, it only works through the process of *self-negation*, which is always in danger of not liberating from the oppressive powers of society, but destroying the *very existence* of the society for which the transformation of human subjectivity was introduced in the first place. If the life of the psyche, for Butler, is essentially the *subjection* to the suppressive powers of a society that hides its own contingency of the play of powers behind Reason, Logos, and the Law, then the human subject is always the outcome of this subjection. If it is the power "that first appears as external, pressed upon the subject, pressing the subject into subordination, [that] assumes a psychic form that constitutes the subject's self-identity,"[104] then the subject in its performativity is itself "the effect of subordination."[105]

In *this* dialectic the subject-being is, at the same time, the *condition* of its own subjection to oppressive powers *and* its *effect*, creating the very self-identity from which (through its self-perpetuation) the powers of subjection gain their force.[106] This marks the grand in/humanism, as can be seen in Butler's conversations with Foucault, Lacan, and Žižek. Human subjectivity always is trapped in the paradox of its own existence—namely, to be based on the very powers that oppress it in creating it. Human culture, even in its form of subversive transformation, is only possible as the exclusion of its constituting factors in the hiding of its own becoming and in the perpetuation of its own continuity. There is something that *must be excluded* to allow for human existence—"the Real"—and it haunts and threatens to destroy it at the same time.[107]

Introduction: Negotiating Becoming 21

In surprising ways, Deleuze and Whitehead enter this picture of the inhuman dialectic of power. Deleuze's analysis of a fluent medium of constructive powers that create subjects of human self-identity—but always only in its process of self-destruction—comes very much to the same conclusion. In *Anti-Oedipus*, this inhuman medium appears, e.g., as the *Capital*,[108] as the unproductive fluid of self-production, as the "full body without organs"[109] that, instead of arising with its productive organs/organisms, works in the mode of "inscription"[110] by which that which is produced but is itself "unproductive" is given a productive energy—*from which* the becomings seem to be granted their own *productive origin* of becoming. The "*full* body without organs" is "the Real" that has to be fulfilled and excluded at the same time. It creates and destroys its subjects by subjection and foreclosure.

Whitehead's social view of becoming, on the other hand, is readily predisposed to harbor the same implications. Although his performative view of series of becoming is mostly used to deconstruct "identity" as the substantial continuity of what is really vibrating patterns of repetitive perpetuation, his understanding of societies of occasions of repetition is precisely about the social influence that initiates the becoming of new repetitive events of such societies.[111] As with Butler's internalization of social norms and their rationalizing, regulatory power, which creates the human subjects in their identity, Whitehead's occasions rise out of their *internalized inheritance of social norms*.[112] Human societies then, which do not allow for a performative deconstruction of their modes of inheritance (of instinct and reflex), will create *conforming* (subjected) subjects as their expression.[113]

Even if the performative character of this process of becoming-society is realized, its recognition does not lead to any utopian liberation from social inheritance and repetition of oppressive norms. To the contrary, *because*, for Whitehead, subjects are not *constructive* of their own conditions (as he saw Kant assuming), but are *constructed* by the "objective data" when they "pass into subjective satisfaction,"[114] this leads him to a very disturbing conclusion: subjection—although in its contents arbitrarily inherited—is *necessary*, because "a persistent community of persistent organisms" can only perpetuate and, hence, exist as society over time, through "the environmental influence in the shape of instinct"[115]—the pressure of inheritance. On the other hand, any "major advances in civilization are processes which all but wreck the societies in which they occur."[116] The very process of stabilizing that creates the substantialized human subject allows it to exist and, at the same time, hinders its liberation from subjection because its liberation would destroy its own basis of existence. Where "individual springs of action . . . escape from the obligations of social conformity" the "decay of secure instinctive response" has to be replaced by "various intricate forms of symbolic expression," creating new forms of "imperative . . . conformation."[117]

For Whitehead, too, there is no utopian outside to this trap: *Symbolism* mediates subjection as subject-forming. While the powers of inheritance allow for the perpetuation of a society (identity-formation, stabilization, naturalization), they always fall back on instinctive or reflexive internalizations of these powers, thereby creating human subjects in their substantiated form. To destroy, or to liberate from, these powers of subject-formation means to destroy the "common symbolism" that was "leading to common actions for usual purposes" so that such a "society can only save itself from dissolution by means of a reign of terror."[118]

In consequence, the grand in/humanism of all three thinkers, if it undermines a human ability to act on human identity, does so not by *destruction* but by laying free the *conditions* for reconstruction and political resistance against the inhumane consequences of humanism. The genealogical "method" does not destroy *what is* (the being of the subject), but it deconstructs it in *how* it *comes to be* (the becoming of subjection); it reveals the mechanisms the humanist subject *implies* to generate its being (substantiation) and the powers it exploits to *hide* its own becoming in order to reach and sustain a "perfect" integrity and a "total" integrality. The *disclosure* of becoming in the metanoetics of Butler, Deleuze, and Whitehead *itself* is a reserve for transforming being, subjectivity, and undeconstructed humanism. Their grand in/humanism is not the expression of the waste of human existence *as such* and the proclamation of post-human existence *per se* but the deconstruction of the destructive powers of undeconstructed subjectivity as long as its performative construction remains hidden. Performing its "disintegration," however, sets its mechanisms into the context of their own *contingency*, allowing us to act on its hidden demands for "natural" (necessary) perpetuation.

Transgression (Grand In/humanism 2)

> The fundamental gesture of poststructuralism is to deconstruct every substantial identity, to denounce behind its solid consistency an interplay of symbolic overdetermination—briefly, to dissolve the substantial identity into a network of non-substantial, differential relations.[119]

Following Žižek's account of the post-structuralist deconstruction of the human subject, we must ask whether this "method" is only to apply to cultural, social, and psychological reconstructions of in/humanism or whether it also must be said of its ontological constitution. If, with Butler, there is a mutual determination of both the cultural deconstruction of ontology as the mode of application of in/humanism and of the ontological implications of such a deconstruction *itself*,[120] we will understand that the grand in/humanism also appears as the deconstruction of *human privileges in the chaosmic environment* of which human subjectivity becomes just another expression. Although generally beyond Butler's interest, this environmental reconstruction of subjectivity within a chaosmic milieu is most important to Deleuze and Whitehead. If the Chaosmos, for both, is the (musical) play of (self-)constructing complexities of vibrating patterns that, at a certain point, allow also for human subjectivity to appear, this process of complexification is also the *performative* "ground" of human existence. In other words, the chaosmic dis/harmonies of construction *permeate* human subjectivity *totally* and without reserve. Human subjectivity is in environmental "continuity" with that which—seen from its interior substantiation—seems to be its excluded exterior: "women," "nature," the "perverse," the "other," the "ape," "matter," "stardust." And the reduction of the excluded exterior to "the Other" (of pure form, immaterial soul, social normality, heterosexual difference) is nothing but another form of the mechanism of the excluded "Real" (= grand in/humanism 1).

Alain Badiou's criticism of this post-structuralist (and process) account of the death of the human(ist) subject, however, postulates this move to be extremely unfortunate because it equals the loss of two human abilities that define *humanitas*. First, post-structuralist accounts of the human subject are unable to ascribe *unity* and *identity* to human action, which would allow for decisions to be accurate on a human level. Second, because of missing identity, post-structuralist accounts of the human subject are unable to establish (or regain) an ethical profile because that would presuppose or imply an *agent* of activity, *able* to act. Both inabilities together—so the accusation—are based on another insufficiency: namely, that the categories employed to conceptualize *especially* human subjectivity are merged with a *general* ontology, which then is exactly unable to differentiate human subjects from a general background.[121] In other words, deconstructive in/humanism cannot account for (or, even more, erase) the *uniqueness* of human subjectivity while its recognition is used to undermine it.[122] But isn't this criticism exactly *presupposing* a substantial human subject?

In the chaosmic world of Deleuze and Whitehead, there is neither a pre-stabilized harmony hinting at any human exteriority from (or superiority to) the process of becoming nor any exceptions to its continuous transformation but only "divergent series" of "endlessly tracing bifurcating paths."[123] This "becoming," in their eyes, "does not occur in the imagination, even when the imagination reaches the highest cosmic or dynamic level" of human subjects and societies. "Becomings . . . are neither dreams nor phantasies. They are perfectly real."[124] They are the "stuff" human imagination is made of, and everything else for that matter. But since becoming "produces nothing other than itself,"[125] *everything is in the process of becoming*—"Becoming-Intense, Becoming-Animal, Becoming-Imperceptible."[126] For both, the Chaosmos is the becoming of becomings; it is "a process, and . . . the process is the becoming of actual entities. Thus actual entities are creatures"[127] of their own becoming. Becoming is a matter of "alliance"[128] or "concrescence"—"the production of novel togetherness"[129]—of multiplicities of becomings, which "is the domain of *symbiosis* that brings into play being of totally different scales and kingdoms"[130] to create ever-new and ever-shifting convergences of becomings—no matter *what* we think it is.[131]

In Deleuze, this horizontal transgression of becoming radically amounts to a "non-difference" of domains: of inside and outside, of body and soul, of "I (*Moi*)" and the Other—all speak univocal—with the "one" voice of becoming![132] All becoming is but a transversal, vibrating shift pictured as *"plica ex plica,"*[133] as process of infinite "folding, unfolding, refolding."[134] With "folds" there is the fluency between intensities and extensities, subjects and objects, space and extension,[135] *chronos* and *aion*.[136] The fold creates an inside that is nothing but a folded outside and vice versa—the universe as origami.[137] Hence, Deleuze's fluent concepts between biology (rhizome) and physics (multiplicity),[138] mathematics (manifold)[139] and music (polyphony),[140] concept and event,[141] human cognition and vibrating fields of elementary particles, Mandelbrot[142] and Whitehead.[143] He embraces them all in order to address the *becoming multiplicities* that represent the cut through all levels and areas of division of the Chaosmos.[144]

> Thus packs, multiplicities, continually transform themselves into each other, cross over into each other. Werewolves become vampires when they die. This is not surprising, since becoming and multiplicity are the same thing. A multiplicity is not defined by its elements, nor by a center of unification or comprehension. It is defined by the number of dimensions it

has. . . . Since its variations and dimensions are immanent to it, *it amounts to the same thing to say that each multiplicity is already composed of heterogeneous terms in symbiosis, and that a multiplicity is continually transforming itself into a string of other multiplicities, according to its thresholds and doors.*[145]

From technological to musical and maritime expressions, from mathematical to physical and aesthetical instantiations, multiplicities *are* what becomes,[146] without ever reaching being beyond becoming.[147] In their *mutability of becoming*, multiplicities form a univocity of voices beyond, before, and under any singled-out humanity, which, in its isolation, is just misplaced substance, a substantialized transcendent objectification of its vibrating pattern *as if* it were the transcendent cause of its becoming.[148]

The same *transgression* between subject and object, matter and form, inside and outside, intensity and extensity, time and space, as it appears in Deleuze, is at work in Whitehead.[149] Moreover, as Deleuze notes in his 1987 lecture, this reconstruction of every-thing as expressions of a vibrating Chaosmos of event-relations (prehensions) is precisely what makes Whitehead *"un grand philosophe, un philosophe de génie"* ("a great philosopher, a genius philosopher").[150] Like Deleuze's "fold," Whitehead's concept of "prehension" and the process of the "concrescence of prehensions" name exactly this fluent relation of inside and outside, subject and object, space and time, *in their becoming* because becomings "involve each other by reason of their prehensions of each other" by which they create a "particular fact of togetherness among actual entities [that] is called a 'nexus'" of which all "else is, for our experience, derivative abstraction."[151]

> A prehension reproduces in itself the general characteristics of an actual entity: it is referent to an external world, and in this sense will be said to have a "vector character"; it involves emotion, and purpose, and valuation, and causation.[152]

It is the transversal vector of the *How* of the relatedness of matter and form, efficacious and final causation, physics and mentality, cause and aim, body and soul, individuality and sociality, events and things, human subjectivity and stones, personal identity and the chaosmic environment, inheritance and novelty—all enveloped in a process of mutual transformation into one another. In Deleuze's appropriation, we could say that *prehension* is the *folding activity* of the Chaosmos *itself*.[153] And, as in Deleuze, the prehensive process expresses all elements and categories involved in being *actual* only *univocally*.

"Actual entities"—also termed "actual occasions"—are the final real things of which the world is made up. There is no going behind actual entities to find anything [28] more real. They differ among themselves: God is an actual entity, and so is the most trivial puff of existence in far-off empty space. But, though there are gradations of importance, and diversities of function, yet in the principles which actuality exemplifies all are on the same level. The final facts are, all alike, actual entities; and these actual entities are drops of experience, complex and interdependent.[154]

Indeed, both philosophers deconstruct human subjectivity as *domains* of becoming in a complex process of environments, all following and creating their own rules, thresholds and doorways, in which they differ only *gradually*, but not essentially, *diffusely* (moving into one another) and not definitely (creating independent realms). While they congregate on different levels and in different regions, the nexus/strings of symbiotic/concrescent multiplicities of this chaosmic landscape are in constant transformation into one another. No wonder that for Deleuze and Whitehead the folds of the soul and that of matter do not fall apart in different ontological realms; anti-dualistically, they are not expressions of substantial forms, but of nexuses/series of complex events of congregated multiplicities. They are not independent (either from other individual instantiations or any "other" of it), but only differently arranged. Their difference is not based on a universal sanctification of human *uniqueness* (in the universe)—sanctioned by God or the Absolute Spirit or the Final Aim of the Universe—but only the wonder of infinite permutations of *diversity*.[155]

In their reconstructing of human uniqueness as part and parcel of the chaosmic nexus of societies of events and of chaosmic strings of becoming multiplicities, both Whitehead and Deleuze are neither interested in a dualistic division of human subjectivity from a per se meaningless world (which they both attack) nor in an ethical reduction of human being to stones but in reformulating the *transcendental conditions* of the *becoming* of human subjectivity, identity and agency.[156] Substantiality of identity, endurance of agency, and the independent incurvature of self-reflection—all this *sameness* without difference "with its permanent characteristics is exactly the irrelevant answer to the problem which life presents. That problem is, How can there be originality?"[157] If it is about *novelty*, then the transformative continuity of human subjectivity, identity and agency is not associated with permanence anymore but with *intensity*. If Chaosmos has a "purpose," for Deleuze and Whitehead it lies in "the evocation of intensities. The evocation of societies is purely subsidiary to this absolute end."[158]

In "seeking intensity, and not preservation,"[159] "the answer [that] explains how the soul [i.e., identity and agency] need be no more original than a stone" *reverses* Badiou's accusation: Whitehead's and Deleuze's grand in/humanism is *not* an integration of human agency and identity into a common ontology that results in their disappearance. On the contrary, Whitehead's and Deleuze's *genealogy of becoming-human* is a dissolution of a privileging (logocentric) distinction and a liberation of the becoming of multiplicity from its bondage to humanism with its undisclosed presuppositions of a *common ontology of substantialism*.[160] While this ontology is structured due to its inherent dualism and totalitarianism that leads to the disappearance of human uniqueness in chaosmic diversity, the genealogy of becoming acts upon chaosmically mediated novelty and intensity. This grand in/humanism is about *becoming multiple*,[161] *becoming minor*,[162] and *becoming discoercive* or "persuasive."[163] This is the in/humanism with which Deleuze and Whitehead fight *any form of totalitarianism* implicit in any undeconstructed humanism of (dualistically) distinct, pregiven human unity and causally effective agency.

Finally, their disintegralism is not unrelated to Butler's *performability*. In her account of the "liberating" effect of the performance of sexual difference, she draws on all forms of performed transgression of gender fixation through strategic essentialism, citation, parody, masquerade, and drag in order to release the *discontinuity* and *contingency* of the substantial fixations. In consequence of Whitehead and in line with Deleuze, Butler encourages us to perform "subversive body acts" that not only uncover the "contingent groundlessness" of any substantiations of human subjectivity, pre-given identity, and free-willed agency, but *enact* the "arbitrary relation between such acts"[164] in order to de-form their repetition in a variety of disintegrating ways.

Contingency (of the Law)

At this point, we face a tension inherent in both modes of in/humanism. While Butler is facing the problem of the *trap* of *exclusion* within the phallogocentric law, which has no outside, before, or beyond, Deleuze and Whitehead have to cope with the accusation of utopianism by tapping into resources *not bound* by the *substantializing* Law. Indeed, both sides may draw on different aspects of the process of substantiation because the "normative force of performativity—its power to establish what qualifies as 'being'—works not only through reiteration, but through exclusion as well."[165] They all may agree on the *genealogical* strategy to uncover *the eraser of becoming* in the being of the law, but they disagree on the *status* of a Beyond that is not (just) part of the law. While Butler—in Lacan's and Foucault's lore—tends to understand the Beyond as a *negation* or *lack*, based on the concept of "exclusion";[166] Whitehead and Deleuze—with Derrida—tend to interpret it as an untapped *plenitude* of multiplicity of becoming-otherwise (only hindered by reiteration).

Yet, things are not that easy, and there is a hidden "transgression" between these views: Whitehead and Deleuze know of the mechanisms of "exclusion" of becoming that allows substantialism to prevail; Butler, on the other hand, undermines her Kafkaesque trap with the very "performability" of the Law that cannot totally erase its own becoming (out of which it is generated) but that in its "foreclosure" always draws on the chaotic element of "contingency" that it excludes. We could say it this way: While Butler is more apt to believe in the power of "cosmos" (*logos/law/phallus*) to *create* the *phantasmagoria* of a Beyond, Deleuze and Whitehead believe more in the powers of chaos always to *effectively* undermine the Law and give way to unpreformed novelty.

In light of the metanoetics of becoming to *deregulate* substance/*logos*/phallus *effectively*, the question is, is the law one of exclusion, negation, and lack, out of which it gains its "omnipotent" power to silence its contingency—which it then sells as a dangerous chaos—or is this law itself a contingent variation of (substantialized) harmonies of a chaotic background? And even if the law is the exclusion of its chaotic underside (its becoming, its contingency, its genealogy), is the Beyond its creature or its fate? And "what" is this Beyond anyway? Is it a name for the ever-excluded, the no-thing beyond any symbolism (of language, the text, the process of signification)? *Must* this Beyond, then, *remain* ever-unnamable (ever beyond the text)—as in Derrida's and Irigaray's account of Plato's *khora*[167]—or is it a *resource* for the metanoetics of becoming (disintegrating and transgressing)—as in Kristeva's account the *khora*?[168] And how do Butler, Deleuze, and Whitehead account for this Beyond of the law of symbolization? A basis for addressing this question may be that all three philosophers are engaged in a deregulation of the law by uncovering and acting upon its *radical contingency* underpinned by a hallmark of their "post-structuralism": namely, by the invocation of a *beyond* of structure. Deregulation is *to face* the fear of the Beyond, to *interfere* in the Symbolic with its Beyond, and to *cut lose* its chaotic multiplicity to appear as the law's "real" contingency.

For Butler, this *engagement* in the Beyond is bound to her Foucaultian heritage of the "discursive production of the subject,"[169] on which the process of the subjection under the law is based because it creates subjective/substantive identity in the first place.[170] It is a highly unstable process that can never reach "perfect" identity due to the psychoanalytic conviction she shares with Lacan, that this identity is based on an *exclusion of the unbearable* that, nevertheless, always haunts and "defines" the Symbolic in its perpetuation and its danger to fall apart. In Lacan's words of the Third Lecture of *Les Psychoses*: "What is refused in the symbolic order returns in the real."[171] In the symbolic discourse, there is always an "imperative" at work that "requires and institutes a 'constitutive outside'—the unspeakable, the unviable, the nonnarrativizable that secures and, hence, fails to secure the very border of materiality." Identity is *impossible* because it is "the consequence of a set of exclusions which found the very subject whose identities [that it is] supposed to . . . represent."[172] This Beyond is "the Real," the excluded, the exclusion of that which creates (symbolic) "reality" (of signification) and, at the same time, guards the threshold to the symbolic order.[173] Butler agrees with Lacan and Žižek that "the 'subject' is produced in language through an act of foreclosure (*Verwerfung*). What is refused or repudiated in the formation of the subject continues to determine that subject."[174] She departs from Žižek, however, in her insistence on the *contingency* not only of the "Law of the Father" as a "universal principle"[175] but of the law that guards the *border* between the symbolic Law and the nonsymbolic Real.[176] In her view, it cannot be fixed; it is unstable and can only be accounted for as a Beyond that is *multiplicity*.

> To claim that there is an "outside" to the socially intelligible, and that this "outside" will always be that which negatively defines the social . . . *seems right, but to supply the character and content to a law that secures the border between the "inside" and the "outside" of symbolic intelligibility is to preempt the specific social and historic analysis that is required, to conflate into "one" law the effect of a convergence of many, and to preclude the very possibility of a future rearticulation of that boundary which is the central democratic project that Žižek, Laclau, and Mouffe promote.*[177]

Although Butler believes with Žižek that "the Real" is produced by the law of exclusion—even in its utopian dimension (its "promise")—Žižek symbolizes its *border* with the "Law of the Father" *with* a law that guards "the Real" from being symbolized. Ironically, in Butler's view, this border-guarding "law" represents a *culturally, invariantly universally necessary exclusion* that allows for human societies to rise in the first place—namely, the "threat of castration." It is understood as "producing the 'lack' against which all symbolization occurs. And yes, this very symbolization of the law as the law of castration is not taken as a contingent ideological formulation."[178] In doing so, Žižek builds "the Real" not only on a *male-dominated exclusion* (castration), but on the *silent* exclusion of the female per se (which cannot be castrated and hence is not symbolized), whereby he also installs "the Real" as the basis for a new phallocentric gender hierarchy. In presupposing this border-guarding law to be universally non-negotiable, the "one" law excludes renegotiations and future inclusions.[179] This is the reason that she contests Žižek's repudiation of the post-structuralist account of a more *contingent* engagement of the Beyond.

> Žižek begins his critique of what he calls "poststructuralism" through the invocation of a certain kind of matter; a "rock" or a "kernel" that not only resists symbolization and discourse, but is precisely what poststructuralism, in his account, itself resists and endeavors to "dissolve."[180]

In other words, while Žižek seems to reintroduce the excluded "negation" as a "rock," i.e., as a "substance"[181] of universal persistence, Butler's insight is that a radical *contingency* of the law of the Symbolic can be postulated only as long as there is the possibility of a *multiplicity of fluent exclusions*! If Žižek is right to detect the post-structuralist tendency to "dissolve" any fixed, law-like border between the law and its Beyond, it is precisely *this* "dissolving" view of the Beyond as *multiple folds of transgression* between the Symbolic and the Real that binds Butler to the chaosmic fluency of the Beyond in Deleuze and Whitehead.

Nevertheless, in order to avoid the short circuit of conflating Butler with Deleuze and Whitehead, we have to name another form of the invocation of the Beyond of which Butler is critical: that of the *khora* as it is found in Derrida, Irigaray, and Kristeva. For Irigaray, Plato's (the father of philosophy's) *khora*—although beyond any category, any opposition (of sexes), hierarchy (of gender) and analogue—came to be seen as the "excluded Real," not as (guided by the) law of castration but as "a substitution for and displacement of the feminine."[182] The whole process of thought, then, was based on this exclusion of the *female*; exclusion of the female as the "unspeakable condition" that "can never be figured within the terms of philosophy proper"[183] but remains always haunted by it. For Butler, three augmentations of this claim have to be made. First, Irigaray herself realized that Plato situated the *khora* as a *limit beyond any symbolization*, the pure outside, so that even his commonly used analogues of "mother," "foster-mother," "receptivity" (awaiting fertilization), and (female) "space" (of fertilization)—stereotypes of female identification—must *not* be taken as symbolizations of the *khora* herself. She remains beyond. She is a pure limit of negation, basically lacking any positive symbolization at all.[184] Second, it was Aristotle, and not Plato, as Butler notes, who used "matter" as a principle of embodiment, in a sense that again leads to the exclusion of the female/mater/matter as the passive formless, expecting the fertilizing (male) form. Plato, however, never used "matter" for the *khora* so as to make her the opposite of form/male and, at the same time the irrational "outside" of the *logos*/phallus.[185] That, however, makes *khora*, in Irigaray's and Butler's eyes, "sterile"[186] and unable to account for embodiment at all.[187] Third, Derrida's interpretation of the *khora* as "surname" of *différance* reinforces the two points: that the *khora* is (absolutely) beyond the Symbolic (discourse, the text) as a *limit*, and it cannot be identified with the excluded female.[188]

This is the basis for Butler's criticism of Kristeva's important interpretation of the *khora* as the nonsymbolic "semiotic."[189] Against Lacan, Kristeva knows of a realm of nonsymbolic, breaking through the *fixed* poststructuralist norm of the strict "discursivity" and "textuality" of all "reality" (beyond which there is only silence or the "the Real").[190] Breaking through the norm of a *strict* limit, which can be approached *only* negatively, she understands this semiotic realm as "that original libidinal multiplicity"[191] of the not-yet-united (suppressed) forces of desires and drives of the motherly body that gives birth to humanity.[192] And it *can* be approached by the disintegration of the *poetic* as it breaks into the symbolic realm of (excluding) consistency.[193] For Butler, this amounts to a violation of her three augmentations: a re-symbolization of the semiotic, an essentialism of the identification with the essence of the female, and a stretching of the strictly negative limit to a field of forces.[194] In a Whiteheadian and Deleuzian context, however, it is interesting that Kristeva's *khora* is *not* created by the symbolic law—it has "an ontological status prior to the paternal law"[195]—but conversely, the law is the expression of a lack: the loss of the free-flowing desires and the impossibility of fulfilling the desire to reunite with the primordial motherly body. Because this desire can *never* be fulfilled, it creates the realm of the Symbolic (language, culture, gender) as its substitute. But the "irrepressible heterogeneity of multiple sounds and meanings" that breaks through with the "plurivocity of poetic language"[196] for Kristeva, holds the boundary between the semiotic and the Symbolic *fluent* where "the semiotic disrupts its signifying process through elision, repetition, mere sound, and the multiplication of meaning through indefinitely signifying images and metaphors."[197]

This is a dilemma: On the one hand, Butler does not follow Žižek's fixation of the border between Symbolic and "the Real" because it violates the radical contingency of the law and installs a new law guarding this border,[198] which again cannot be theorized without being "compelled to refuse or cover over that which it seeks to explain."[199] Therefore, it must *fluently be negotiated*! On the other hand, being beyond all Symbolic, "the Real" must remain a strict negative limit of symbolization because any signification would violate its function of constitutive exclusion on which the Symbolic is based. It cannot be understood even as "resistance against symbolization" because that would "institute a permanently unsatisfiable desire for an ever elusive referent."[200] Both interests contradict one another. Kristeva, however, in engaging the Beyond as *khora*, answers this dilemma differently. While she highlights the contingency of the Law and its border to the excluded with *the multiplicity of the semiotic*, she consequently envisions a "space" of negation instead of an absolute limit that, although it is still the excluded, now is a *force field of foreclosed desires*. It seems to be this direction of thought that not only divides Butler from Kristeva, but also unites Kristeva, more than Butler, with Deleuze and Whitehead. However, what divides Butler from both Deleuze and Whitehead is another important thesis: that the negativity of the excluded is to be interpreted as a *lack of fulfilled desire*—and not as a hidden *plenitude of intensities*.[201]

Pure Affirmation (Chaosmic Deregulation 1)

Deleuze's and Whitehead's interpretation of the realm of *khora* not only differs from Butler's account of a normative performativity of becoming—namely "being" as *negation* of becoming through reiteration and exclusion—but also from Kristeva's account in this *one* important point: It is *not* a lack. It is neither a negation nor a lack! Rather, it is the "space" of a *chaosmic multiplicity* that is always in the process of becoming, or better, *is* the *process of becoming*. For both Deleuze and Whitehead, the deregulation of the law has its resource in the unsurpassable, insuppressible, and primordial *immanence of the Chaotic* in the cosmos of order, which it always exceeds, feeds, and reverses *at the same time*. The "mechanisms" that fuse being out of becoming *and* that deregulate being into becoming are *conflicting* as in Butler, Lacan, Žižek, and Kristeva, but it is a *different* co-creative conflict. It is *not* the haunting of the excluded that forces into reiteration (and suspends it at the same time); it is *not* negation that builds identity and destroys it; it is *not* unfulfilled desire that establishes the Symbolic and undermines it at the same time; it is *not* the Law that creates its outside and is endangered by it at the same time. It is this *performability of becoming* itself that in being radically contingent generates the illusion of "substance" by *repetition*—reiterating difference into a resemblance in the Same—*whereby* it performs an *exclusion* of its own contingency. It is through *the same affirmation* of this performative process that becoming sediments into being *and* deteriorates into becoming. The "movement[s] of the negative and of exclusion"[202] are nothing but secondary phenomena to this performativity if they are disclaimed at all.

It is not that Deleuze doesn't know of the "power of negativity" (which he has studied in Hegel), and it is not that Deleuze was not informed of psychoanalytic theories of repression, desire, and lack (as is obvious with his *Anti-Oedipus*);[203] rather, by following Bergson and Nietzsche, he *directly* attacks both of them as life-negating procedures.[204] The power of negation (and negation of negation), for Deleuze, is nothing but a recapitulation of the incurvature of the Same in itself against which he develops his strong instrument of Difference, difference as the *basis* for performative repetition.

> It is always differences which resemble one another, which are analogous, opposed or identical; difference is behind everything, but behind difference there is nothing. Each difference passes through all the others. . . . That is why eternal return . . . relates to a world of differences implicated one in the other, to a complicated, properly chaotic world *without identity*. Joyce presented a *vicus of recirculation* as causing a *chaosmos* to turn; and Nietzsche had already said that chaos and eternal return were not two distinct things but a single and same *affirmation*.[205]

The "space" of passing vibrations through one another, i.e., the consistent planes of immanence that *mediate* such movements, is Deleuze's version of the *khora*—the Platonic sieve through which "consistency" always remains *contingent* and on the move.[206] She is not instantiating any "form"; she is the *field* of "divergent series" of "impersonal and pre-individual singularities,"[207] a *virtual* field of potential actualizations,[208] nothing abstract, rather a sheer *multiplicity of movements* into one another. It is a *plenitude of manifolds* folding, un-folding, de-folding. Nothing is missing, no negativity, no lack of anything, no suppressive and constitutive exclusion, instead—*pure affirmation of manifoldness*.[209]

One of Deleuze's most telling concepts for this process of chaosmic deregulation (as basis, implication, and critique of, as well as counter-activity against, any substantialism) is "the glorious body without organs"[210] he encounters with Nietzsche's Dionysus. Through the many transformations this concept undergoes from *The Logic of Sense* to *A Thousand Plateaus*, the most remarkable in our context is his imaging of the body without organs (BwO) to be *the process of becoming itself* as an active process of transgressive deregulation of being.

> The BwO: it is already under way the moment the body has had enough of organs and wants to slough them off, or loses them. A long procession. The *hypochondriac body*. . . . The *paranoid body*. . . . The *schizo body*. . . . The *masochist body*. . . . Why such a dreary parade of sucked-dry, catatonized, vitrified, sewn-up bodies, when the BwO as also full of gaiety, ecstasy, and dance? . . . Is it really so sad and dangerous to be fed up with seeing with your eyes, breathing with your lungs, swallowing with your mouth, talking with your tongue, thinking with your brain, having an anus and larynx, head and legs? Why not walk on your head, sing with your sinuses, see through your skin, breathe with your belly: the simple Thing, the Entity, the full Body, the stationary Voyage, Anorexia, cutaneous Vision, Yoga, Krishna, Love, Experimentation. Where psychoanalysis says, "Stop, find your self again," we should say instead, "Let's go further still, we haven't found our BwO yet, we haven't sufficiently dismantled our self." Substitute forgetting for anamnesis, experimentation for interpretation. Find your body without organs. Find out how to make it. It's a question of life and death, youth and the old age, sadness and joy. It is where everything is played out.[211]

It is where we become immanent and cut the powers of multiplicity loose, where the chaotic element of connectivity can play out under, against, and in taking away, the substitution of chaosmic plenitude with law, *logos*, and cosmic order that we discover the process of becoming in its most pure and also most dangerous modes. In *affirming* this flow of transgressive immanence, we find fullness and emptiness at the same time: the fullness of the manifold, and the emptiness from any transcendent regulation that imposes an order on this multiplicity by negating its inconsistent diversity and disintegrative mobility.[212] The negation of the law is the anxiety (of losing being); the fixation of the law is the caretaker of security: reiterated is the repetition of the same/subject/substance; excluded is multiplicity in the name of the Same, and difference is muted in the name of identity.[213]

In affirming multiplicity and fluency, however, things are not ordered "in the desire to accommodate negativity,"[214] but they are "affirmed *through* their difference."[215] In refusing "to the spirit of the negative the right to speak in the name of philosophy," a "pluralism lined with multiple affirmation" and a body of "the joy of the diverse"[216] arises. *This* BwO is

Introduction: Negotiating Becoming

not the place of a hidden lack and exclusion of unfulfilled desires; it becomes the *fullness of intensities*.

> A BwO is made in such a way that it can be occupied, populated only by intensities. Only intensities pass and circulate. . . . The BwO is a *field of immanence* of desires, the *plane of consistency* specific to desire (with desire defined as a process of production without reference to any exterior agency, whether it be a lack that hollows it out or a pleasure that fills it).[217]

Instead of unfulfilled desires that feed the structure of lack and create the excluded "Real" as petrification of the very law—the "rock" of "the Real"—that the exclusion tries to justify, it is, indeed, precisely the (dangerous) "dissolution" of the boundary between the law and its excluded multiplicity of directionless desires (feared by Žižek) that makes the boundary fluent (not guided by any law). Deleuze accuses psychoanalysis of such procedures because it "even found new ways to inscribe in desire the negative law of the lack, the external rule of pleasure, and the transcendent ideal of phantasy."[218] The exclusion is that of intensities, in their own unguarded multiplicity, of flowing into one another. Conversely, in the BwO,

> everything is allowed: all that counts is for pleasure to be the flow of desire itself, Immanence, instead of a measure that interrupts it or delivers it to the three phantoms, namely, internal lack, higher transcendence, and apparent exteriority. If pleasure is not the norm of desire, it is not by virtue of a lack that is impossible to fulfill but, on the contrary, by virtue of its positivity, in other words, the plane of consistency it draws in the course of its process.[219]

Yet, *because* for Deleuze (as for Butler) one "can never reach the Body without Organs" because "it is a limit" (*other* than Butler), now it is really a *fluent* limit, not guarded by any "law of lack," and not entrapped in its own negativity (which excluded it from itself). The BwO is and always remains something "you are forever attaining."[220] Here, Deleuze differs from Kristeva's semiotic body, which never can and never should be "attained"—or only attained for the price of "psychosis"[221]—but always has to be substituted by the Symbolic.[222] The multiple desires (of the Mother) have to be sealed forever and can only break into the realm of the paternal law by poetically "destroying or eroding the Symbolic."[223]

If there remains "negativity" in Deleuze—as the phrasing "body *without* organs" suggests—it is more akin to Derrida's account of negativity as *medium* of multiple desires to form freely without the skin of the organizing *logos*. It is a "negativity" that means "richness"[224] and indicates a "multiplicity of sexually marked voices," a "mobile of non-identified sexual marks whose choreography can carry, divide, multiply the body of each 'individual,' whether it is classified as 'man' or 'woman.'"[225] This is the negativity of the BwO: to be *empty* and *therefore* "full" at the same time, but never in the sense of being "fulfilled" ("presented") as in the "metaphysics of presence"—in which we can only find the *full* BwO[226] or the body *with* organs.[227] It is this "negativity" that subverts the symbolic law with the *affirmation of multiplying intensities*. Still, the BwO remains a *limit*; it is dangerous to "fulfill" and its transgressions might deregulate into deteriorating dissolution. It remains the *khora*, the unattainable, the Beyond, but now it also has become the *medium of the fluency of the body*.

Mixtures (Chaosmic Deregulation 2)

There are striking resonances between Deleuze and Whitehead: Whitehead's account of the *khora* as the "medium of intercommunication";[228] his understanding of the process of becoming as flow of "intensities" and "feelings";[229] his trust in *affirmation*—"(positive) prehension"—as the basic expression of this process;[230] his insistence on the multiplicity of events in a chaotic nexus[231] with its shifting formations of laws;[232] his "groundless grounding" of the process on self-creativity as self-affirmation of becomings prior (but not outside) to any binding law of inheritance or repetition.[233]

Like Deleuze's "chaosmos"[234] with its fluent limit of performativity of becoming, Whitehead's "cosmological" account of becoming is based on the *limit* of the "the origin of the present cosmic epoch"—or any cosmic epoch (as the institution of a certain multiplicity of contingent laws)—which "is [to be] traced back to an aboriginal disorder."[235] The chaotic nexus[236] is not bound by any law, but only by contingent mutual prehensions.[237] Cosmic evolution, then, is the process by which complex societies are formed, "informed" by common laws (with mechanisms of external pressure and internal acceptance). Yet there is "no reason, so far as our knowledge is concerned, to conceive the actual world as purely orderly, or as purely chaotic."[238] In Whitehead's point of view, *the process of becoming is a mixture of chaos and law*.

This mixture of Chaosmos is always a "bewildering complexity"[239] of opposing movements. As in Butler, it is guided by processes of contingent performability, creating norms of "being" issuing structured "societies" through *reiteration* (inheritance) and *exclusion* (simplification).[240] In this context, law appears as a "set of dominant societies in certain ordered interconnections" that furthers complexity as harbouring *intensity*, but there is also "an admixture of chaotic occasions which cannot be classified as belonging to any society."[241] These "non-social actual entities," however, while they "constitute" the "element of chaos,"[242] also answer—from the perspective of the Law—*triviality*.

> It follows from this doctrine that the character of an organism depends on that of its environment. But the character of an environment is the sum of the characters of the various societies of actual entities which jointly constitute that environment. . . . Apart from the reiteration gained from its societies, an environment does not provide the massiveness of emphasis capable of dismissing its contrary elements into negative prehensions. Any ideal of depth of satisfaction, arising from the combination of narrowness and width, can only be achieved through adequate order. In proportion to the chaos there is triviality.[243]

Yet for Whitehead, as for Deleuze, the same performability of becoming—*because* it is based on the groundless difference Whitehead names "creativity"[244]—*undermines, reverts, and disintegrates* the law by originating complexity and intensity. In this perspective—namely, that of the chaotic nexus *underpinning* any order as its contingent performability—it is the transgressive movement of "the non-social occasions" to converge into "entirely living nexus" that *constitutes* intensity through originality. Here, as in Deleuze, the chaotic nexus is the high limit expressing the *intense complexity of Life, which is based on originality, disintegration and transgression, rather than repetition, reiteration, and exclusion.*

> The complexity of nature is inexhaustible. So far we have argued that the nature of life is not to be sought by its identification with some society of occasions, which are living in virtue of the defining characteristic of that society. An "entirely living" nexus is, in respect to its life, not social. Each member of the nexus derives the necessities of its being from its prehensions of its complex social environment; by itself the nexus lacks the genetic power which belongs to "societies." But a living nexus, though non-social in virtue of its "life," may support a thread of personal order along some historical route of its members. Such an enduring entity is a "living person." It is not of the essence of life to be a living person. Indeed a living person requires that its immediate environment be a living, non-social nexus.[245]

Flowing freely through the bodies of law, these "outlaw" nexuses further complexity, not triviality (beyond and subversive to any fixed law); however, they also dangerously disintegrate any substantial subjections under the law, which now appear as "simplification in the successive phases of the concrescence."[246] Personal unity, the soul, the unified subject, consciousness, mind, and reason—all appear to be "the outcome of a complex process of massive simplification which is characteristic of higher grades of actual entities,"[247] against which the chaotic nexus "limits . . . such unified control," allowing for "dissociation of personality, multiple personalities in successive alternations, and even multiple personalities in joint possession."[248]

It is this specific approach to the *mixture* of chaos and cosmos that differentiates Whitehead from Butler and Deleuze. Chaosmic deregulation in Whitehead is created by the *paradoxical interplay of intensity and triviality* as played out in the mutually limiting and delimiting moments of the performative process of becoming: complexification as subjection to law *and* complexification as liberating the chaotic nexus in the evolution of Law; simplification as trivialization through the chaotic nexus *and* simplification as highly structured avoidance of the chaotic interplay.

> By this transmission the mental originality of the living occasions receives a character and a depth. In this way originality is both "canalized"—to use Bergson's word—and intensified. Its range is widened within limits. Apart from canalization, depth of originality would spell disaster for the animal body. With it, personal mentality can be evolved, so as to combine its individual originality with the safety of the material organism on which it depends. Thus life turns back into society: it binds originality within bounds, and gains the massiveness due to reiterated character.[249]

While the law, for Whitehead, becomes a necessity for the development of the complexity of the bodily evolution, societies, and cultures, it is, at the same time, the limitation, reiteration, and exclusion of the multiplicity of intensities it harbors and supports. And while the chaotic nexus is the expression of the limit of absolute intensity, without the canalization of repetition, inheritance, reiteration, exclusion, and suppression of its chaotic non-regulative emptiness, it will deteriorate into pure triviality.

This *mixture* is the reason that Whitehead, against Deleuze and with Butler, has a "positive" function for *negation* (although not dialectical) and *lack* (although not of desires), which is situated precisely on the "suture" between becoming and being, the law and the Beyond, event and substance. It is their complication, their mutual disturbance, their paradox.

Negation is important to allow becomings to become *what* they are (the becoming of *something*); they allow for *different* traces of differentiation; they generate structures of inheritance; they account for the *evolution* of life-forms to develop at all. In a "negative prehension," the concrescent occasion of becoming *excludes* what it cannot integrate in order to survive as finite symbiosis.[250] In its definiteness, it is a *lack* of a higher power of integration.[251] While for itself this exclusion instantiates different forms of negation of higher modes of integration—mutual hindrance, aesthetic destruction, anesthesia[252]—the *effect* of such an excluding negation and lack of symbiosis is a *positive* one.[253] It remains haunting the integrity of the event and the nexus in which it is vibrating.[254]

While it is only in the later Butler that the non-presence of a subject to itself is not just based on the *lack* of exclusion but becomes the expression of an *abundance* of performative self-account,[255] for Whitehead the basic drive of higher symbiosis was never negation or lack, but always the *power of intensities* in their multiplicity to attain recognition beyond themselves, i.e., in the *novelty* of a new event of concrescence.[256] The higher such symbiotic concrescence in its *less repressive* "distribution of intensities,"[257] the more unrestricted the ability to withstand the reduction of opposition into simplification.[258] The more heterogeneous the ability to encompass (envelope) difference, opposition, and incoherence, the higher the *intensity* of the process and the more complex the *harmony* of the nexus in which it vibrates.[259] In its most unrestrained assemblage, the event of becoming becomes an event of an "entirely living nexus,"[260] i.e., a "non-social nexus" that "answers to the notion of 'chaos,'"[261] its life being "the capture of intensity."[262] Indeed, it is the *affirmation of becoming multiplicities* that is the whole aesthetic self-justification of the process of becoming itself: *the intensity of immanent self-creativity in nexus of discordant harmonies*.[263]

With Deleuze, then, Whitehead trusts the power of affirmation. Like the BwO, Whitehead's "entirely living nexus" represents the disintegration, transgression, and dangerously intense performance of a nexus of events that is *based* on the *chaotic nexus* (which is the Chaosmos itself) that is primordial to, but always only immanent in, all cosmic orders. In contrast to Deleuze, however, Whitehead allows societies (the reign of the law) also to *harbor* and *protect* chaotic offspring.[264] With Deleuze, Whitehead understands vibrations, i.e., "pulses of emotion,"[265] to be the basic expressions of the affirmation of intensity and harmony. In opposition to Deleuze, he views negation to be an *integral* part of the fabric of vibrations.[266] With Deleuze, although polemically, Whitehead could be understood to entertain negation as a necessary ingredient in the development of the law—the "'affirmation-negation' contrast"[267] as a basis for the performative constitution of any higher forms of subjectivity (as, e.g., for human consciousness) and, hence, for the subjection under the law. But against Deleuze, Whitehead's primary meaning of negation is not lack or exclusion of unbearable intensity for the reiteration of the Same, but "alteration" in becoming, i.e., *affirmation of novelty* in the process.[268] Becoming is a process of decisions taken to *affirm intensifying alternatives* rather than functioning as a reductive simplification of complex diversities.[269]

It has been suggested that there is a high affinity between Whitehead's layout of the process of becoming and Kristeva's semiotic realm of "prepaternal causality."[270] Indeed, it is a "rhythmic presymbolic process," "which cries out for interchange with Whitehead's odd doctrine of 'causal feelings'"[271] both of which are "located" at the pre-symbolic limit herself—the *khora*. And because of the mixture of law and Beyond in Whitehead and his account of his contrast of affirmation and negation, the resemblance might be even more striking than it is for Deleuze.[272] Indeed, Whitehead's *whole* deconstruction of the history of philosophy is to lay free the *exclusion* of the pre-symbolic realm of becoming—which he terms "causal efficacy"—under the guise of the controlling "metaphysics of presence"—he terms "presentational immediacy."[273]

> But we must—to avoid "solipsism of the present moment"—include in direct perception something more than presentational immediacy. For the organic theory, the most primitive perception is "feeling the body as functioning." This is a feeling of the world in the past; it is the inheritance of the world as a complex of feeling; namely, it is the feeling of derived feelings. The later, sophisticated perception is "feeling the contemporary world." Even this presentational immediacy begins with sense-presentation of the contemporary body. The body, however, is only a peculiarly intimate bit of the world. Just as Descartes said, "this body is mine"; so he should have said, "this actual world is mine." My process of "being myself" is my origination from my possession of the world.[274]

Whitehead was on his way to discovering one of the most cherished insights of post-structuralism—that the substantialism of the law is based on *one exclusion*: that of the multiplicity of becoming in its diversity, vibrating divergence, concrescing symbioses, and fluent performability. Here, Whitehead's claim is very much in accordance with Derrida's deconstruction of fulfilled presence (and its inherent logocentrism) and the "traces" of the multiplicity beyond, with Butler's performability and its heavy baggage of reiteration, with Irigaray's primordial exclusion of the female, with

Kristeva's poetic disturbance of the Symbolic by the unregulated drives and desires of the mother, and with Deleuze's BwO in its deregulated transgression. Yet, Whitehead's account of the pre-symbolic realm differs from all of them due to his *specific* account for *the mixture of Chaosmos*.

> The bonds of causal efficacy arise from without us. They disclose the character of the world from which we issue, an inescapable condition round which we shape ourselves. The bonds of presentational immediacy arise from within us, and are subject to intensifications and inhibitions and diversions according as we accept their challenge or reject it.[275]

Whitehead's presentational immediacy resonates with Derrida's "metaphysical presence" regarding the inherent logocentrism: in presentational immediacy, a contingent togetherness of elements is sedimented as necessary law (as fulfilled presence of the *logos*). But while presentational immediacy allows us to discover "necessary" structures of mathematical, logical, or ontological order, they are, in fact, *contingent* forms of projections on the world[276] in order to control the multiplicities of causal efficacy.[277] Paradoxically, however, i.e., according to his *mixture* of the Chaosmos, Whitehead understands the appearance of presentational immediacy as an important *evolutionary accomplishment*, allowing for *freedom* from the bounds of inheritance of causal efficacy,[278] rooted in the process of becoming as the process of *creative self-production* itself.[279] Then, again, the price for higher intensity is also higher simplification, i.e., exclusion of divergent multiplicity.

As with Butler, "causal efficacy" is Whitehead's concept for the performability of becoming insofar as it initiates "being" (by performing reiteration) and overthrows it (deregulation). It expresses the basic relation of prehension as the "conformation"[280] of the (past) world to any new event of togetherness, i.e., to be a transfer of energy that energizes and bounds to reiteration.[281] It is *contingent*, i.e., it has no pre-given, transcendent structure it executes and is, therefore, "incapable of rationalization."[282] But, as a realm of heavy feelings of causality, compulsion, and reiteration, causal efficacy—contrary to Butler and Derrida—*needs* the *deliberate presentations* of presentational immediacy to free its performance from its causal "fate."[283] It is in a paradoxical dialectic of necessity and freedom, in which the law—in its deconstruction—seems to have become a medium for the *deregulation* of reiteration and exclusion.

With Irigaray and Kristeva, the *excluded* causal efficacy is the realm of instincts, desires, and drives that can be approached only when we lose control of presentational immediacy,[284] in which case it appears "insistent, is vague, haunting, unmanageable."[285] But against Kristeva, and with Deleuze, it is not lacking anything; it needs no transcendent rule. It deregulates into the acts of a BwO when we "find ourselves in a buzzing world, amid a democracy of fellow creatures."[286]

The most intriguing element of Whitehead's account of the pre-symbolic, however, that differentiates him from all of these approaches, has not been named yet. His theory of the pre-Symbolic and the Symbolic, as elaborated in his *Symbolism*, postulates neither a *negative limit* against which the Symbolic is the mourning of the excluded semiotic, nor *one* realm of "subversive multiplicity of drives"[287] against which the Symbolic is *another* realm. While the former would be a self-exclusion of the limit as unspeakable Beyond and the latter would imply a problematic dualism of realms with a fluent (overlapping) border "between" them, Whitehead understands *both* causal efficacy and presentational immediacy as *mutually immanent aspects of the pre-Symbolic*—the Symbolic has not been even named yet! And this Symbolic is *not a realm at all*, but nothing other than *the fluent relation between the two pre-symbolic aspects of causal efficacy and presentational immediacy*;[288] Symbolism is the "symbolic reference"[289] of, and the "symbolic transference"[290] between, causal efficacy and presentational immediacy.

> It is the thesis of this work that human symbolism has its origin in the symbolic interplay between two distinct modes of direct perception of the external world. There are, in this way, two sources of information about the external world, closely connected but distinct. These modes do not repeat each other; and there is a real diversity of information. Where one is vague, the other is precise: where one is important, the other is trivial. But the two schemes of presentation have structural elements in common, which identify them as schemes of presentation of the same world. There are however gaps in the determination of the correspondence between the two morphologies. The schemes only partially intersect, and their true fusion is left indeterminate. The symbolic reference leads to a transference of emotion, purpose, and belief, which cannot be justified by an intellectual comparison of the direct information derived from the two schemes and their elements of intersection. The justification, such as it is, must be sought in a pragmatic appeal to the future.[291]

This constellation may allow for a distinctly Whiteheadian niche in the post-structuralist landscape of becoming. Against the presumption that the process of becoming *itself* is pre-symbolic—in its non-regulated forces ("the semiotic")—and becomes symbolic in its regulation-performing sediments ("the law"), for Whitehead, "logocentrism" is not itself the essence of symbolism, but has its "roots" in one mode of "direct recognition"[292] of the world of becoming (presentational immediacy). The process of "normativization"—be it reiteration or exclusion—can never be isolated from the pre-symbolic process; rather the struggle between regulation and deregulation is of its essence. The symbolic, then, is not a "realm," but a *relation*. The Symbolic *is* the ever-fluent border and transfer *between* the aspects of the pre-Symbolic. *It traverses, and is produced by, the pre-symbolic difference.*[293]

> I shall also endeavour to illustrate the doctrine that all human symbolism, however superficial it may seem, is ultimately to be reduced to trains of this fundamental symbolic reference, trains which finally connect percepts in alternative modes of direct recognition.[294]

If, however, the Symbolic arises from a *pro/found difference in the semiotic* and establishes itself *as* transgression, it is nothing we have to *resist* with "the Real" (as Žižek suggests) and nothing we have to *subvert* with the *khora* (as Kristeva suggests)—Butler, rightly, has criticized both approaches!—but, with Deleuze, it is something we have to *attain* in making it *fluent*. It is "in its flux" of the pre-symbolic difference that "a symbol"[295] will open for the multiplicity of intensities, disintegrate the substantiations of the pre-symbolic performance of "conformation," and deregulate the self-erasing projections of the contingency of pre-symbolic "presentations." In affirming a *fluent symbolic body*, the pre-symbolic difference will contingently attain the greatest possible multiplicity of intensities by *infinitely becoming dis/harmonious*. But as in Deleuze, the attainment of this fluent Body of Intensity is *impossible*! Yet, trying is not futile, either! It is the essence of being *in the process of becoming*—a *metanoia*, reverting exclusion and reiteration, deregulating *being*.

Impossible Event?

At this point in negotiating Becoming with Whitehead, Deleuze, and Butler, with all their divergences and occasional coalitions, one element remains to be named that strictly seems to divide Whitehead from the post-structuralist approaches of Butler and Deleuze—Whitehead's invocation of a concept of "God" in the process of becoming. It is, indeed, *the* scandal of his metanoetics of becoming that—in the eyes of many—leaves his philosophy on the *other* side of the Nietzschean divide, the modern side, and positions Deleuze and Butler on this side, the "truly" postmodern, "truly" naturalist, "truly" pluralist side.[296] Isn't it the death of God that initiates the death of the subject? Isn't it the deconstruction of the divine that opens the infinite sea of becoming in the first place? Isn't it the invocation of transcendence that *hinders* true becoming from unfolding?[297] If there is a Beyond, isn't it named already: "the Real," the semiotic, the *khora*? And isn't this Beyond the exclusion on which we build our cultural integrities, instead of being its "savior"?

The relations of our three philosophers to religion, God, and, expressions of the Divine are equally complicated. We could ask to what extent an "exclusion" of Deleuze's Catholic education has influenced his account of *immanence* of which he firmly says that whenever "there is transcendence, vertical Being, imperial State in the sky or on earth, there is religion; and there is Philosophy whenever there is immanence."[298] We know of Butler's complex relationship to her Jewish inheritance[299] with her sympathy to "the particular conviction of postwar Ashkenazi Jews"—mediated through the Shoah "that had destroyed the belief in God"—"that God had died or had himself [*sic*] been annihilated in the course of the twentieth century."[300] Whitehead, on the other hand, always struggled with the "naive trend of Semitic monotheism, Jewish and [Islamic] . . . towards the notion of Law imposed by the fiat of the One God."[301] He was reluctant to accept the idea of a personal God[302] and was horrified by the "concept of a definite personal individual entity"[303] in the heavens and especially by its Christian version.[304] Whitehead's relationship to religion was not naïve; rather, he was disillusioned by the "the horrors produced by bigotry"[305] and often saw religion as "the last refuge of human savagery."[306]

Nevertheless, Whitehead—of all the others—introduced the concept of God in his world of becoming.[307] There are at least three ways to approach this odd fact after all that has been said about becoming, or rather, three questions to be asked: *Where* is the "place" for the Divine in Whitehead's Chaosmos? *How* does Whitehead's notion of God fit into the post-structuralist sensitivities of the Chaosmos? And *why* does Whitehead's "God" not fall under the ban of the Divine in Butler's and Deleuze's account of becoming? I will begin with the last question.

Deleuze exclaims: "*to be done with the judgment of God!*"[308] The context is the exploration of the BwO, out of which to construct a transcendence really is to destroy the immanent multiplicity and to transubstantiate it into a lack of aim that has to be remedied from outside—the great organizer.[309] This God becomes the expression of substantiation *per se*, the "*Omnitudo realitatis*, from which all secondary realities are derived by a process of division."[310] No wonder Deleuze's discussion of Whitehead appears in the context of Leibniz's God of pre-stabilized harmony who "calculates and chooses," thereby instantiating "a negative use of divergence of disjunction—one of exclusion," whereby God *replaces* the "pure event" in which "divergence and disjunction are . . . affirmed as such"[311] by a totality of decisions taken *for* all monads.[312] But the pure event,

> which traverses the divergent as such, this aleatory point which circulates throughout singularities, and emits them as pre-individual and impersonal, does not allow God to subsist. It does not tolerate the subsistence of God as an original individuality, nor the self of a Person, nor the world as an element of the self and as God's product. The divergence of the affirmed series forms a "chaosmos" and no longer a world; the aleatory point which traverses them forms a counter-self, and no longer a self; the disjunction posed as a synthesis exchanges its theological principle for a diabolic principle.[313]

While Deleuze thinks that "Leibniz was unable to grasp, hindered as he was by theological exigencies,"[314] this pure event, surprisingly, Deleuze realizes that Whitehead's God is *not* the transcendent One beyond, suppressing and directing the multiplicity of the world of becoming, taking away its affirmative process of difference and divergence.[315] On the contrary, in Whitehead's "Chaosmos,"

> even God desists from being a Being who compares worlds and chooses the richest compossible. [God] becomes Process, a process that at once affirms incompossibilities and passes through them. The play of the world has changed in a unique way, because now it has become the play that diverges.[316]

Obviously, Whitehead's God is *not* the pinnacle of the monotheistic law, which Butler deconstructs as the final One in which the whole process of exclusions of becoming finds its unchangeable ground and justification. It is in her criticism of *any* kind of transcendent unification (even of the monolithic "'paternal Law' in Lacan, as well as the monological mastery of phallogocentrism in Irigaray") that she thinks they all "bear the mark of a monotheistic singularity that is perhaps less unitary and culturally universal than the guided structuralist assumption"[317] totalizes. It is in this regard that Whitehead aggressively attacks the assumption of any transcendent One beyond the "mutual immanence" of all elements in the Chaosmos,[318] because, for this "monotheism,"

> the nature of God was exempted from all the metaphysical categories which applied to the individual things in this temporal world. The concept of him

was a sublimation from its barbaric origin. He stood in the same relation to the whole World as early Egyptian or Mesopotamian kings stood to their subject populations. . . . In the final metaphysical sublimation, he became the one absolute, omnipotent, omniscient source of all being, for his own existence requiring no relations to anything beyond himself.[319]

Thereby, Whitehead's God does also not fall into the trap of the Law in the form of the "guilt" Butler is subscribing to the invention of the Divine in the form of Benjamin's "divine violence"[320] that intervenes from *beyond* the Law. While for Whitehead, this beyond in his caricature appears as the pure power of the despot. Although this pure power is meant as the shock of guilt from beyond the Law, it is, in fact, nothing but the "purification of guilt." In other words, based on the introduction of God as the isolator of guilt *beyond* the Law, for Butler this Divine act is already an illusionary effect of the Law that "inflicts a suffering that is, through law, attributed to the subject as his or her own responsibility."[321] In the context of Butler's account of Divine violence, Whitehead's classical theistic description of Divine is the sublimation of the Law, of which even the image of the despot is an effect and for which "transcendence" is not a way to escape.

How then does Whitehead's "God" resonate with the post-structuralist presuppositions of multiplicity, divergence, and immanence? In short, God is not the *origin* of the process of becoming—because "process is ultimate"—but is its "primordial, non-temporal accident."[322] God is conceptualized as "creature of creativity"[323] or even as the "primordial superject of creativity."[324] In understanding God as "the 'superject' rather than the 'substance' or the 'subject,'"[325] the process of becoming is not reflected in the One/Subject (*ego cogito ergo sum*) but is the *effect* of the process of becoming; not the pre-given unity of the subject but the "emergent unity of the superject."[326] If God is not vertical Being—"the fixed individuality of an infinite Being (the notorious immutability of God)"[327]—but an *accident* of Becoming, God is also not the expression of the series of reifications and exclusions held to be responsible for the illusion of Being.[328] If, indeed, there is no doer behind the deed, even for the becoming that is God, God should be understood as a *primordial consequence*[329] of the process of prehensive relationality and concrescing symbiosis and, hence, in a sense as *the limit that is pure becoming itself*.

The concept of the *limit of pure becoming*—like that of the "pure event"[330]—would be the *infinitely attained BwO*. In order to fulfil the post-structuralist sensitivities of the metanoetics of becoming, this BwO would be a body of *pure intensity* (its free fluency) and *infinite dis/harmony* (of fluent divergences and convergences). It would be the *limit* of what can never be attained: the body of *pure affirmation*. In fact, this is without a doubt precisely Whitehead's concept of God: being the "absolute standard of such intensity" ("which is neither great nor small") and which, because it is *the* limit of becoming, "arises out of no actual world";[331] being the "Harmonies of harmonies";[332] "tragic Beauty"[333] with all the tensions that arise out of the *absolute affirmation of the whole process of becoming* whereby God is "limited by no actuality which [God] presupposes" but rather is infinitely "devoid of all negative prehensions."[334] In other words, there are no restrictions, exclusions, negations, or suppressions in God by which God instantiates "guilt" as the basis for responsibility.[335] God is the affirmation of (even) "the tragic intensity of feeling"[336] in their divergences, the "understanding of tragedy, and at the same time its preservation."[337] God is *the limit* of the Event of Becoming, the *impossible* Event "in which we understand this incredible fact—that what cannot be, yet is."[338]

Finally, where is the "place" for the Divine in Whitehead's Chaosmos? While it is often assumed that Whitehead introduces God at least "somehow" in restating Leibniz's pre-stabilized harmony—implying negation, exclusion, and reduction to be the activity of God[339]—this is wrong.[340] Conversely, if it is true that for Whitehead "God is the organ of novelty, aiming at intensification,"[341] the *meaning* that is assumed to be "introduced" in the process by God *cannot* be any transcendent law.[342] As for Deleuze, the transcendent law of the vertical Being is but the erection of substantivism "fashion[ing] God in the image of an imperial ruler, . . . in the image of a personification of moral energy, [and] in the image of an ultimate philosophical principle."[343] On the contrary, God must be the *infinite process of intensification itself*.

The limit of pure becoming is not fixed, but is, itself, the process of the becoming (out) of (and for) these intensities.[344] This is the reason that, for Whitehead, the "immanence of God gives reason for the belief that pure chaos is intrinsically impossible."[345] It does *not* mean that God is (preordained) order against chaos, but it means that the limit of the process of becoming is not Chaos *itself* (in its triviality of "non-difference"), but—*as* its limit—is *pure intensity*. "Thus God's purpose in the creative advance is the evocation of intensities. The evocation of societies is purely subsidiary to this absolute end."[346] This is the "foundational process of creativity"— "seeking intensity, and not preservation"—in which God as its primordial accident is indifferent alike to preservation and to novelty. [God] cares not whether an immediate occasion be old or new, so far as concerns derivation from its ancestry. [God's] aim for it is depth of satisfaction as an intermediate step towards the fulfilment of his own being. His tenderness is directed towards each actual occasion, as it arises.[347]

It is this *limit* of intensity by which the process of becoming never reaches Being but instead "is thus passing with a slowness, inconceivable in our measures of time, to new creative conditions, amid which the physical world, as we at present know it, will be represented by a ripple barely to be distinguished from nonentity"[348] In a sense, this limit, although not quite as the Ashkenazi would believe, always can be approached only in its *"vanishing" into immanence*. In one of the most radical formulations, Whitehead states that

> there is nothing in the Universe other than instances of this passage and components of these instances.... Then the word Creativity expresses the notion that each event is a process issuing in novelty. Also if guarded in the phrases Immanent Creativity, or Self-Creativity, it avoids the implication of a transcendent Creator. But the mere word Creativity suggests Creator, so that the whole doctrine acquires an air of paradox, or of pantheism. Still it does convey the origination of novelty.[349]

If, for Deleuze "all BwO's pay homage to Spinoza,"[350] with Whitehead's Body of Pure Becoming, the "substratum of Deistic infinitude"[351] is gone, and Spinoza's "immanence is not immanence to substance" anymore, but "substance and modes are in immanence."[352] Indeed, Whitehead—as does Deleuze—understands his philosophy to be "closely allied to Spinoza's scheme of thought," although his "morphological description is replaced by description of dynamic process" so that "Spinoza's 'modes' now become the sheer actualities"[353] of which "creativity" becomes the ultimate and God its primordial accident. This shift is crucial for the understanding of the "function" of the Divine in Whitehead's Chaosmos:

> In monistic philosophies, Spinoza's or absolute idealism, this ultimate is God, who is also equivalently termed "The Absolute." In such monistic schemes, the ultimate is illegitimately allowed a final, "eminent" reality, beyond that ascribed to any of its accidents. In this general position the philosophy of organism seems to approximate more to some strains of Indian, or Chinese, thought, than to western Asiatic, or European, thought. One side makes process ultimate; the other side makes fact ultimate.[354]

In this *ultimate* Chaosmos "the function of God"—as *limit* of becoming—might be more "analogous to the remorseless working of things in Greek and in Buddhist thought."[355] Nowhere else does this become more obvious than in two texts arguably understood as the philosophical "testaments" of both philosophers: Whitehead's "Immortality" (1941) and Deleuze's "Immanence: A Life" (1995). Here, Deleuze's empty BwO appears as the limit of pure becoming: as the realm of the virtual or of the pure event. Yet, isn't this "pre-reflective impersonal consciousness . . . without a self"—which is the pure "flow of absolute consciousness" that allows for "the passage from one to the other as becoming"[356]—like the primordial aspect of Whitehead's God?[357] And isn't this "absolute immanence"[358] of the pure body of intensities—which "is itself virtual" with all "the events that populate it [as] virtualities"[359]—like the consequent aspect of Whitehead's God?[360] And isn't mutual determination—where "events or singularities give to the plane all their virtuality, just as the plane of immanence gives virtual events their full reality"[361]—like Whitehead's mutual creativity of the multiplicity of events with God's immanence?[362]

In Whitehead's text, "Values" resonate with the "Virtuals" of Deleuze. These Values are situated in a "World of Value" in mutual immanence with the "World of Active Creativity."[363] This virtual "World of Value exhibits" the notion of God *insofar* as the "existence of God is founded in Value" as the "essential [not actual] unification of the Universe"[364]—the actual unifications being the events in their self-creativity. As in Deleuze, they are subjectively unpossessed (without a self), but are situated in an impersonal unconsciousness of God.[365] Within the "totality of the universe,"[366] however, both Worlds are but "abstractions from the Universe." It is a Chaosmos, not tainted by God, but an infinite process of the mutual immanence of "coordinated value" with "the multiplicity of finite acts"[367]—"God" indicating the *limit* of the *most intense dis/harmony of the Chaosmos*.[368] It seems that, while there remains a certain divine trace of immanence in Deleuze, Whitehead's "God" names the impossible event, the limit of pure becoming, that leaves traces in the immanence of the process of becoming . . .

Maybe this book evokes such an impossible event: the togetherness of Whitehead, Deleuze and Butler, the togetherness of negativity and affirmation, of chaos and Law, of difference and process, social construction and metaphysical deconstruction of universality, of humanity and beyond humanism, of suffering and becoming. Maybe the chaosmos is a complexity in which the voices of these three thinkers will be the difference, the multiplicity, and the affirmation of its secret, the secret that has its becoming and in which all becomings are secrets.

PART ONE

Negotiating Events and Multiplicities

CHAPTER 1

Whitehead, Post-Structuralism, and Realism
Keith Robinson

Post-structuralist thinking locates itself in the problems and predicaments of representation. In the critique of concepts like "ground," "presence," and "subject," etc., various post-structuralisms have moved beyond the desire to locate the given in representational structures. This has taken a variety of forms. For the sake of brevity I will suggest there are two main logics or trajectories. The first is governed by what we might call the logic of "transcendence." We can gloss this view in terms of the (later) Heideggerian idea that the event of being is a unique otherness that cannot be captured in philosophical concepts. Philosophy must become a "poetry of thinking" in order to express the other. Derrida develops this "transcendent" trajectory by showing that there is no simple choice between staying within metaphysics or "twisting free" of it. The closed representational structures of metaphysics always already and necessarily are opened up by a transcendence that functions as their condition of possibility and impossibility. They "deconstruct" themselves. This is the aporetic condition of philosophical thought. The critiques of these forms of post-structuralism are well known and range from the claims of "idealism" and "textualism" to accusations that concrete lived experiences are reduced to an abstraction in the "prison house" of language or to a product of "sign systems."[1]

Another trajectory, which operates through what we might call a logic of "immanence"—and therefore arguably avoids the criticisms of the transcendent view—escapes representational structure by positing the event of the given as nothing but itself, as not immanent to anything but itself.[2] In this trajectory, immanent sub-representational, genetic, or genealogical factors are appealed to in order to account for the given. In this line of post-structuralism the real or the other of reason is not sequestered in some inaccessible transcendence but can be expressed through "concepts," "intuitions," "images," or, indeed, perhaps even "Ideas" and "categories," albeit "open," incomplete, or differential categories. In this view, such categories or images tend to be theorized in relation to new conceptions of "matter" in the shape of "incorporeal materialism" or the so-called "materiality of the signifier."

I would suggest, however, that the debates within these two trajectories of post-structuralism can be understood usefully not in terms of idealism or materialism, social constructivism or essentialist realism, but in terms of forms of "non-" or "anti-" realism and types of nonessentialist realism.[3] The transcendent (Heideggerian, Derridean, and Levinasian) trajectory corresponds more with a range of "anti" or "non-realist" positions while the immanent (Nietzschean and Deleuzian) trajectory corresponds more with various forms of nonessentialist "realism." Although Whitehead is rarely thought of as a post-structuralist, he is often described—and describes himself—as a "realist."[4] In this chapter I want to explore three basic problems: first, whether Whitehead can be seen to be working within either of the post-structuralist trajectories outlined above. Second, I want to examine the nature of the "realism" to which Whitehead appeals as well as the idea, stated in *Process and Reality*, that the philosophy of organism might be the transformation of idealism onto a realist basis. Finally, I want to look at the connection, if there is one, between the first two problems. My argument will be that Whitehead can be seen as contributing fruitfully to debates within post-structuralism on the basis of an immanent and realist process ontology. Indeed, "post-structuralism" and the debates that surround it would benefit from being recast in the form of more general questions relating to the redefinition of the concepts of "realism" and "anti-realism," bringing another neglected version of post-structuralism to bear on the main traditions of western philosophical epistemology, metaphysics, and ontology. In the first section below, I will briefly sketch out two lines that emerge from Kant and feed into post-structuralism. In the second section I will try to characterize Whitehead's relation to metaphysics and show why Whitehead is best situated in the "immanent" line of post-structuralism by analyzing his transformation of the concepts of ground, subject, and presence. Given the context of the first two sections, in the final section I will lay out Whitehead's unique form of pluralist or process realism.

Kant: Idea and Concept

The two trajectories of post-structuralism outlined above can be traced back, in their modern form at least, to Kant and can be found together in the Kantian epistemological settlement over the delimitations of metaphysics. Kant famously tried to secure an empirical realism via a transcendental idealism as the only way to make progress in metaphysics. Transcendental critique is precisely a reflection on empiricism's own condition. Empirical realism is real for a cognizing subject and transcendental idealism posits what is presupposed in the subject's point of view. For Kant, this means two things: First, external objects can be perceived and exist independently of us: they are empirically real. However, second, these real objects in space and time are relative to the a priori forms of experience, a set of necessary conditions that must be obtained if experience and the world are to have the character that they do for us. Our experience of the world as empirically real is possible because the conditions are transcendently ideal. Knowledge that transcends the bounds of these conditions is impossible.

Knowledge is thus restricted to cognition and there are two sources of cognition, namely, sensibility and understanding. Corresponding to the faculties of sensibility and understanding are the two types of cognition given by intuitions and concepts. In addition to sensibility with its intuitions and the faculty of understanding with its pure concepts or categories conditioning possible objects of experience, Kant posits the faculty of reason and its "pure Ideas," which *refer* to the totality of experience without themselves *being* objects of experience. If reason is free from the determinations of sense, it also actively incites us to make inferences about the world that transgress the boundaries set by the understanding. This, for Kant, leads knowers into inevitable illusion through mistaking an Idea of reason for an object of understanding, which leads to Kant's famous "paralogisms" and "antinomies." For every conditioned state the understanding supplies the conditions, but the faculty of reason supplies an extended syllogistic inference, which strives for complete explanations and so is led to search for the unconditioned beyond the bounds of sense. For each form of syllogistic relation (categorical, hypothetical, disjunctive), there is a corresponding Idea that represents the unconditioned totality of conditions necessary for any conditioned form. These are the Ideas of Self, World, and God. For Kant, the categories of experience do not apply to these transcendent Ideas. Rather, they are "transcendental illusions" that, although natural and unavoidable, result from illegitimately applying categories to things in themselves.

Kant's response to this predicament is to recognize that the Ideas of reason here are not constitutive but regulative, providing, in the first critique, a heuristic guide to the understanding in the way the focal point of an image in a mirror unifies and directs without causally influencing (in contrast, in the second critique the Ideas play a more important role as a priori principles of practical reason). Thus, on the one hand the original Kantian inspiration in the first critique was a rethinking of the transcendental as a philosophy of immanence. Critique ought only be governed by immanent criteria. On the other hand Kant showed that whenever reason leaves experience behind it is necessarily beset by the illusions of Ideas—transcendent illusions beyond the limits of experience that can be thought as legitimate Ideas but not known. Here Kant was borrowing and transforming Plato's notion of the supersensuous Ideas, as well as purging the Aristotelian "idea" of its empiricity, removing their status as exclusive forms of real being in the first critique (only phenomena can be known) but extending them as transcendent heuristic devices of reason that help shape and guide the work of the understanding. In its "legitimate" use, an "idea in the Kantian sense" is "orientational" with regard to the understanding, imposing unity and necessity upon the totality of experience.

Thus, Kant makes an important distinction in the first critique between the categories of the understanding, which are immanent conditions of cognition, and the Ideas of reason, which are transcendent objects of thought. Depending on whether emphasis is placed on the Idea or the concept, the post-structuralist response to the Kantian legacy can be traced back to this distinction. These two lines from Kant—the line of the understanding and the line of reason—develop into the two main trajectories of post-structuralism: the one more "idealist," transcendent and "deconstructive," the other more "materialist," immanent and "genealogical"; the one operating more as a non- or anti-realism in which the "noumenal" is "otherwise than being," unknowable and inaccessible; the other a "realism" in which the phenomenal-noumenal distinction is abandoned and the real is accessible "all the way down"; the one a going beyond or an "overcoming" of metaphysics; the other a creative reversal into an immanent, or more material "metaphysics." From this very rough and basic outline we can see how these two streams feed into the more prominent contemporary forms of post-structuralism. It is perhaps the later Heidegger's work more than any other that connects the "transcendent" and "anti-realist" strains of post-structuralism out of which we can trace a good deal of Derrida's and Levinas's work, and it is in Nietzsche, Foucault, and Deleuze that we can find a more "immanent," materialist, and realist commitment. I want to suggest that Whitehead's later metaphysics of process is appropriately situated within this latter group, offering an immanent and realist conception of the relation between ideas, concepts, and intuitions.

Post-Structuralism and Metaphysics

As is well known, Heidegger traces metaphysics and the "forgetting" or "oblivion" of Being back to an "originary" Greek moment and the positing of the *eidos* as Being. Just as Kant pointed out the illusory character of the Platonic Idea in the first critique, Heidegger pointed out what he calls the "fictioning essence" of the Idea in Greek thought. He says, "what in Greek would be referred to as Idea—thus created, is originally fictioned." The "Idea" for the Greeks is the fiction of the "supersensuous," the true being that lies above. This is the inauguration of metaphysics as the attempt to offer a ground of being in the forgetting of the question of how the givenness of this ground is possible. For Heidegger, metaphysics, in its interpretation as "Idea" or other metaphysical "names" of beings (*energeia*, *actualitas*, substance, Will, etc.), thinks in the oblivion of Being. Indeed, Heidegger famously argued that even Nietzsche's "reversal of Platonism"—insofar as that amounted to the idea that the "sensuous stands above all"—also remains within the formal structure of metaphysics, i.e., remains within the Platonic fiction in ignorance of its own ground as "fictioning essence." The sensuous is, on this reading, the true being opposed to the fiction of the counterfeit. Instead of fictioning the supersensuous as the "true," Nietzsche fictions the "sensuous" as its replacement. Thus, for Heidegger, Nietzsche is the "last metaphysician." Although Heidegger recognizes Nietzsche's suspicion of the Platonic Idea as ground and the antinomial values anchored by it, this suspicion for Heidegger is all too late.

The logic of Heidegger's claim regarding Nietzsche holds us to an "either/or," or what Deleuze and Guattari call an "exclusive disjunction," a "double pincer" in that we either remain within the structure of the opposition of metaphysics or we break with the structure, "transgress," overcome, "twist free," etc., in order to "follow the movement of showing" and inhabit the realm of the transcendent where the "event" of being is experienced as that which cannot be "said" but only shown. Heidegger's later thought of *Ereignis*, or the event of the ontological difference, attempts to step outside and escape metaphysics yet the double pincer ties us more deeply to the fictionally redemptive and transcendent power of classical metaphysics where we are restored to what Heidegger called "ontotheology" or what Derrida called the "metaphysics of presence."[5]

This seems to be Derrida's own assessment in his deeply ambiguous reading of Heidegger even as he appropriates and develops what he calls the "Heideggerian breakthrough." Derrida's "deconstruction" demonstrates how the play of "undecidables," or "quasi-transcendentals" as he calls them, prevents any simple return to or recuperation of the fiction of some simple presence since we must remain bound to the task of a constant "vigilance," making visible the constant self-undoing of the metaphysical text. These undecidables prevent the restoration of the structure of either/or or any simple immanence by opening it to a quasi-constitutive transcendence. From Plato to Heidegger, Derrida's texts work through and expose the role of these "Ideas in the Kantian sense," or non-concepts ("*pharmakon*," "supplement," etc.) in making the thought of the metaphysical tradition possible while eluding, disrupting, and limiting that thought. For Derrida, we are bound to this aporia of the Idea as a closure without end.

However, there is arguably a deeper thread in Derrida's work that connects him back to Heidegger and the theme of transcendence. This thread comes increasingly into view when the so-called "ethical" and "theological" registers become more prominent in his work. As is well known, Derrida presents the "aporia" as that which precedes and determines the transcendental and the empirical, acting as both their condition of possibility *and* impossibility. In Derrida's later work there is a tendency sometimes to present this aporia as completely transcendent to the empirical, untouched by *any* passage through the sensible. In his work on "messianic structure," for example, there is an appeal to an utterly transcendent future that will absolutely never arrive. Or, in the "structure of the promise," the very condition of experience is a promise that has always already been made in an absolute and immemorial past. In these formulations of the aporia this absolute temporality that precedes any past and exceeds any future appears so irreducible to and detached from the empirical that it risks losing the tension (both/and) that sustains the aporetic structure itself. Whether "meditative thinking" and *Gelassenheit* in Heidegger or the "aporetics of the undecidable" in Derrida, these modes of thought are responses to the transformation of the Idea or being in their thinking and are examples, in my view, of the continuation of the transcendent trajectory in a post-structuralist context.

There are a few post-structuralist thinkers, however, who do not seek the possibilities for a transcendent "overcoming" or "deconstruction" of metaphysics but rather seek to develop the internal conceptual resources of the metaphysical tradition by opening them to their potential for becoming and creativity. These thinkers recognize the extent to which the metaphysical tradition already offers the resources and philosophemes for creatively "making a difference," already offers the potential, indeed, for an immanent transformation of metaphysics. Deleuze, for example, attempts, over and against any transcendent articulation, to offer a fully immanent conception of the Idea expressed through a field of differences. Deleuze's objections to Heidegger in *Difference and Repetition* revolve precisely around the continuing presence of transcendence in the Idea and the subordination of Being—or ontological difference—in relation to the identity of representation.[6] For Deleuze, as soon as there is transcendence, we divide being, and the real is taken from us. Deleuze is insistent, however, that virtual differences and becomings are fully real only as a function of immanence. As Deleuze says in *Difference and Repetition*, "difference is the noumenon closest to the phenomenon."[7] It is not the given but that by which the given is given. And for Deleuze we have the conceptual means to reach into the noumenal, to the sub-representative, and all the way to the Idea. Thus, Deleuze replaces the representational ground of metaphysical realism with what we might call the groundless ground of "ontological constructivism" or, as Deleuze calls his own work, "transcendental empiricism." Here an "internalist"[8] and genetic account (difference is only internal difference, the real is differentiated internally from itself: virtual/actual) of ideal or "virtual" conditions (*"real without being actual, ideal without being abstract"*[9]) is fused with the actualities of the real: Constructivism is realism and the real is constructed.

Whitehead's thought is important here since, like Deleuze, he is not interested in the idea of a "going beyond" or the contortions involved in remaining within the determinate oscillations of the aporetics of "undecidability." Whitehead's relation to the metaphysical tradition is often thought to lie in his famous yet rather sober view of the history of philosophy as a series of footnotes to Plato. However, this needs to be placed alongside Whitehead's other, lesser-known, but more interesting conception of the history of philosophy as a series of "depositions" in need of imaginative "coordination"[10] or experimentation to generate new alternatives. The history of philosophy in this view could be construed as a series of emplacements within a territory or deposits within stratified or embedded layers. The philosophical task would then be to loosen the sediment, disturb it and transform it, re-awaken another formerly imperceptible layer within it, or, in the idiom of Deleuze and Guattari, we might say the task is to activate a movement of "deterritorialization," create "lines of flight," and so on. In my view this is precisely what Whitehead is doing when he argues that the depositions of the great philosophers "must be construed with limitations, adaptations, and inversions, *either unknown to them, or even explicitly repudiated by them.*"[11] Thus, the Whiteheadian reading operates in the critically challenging and often creatively destructive space of alternatives left unsaid by the author, pursuing their repudiations and adaptions and fictioning them for new ends and problems. This is close to the rationale of some of Heidegger's better readings of great philosophers in the tradition. For example, in his interpretation of Kant, Heidegger's thought pursues a "retrieval" where, if one merely gives back what the author says, then one does not arrive at a more fundamental "laying-out" (*Auslegung*) of what the author was "unable to say" but "had wanted to say," and remains "unsaid in and through what has been said." Equally, Deleuze's own interpretation of Kant was based around a working back to that which an author "does not say in what he says, in order to extract something that still belongs to him, though you can also turn it against him."[12]

Whitehead's own readings of the "unsaid" in the history of philosophy—and as we will see in his reading of Kant—endorse this idea of a rich, critical, and yet creative transformation of the metaphysical tradition in order to invent from the concepts deposited there a kind of "*becoming*" of thought. This becoming or "untimeliness" of thought for Whitehead, as for Deleuze, could be said to operate according to a certain "doubling" and "falsifying," requiring a "redesign" and "dramatization" of the concept, a "method" for expressing the novelty and concrete "essence" or "multiplicity" of the Idea in the actual. This style pervades Whitehead's readings of individual philosophers and the broader sweep of his understanding of the history of philosophy, especially its moments of transformation. Whitehead's own use of individual philosophers in the history of philosophy, like Deleuze's, is dynamic and dramatic, restaging concepts in relation to contemporary problems and releasing them for new becomings. When Whitehead says "a new idea introduces an alternative; and we are not less indebted to a thinker when we adopt the alternative he discarded,"[13] we think he distinguishes the history and representation of a concept from its "virtual" potential for becoming and creation. Whitehead's readings of the metaphysical tradition, like Deleuze's, operate on the basis of creating alternative becomings and relinkings in thought, releasing completely new concepts and new readings of existing concepts from the history of philosophy. Like Deleuze, Whitehead's way of escaping the history of philosophy was by creating from it, pushing thinkers toward new becomings and "immortalizing" their concepts in new ways.

In other words, for Whitehead, the end of metaphysics is, as Deleuze and Guattari say, "pointless, idle chatter" just as positing a distinction between the "end" and the *closure* of metaphysics is unnecessary. Indeed, I want to argue that Whitehead might be considered a "post-structuralist" philosopher in the mold of Deleuze working out of an immanent tradition of metaphysics. One way to understand this is by looking in more detail at the way in which Whitehead creatively transforms the Kantian legacy (as Deleuze does also). This is a somewhat unusual claim in the context of the dominant Anglo-American reception of Whitehead's work, especially if one considers his own well-known references to pre-Kantian modes of philosophy. However, as I have argued elsewhere,[14] the key context for understanding the development of Whitehead is to refuse to read Whitehead as simply a pre-Kantian metaphysical realist. If Whitehead is read as exclusively pre-Kantian, then he is an anachronism (and the Anglo-American philosophical tradition's treatment of Whitehead is vindicated). Rather, Whitehead's pre-Kantianism plays much the same role in his thought as it does in Deleuze: a way of approaching and confronting the aporias of Kantianism as preparation for the laying out of an essentially post-Kantian philosophy of creativity and becoming. Whitehead is a deeply post-Kantian philosopher in much the same way that Deleuze is post-Kantian. We could say, crudely, that Whitehead's ontology is a fusion of pre-Kantian metaphysics with post-Kantian "constructivism." The concept that Whitehead returns to again and again to articulate this fusion, or transformed relation to the tradition, is "*inversion*": Whitehead inverts the pre-Kantians toward a principle of constructive or synthetic activity just as he inverts Kant's epistemic conditions toward a principle of ontological conditioning. Thus, although Whitehead's constructivism is dependent in part upon a Kantian principle of synthetic activity, his "pre-Kantianism" nevertheless steps over any mere anthropological or cognitive constitution toward a transcendental principle of ontological constitution.

Such a reading becomes more plausible when we consider the self-conscious way in which Whitehead rethinks metaphysics by universalizing notions of act, process, and product as the event of being itself, just as one might say that Heidegger universalizes the "it" that gives being and time in the event of Appropriation (*es gibt*), that Derrida universalizes the aporia of time, or that Deleuze generalizes difference as repetition. In Whitehead, fixed representational structures or general concepts are abandoned in favor of "imaginative generalizations" of the real as self-actualizing, as producing itself incompletely through the realization of its own processes. Thus, as we will see below, the concepts of "ground," "subject," "presence," etc., and the relations between them, are completely redefined in accordance with Whitehead's "temporalizing" analysis of the condition of actual occasions.

For example, the concept of ground in Whitehead cannot be understood as in a relationship of reference, resemblance, causality, or representation to what it grounds. Rather, the real is grounded by nothing other than the immanent becoming of novel, actual occasions internally constituting their own temporalized order and nature. Like Heidegger, Derrida, and Deleuze, Whitehead self-consciously attempts to rethink the concept of ground in the context of the question of ontology or being. The real is "groundless," or the real is self-grounding—both can be taken here as equivalent expressions for Whitehead. Thus, for Whitehead, there is no "being" that grounds beings: There is only the process and becoming of being. The question of the "ground" in Whitehead changes according to the movement and development of Whitehead's metaphysical texts but there are significant continuities in the way in which the question of ground appears. In the development of Whitehead's thought, the emphasis in groundless actualization is increasingly towards the individualized, atomic, or epochal nature of actualization. This is not an individualized being but the individualization or atomicity of existence as a condition for anything to be at all.

The thought of ground in Whitehead is thus bound up with the problem of the condition and unity of being, a structure whose unity is given in *Process and Reality* as what might be termed the differentiated teleology of actual occasions. Rather than any Aristotelian primary substance, unity in later Whitehead is given by a groundless process of actualization, each time unique and unrepeatable. In the seriality of this process, each successor occasion is related to its antecedent occasions as a stage or phase, each grounded, conditioned, and unified in part by the other. This process continues, as Whitehead says, to "the crack of doom." Whitehead expresses this idea of unitary relatedness in the form of a principle: "that the potentiality for being an element in a real concrescence of many entities into one actuality is the one general metaphysical character attaching to all entities actual and non-actual; . . . In other words it belongs to the nature of a 'being' that it is a potential for every 'becoming.' This is the 'principle of relativity.'"[15]

The question of the ground of being as becoming is articulated in Whitehead through the problem of relational unity and can be redescribed as the issue and problem of "subjectivity." It is well known that for modern philosophy the concept of the subject functions as a ground and unifying principle of knowledge, the "subjectivist principle" or "bias" as Whitehead calls it. This is the view that conscious experience is the ground or foundational "substance" of experience. In Descartes, for example, the subject is the unifying ground within the world whereas for Kant the subject is transcendentally ideal—the very logic that gives a world to a subject and makes experience possible. However, for Whitehead, the subject no longer can function metaphysically as a *hypokeimenon*, an underlying permanent foundation or fixed substance as in the modern Cartesian and Kantian traditions. With the subject of consciousness as foundation, the datum in the act of experience can be described purely by reference to universals and all the standard epistemological problems return (e.g., problems of skepticism and how a subject can step outside of its "point of view" or conceptual scheme to validate its view of the object). For Whitehead, one finds this set of problems in the Cartesian subject that represents a world and in the Kantian subject that gives the conditions for the possibility of representing a world. If Descartes' subjectivism requires balancing with an objectivism, so Kant's subjectivism needs transforming because his "transcendental unity of apperception" that accompanies representations secures only an "apparent" objectivity since it is based on a "datum" of disconnected sense impressions given shape by conceptual form.

Whitehead wants to retain the "subjective bias" of Descartes but with an "objective" element elaborated in terms of "conditions." However, these are not Kantian conditions of cognitive representation as such but conditions for the immanent actualization of the world. As Whitehead says, without the experiences of subjects there would be "nothing, nothing, nothing, bare nothingness."[16] Thus, if there is something of a critique and "deconstruction" of the subject in Whitehead, there is also a "construction" or a "reformation." The "reformed subjectivist principle" operates as an extension or "enlargement" of subjectivity and functions as the condition of all actualization. Equally, we could say as Whitehead does that his notion of subject is an "inversion" of Kant's subject. Whitehead says, "for Kant the process whereby there is experience is a process from subjectivity to apparent objectivity. The philosophy of organism inverts this analysis, and explains the process as proceeding from objectivity to subjectivity."[17] Thus, we could say that the subject in Whitehead is actualized from experience and is a generalization of the conditions of cognition in Kant or an "ontologizing" of the Kantian epistemological subject. Whitehead's reformed subject does not prescribe the structures of the world in advance as in Kant since the determinability of such structures involves novel synthesis.

Kantian determination does occur famously through synthesis also and one could argue that the character of experience for Kant *and* Whitehead takes the form of "judgment" (in Whitehead's case the "decisions" made regarding "data" in the concrescence) but in each case the mode of determinability is different. For Kant, the synthesis of judgment is the bringing together of terms of assertion in the structure of propositional or cognitive knowing. In Whitehead, however, synthesis comes before any cognitive judgment and is defined and constructed as part of the complex process of the serial actualization of things ("concrescence") just as in Deleuze the "dramas" of individuation come before any *logos*. For Whitehead, the synthesis that assembles perceptions into an objective world isn't an "ideal" or purely logical formal power, a mental or subjective form that makes representation of the world possible. Rather, space and time for Whitehead are assembled and actualized within the process of self-realization. Actualization here is a synthetic activity that involves the realization of its own spatio-temporal extensiveness. One perhaps could make a case here for Whitehead's subject as simply a prehensive relatedness before *logos* or judgment in the Kantian sense, perhaps close to what Heidegger called a "saying-gathering" as disclosure of the world, but Whitehead's subject of actualization gives the conditions of disclosure and "judgment" as a serial relatedness.

Thus, the nature of this "relatedness" is non-conceptual and non-cognitive. Space and time relate to their object "aesthetically," immanently, and creatively. The subject in Whitehead could then be seen as a "prehensive" relatedness, a bare relatedness towards and away from the world, a basic way of appropriating the world, of being involved with it, before any actualized "presence." Representation and spatialization follow only with *logos*. Prior to any immediately present or objective presence that can then be represented, for Whitehead there is a more "originary" condition of relatedness, of disclosive "feeling," of something passing on, and this moment of presencing is tied to the world as "lived" but not as a separate thing or object over and above a subject, but as a pure relatedness, grasping, or taking in. This more primordial "receptivity," sympathy or capacity to be affected is guided by what Whitehead call the "subjective form" of feelings, the way they are felt or how they affect the subject. Thus, redefining the form/matter, concept/intuition couples after Kant is something that Whitehead, like Deleuze and Heidegger, attempts to do by focusing on the implicit "aesthetic" genesis, order, and organization of experience, with experience here understood as enlarged and not simply equivalent to human experience.

Thus, the various traditional names for causal and productive metaphysical structures—like "ground" or "subject"—that refer away from themselves to some fixed point and that function as the "ontotheological" reduction of Being to beings in the Heideggerian critique or the Derridean deconstruction of "logocentrism" are abandoned or reworked in Whitehead's texts as immanent components of the real, elements of the "one genus" that differentiates itself. This whole operation takes place under an "inverted" and revised "transcendental aesthetics" or a "critique of pure feeling." However, at the core of the post-structuralist critique of Western philosophy lies the deep suspicion of the metaphysical organization of time as "presence." Indeed, Whitehead's critiques of "bifurcation" and the exposure of various "fallacies" (of "misplaced concreteness," "simple location," "the static fallacy," etc.) place just as much importance on the critique of time as presence as any found in Heidegger or Derrida, but without a need for the concept of the "end" or what Derrida has called the "closure" of metaphysics. For example, Whitehead's opposition to some systems of thought is based on their dependence upon what he calls a "vacuous actuality" premised on an unchanging subject of change. Vacuous actuality is the notion of a "thing" simply present yet devoid of subjective immediacy and bound to the idea of a substance within which qualities inhere.

These notions are correlated with what Whitehead calls perception in the form of "presentational immediacy," where what is immediately present to the senses—a patch of red, for example,—presents itself in its immediacy and clarity but silently and without any indication in itself of its relatedness or significance to the past or future. In *Science and the Modern*

World, Whitehead finds the seeds of this critique of metaphysical presence in Berkeley's analysis of "simple location." For Whitehead, "this idea [of simple location] is the very foundation of the seventeenth century scheme of nature"[18] at which Berkeley had already begun chipping away. In the "seventeenth century scheme," materialism construes nature as made from indivisible atomic units or particles of matter that are simply located in relation to each other. On this view, matter is expressed in spatio-temporal relations existing at a definite finite region of space and a definite finite duration of time, excluding any reference of those relations to other regions of space and other durations of time. For Whitehead, the idea of bits of matter as externally related to each other in an instant of time and space is not false but an abstraction from a much more complex set of interrelated events. For Whitehead, the "Berkeleyan Dilemma," as he puts it, is that "perceptions are in the mind and universal nature is out of mind."[19] As we have seen, Whitehead repudiates such notions with his concepts of "causal efficacy" and "prehension" and the appeal to a primary relatedness or "feeling."

Like Heidegger and Derrida, Whitehead also traces these criticisms of presence back to Greek metaphysics. Aristotle's "primary substance" is for Whitehead a classic example of a metaphysical presence that functions as a fixed foundation or substratum underlying experience. In this, Aristotle merely carried over the "subject-predicate" prejudice from language into his logic and his metaphysics. In *Process and Reality*, Whitehead says that the admission of an idea of "permanent stuff" that only undergoes change in respect to its qualities and accidents but remains self-identical has "wrecked the various systems of pluralistic realism."[20] I would like to suggest that Whitehead's critiques of the metaphysical tradition and the pursuit of an immanent post-structuralist trajectory out of Kant aims at salvaging, reinstating, and developing a new form of "pluralist realism" that, from the Greeks to Kant, has been "wrecked."

Realism

That Whitehead's post-structuralism might involve a commitment to a realist metaphysics is surprising since post-structuralisms typically have been aligned with a range of anti-realisms because of their perceived critique of so-called "common-sense" or "naïve" forms of realism and "correspondence" models of truth that, it is claimed, offer unmediated access to the real. The "bifurcation" of the real has been carried through into the reception of post-structuralism. Concomitantly, the predominant Anglo-American reception of post-structuralist thinkers typically associates them with social constructionist positions opposed to forms of realism. This "straw man" has tended to occlude the extent to which some post-structuralist thinkers have developed more complex realisms. As I have suggested, Deleuze's thought could be described on a realist basis,[21] but he rarely describes his work in this way, although when Deleuze describes his work as a "pluralism" and an "empiricism," it is Whitehead that he invokes.

Whitehead, however, as we have seen, fully embraces the description of his work as realist but in so doing he rethinks the nature of realism in accordance with his constructivist ontology of process. Whitehead retains the realist commitment to existence not of "things" but processes, with actual occasions as the basic, most "real" condition of process. In Whitehead's transformed realism, rather than "things" having an "essence" given by their nature, we can say that the "essence" of process is "objectively" given in nature but that essence is "creativity"—the creation of the new—and so the real is incomplete and radically unfinished. Thus, existence is a matter of the activity of being, an ongoing actualization of creative process. In addition, Whitehead retains a qualified commitment to the realist idea of "independence." For example, in *Process and Reality*, Whitehead claims that his own categories should be viewed as real, independent of our capacity for knowledge. However, there is no brute "given" or set of empirical contents that await categorical form since the categories organize the real as a matter of the conditions of self-actualization. As we have argued earlier, such categories are not conditions of cognition and do not act as a causal "ground" for an independent set of entities. Rather, the categories are fully immanent to what they condition. Thus, the standard realist claim that the world exists independently of mind has no real purchase in Whitehead since his analysis is explicitly based on a redescription of epistemological distinctions like "man and world," "scheme and content," the "given and interpreted" in terms of conditions of actualization. His own analysis is self-referential in the sense that his own categories and their construction exemplify the generalized account of constructive actualization.[22] Briefly contrasting Whitehead's post-structuralist version of realism with Kant's transcendental idealism / empirical realism will enable us to show how Whitehead transforms idealism onto a realist basis.

We can gloss Kant's transcendental idealism in terms of at least three basic components. First, there is the distinction between things as they are in themselves and the appearance of things. Second, there is the notion that we do not and cannot have knowledge of things as they are in themselves. Third, there is the idea that the appearance of things is to some extent and in some sense "mind-dependent." Whitehead does not accept the first component but, as we have seen, offers a transformed version of the other two. Transcendental idealism is unlike traditional idealism in that it implies the subjectivity of space and time as forms of intuition without denying the real existence of objects distinct from ourselves as represented in space and time. Thus, the objective of the transcendental idealism-empirical realism combination is to both deflect skepticism over empirical realism (this is the requirement of transcendental idealism) and show that objects exist independently (empirical realism). Arguably, the Kantian position here in attempting to reconcile a range of inherited tensions merely deepens the bifurcation of the real and contains the seeds from which various modern versions of *both* realism and anti-realism will grow. Kant's position avoids "direct" or "metaphysical realism" and simple or traditional idealism but attempts to combine at another level variants of both realism (objects exist in space and time) and anti-realism (objects in space and time are mind-dependent) that leaves bifurcation open.

In contrast, Whitehead's position retains transcendentalism but fuses it with a philosophy of being or existence. This enables Whitehead to circumvent bifurcation by serializing occasions as the actualization of the real. Ideality and reality are not fundamentally opposed but are phases within the process of construction. The claim that knowledge is ideal, "situated," or mind-dependent is reconciled here with the claim that knowledge is defined in terms of objects distinct from the subject. Thus, for Whitehead, empirical realism can only be legitimated on the basis of what we might call a pluralist or "process realism" of self-constructing actualizations. Actuality is the process of self-realization and its conditions are real independently of our ability to know. Like Kant, Whitehead's realism clearly cannot be a traditional metaphysical realism and, like Kant, Whitehead is concerned with the nature of "critical" access to the real rather than any presuppositional or merely metaphysical access.

What Whitehead calls his "critique of pure feeling" is constructed around a reworking of the "transcendental aesthetics" section of Kant's first critique—what Whitehead, in relation to Kant, famously called a "distorted fragment of what should have been his main topic."[23] Whitehead's critique follows the Kantian idea that space and time are self-constructing conditions but, rather than talking of "pure intuitions" that "introduce an order for chaotic data,"[24] Whitehead elaborates the idea that actual occasions are "structures" that require both "pure" potential and the actual world. Here Whitehead develops his notion of the "extensive continuum" as that formative, relational, and indeterminate element that connects that which is experienced with that which experiences. Actual entities are said to "atomize" the continuum and in this process of atomization they actualize the potential of the continuum via a process of "temporalization."[25] Thus, actual entities are extended but their extensiveness is a self-actualizing condition of their own becoming, luring out potentials in their process of actualization. This whole schema of temporalization resembles and replaces the work attributed by Kant to the forms of intuition but it is no longer exclusively "pure" since it is also "derived from the actual world *qua datum*."[26] Thus, space and time are immanent conditions of their own realization and so, in this sense, are Kantian "constructs," but their realization is simultaneous with the realization of actual occasions.

Whitehead, then, replaces any appeal to realist "essences," universals, or Kantian a priori structures with an account of form as processual conditions of temporalization by positing an indeterminate abstract space-time (extensive continuum) that submits its elements to creative actualization. This abstract yet real space forms an "intrinsic genesis" (to use Deleuze's words) of actuality, a genetic production or construction of the real. In challenging and transforming the various "doubles" of modern philosophy (dualism-materialism, idealism-realism, transcendental-empirical), Whitehead renews metaphysics by developing an immanent post-structuralism in the context of pluralist realism.

CHAPTER 2

Nomad Thought: Deleuze, Whitehead, and the Adventure of Thinking

Jeff Bell

A central concern of Deleuze's thought was to enable the "insertion of art into everyday life," and this "aesthetic problem," as Deleuze calls it, has become more pressing "the more our daily life appears standardized, stereotyped and subject to an accelerated reproduction of objects of consumption."[1] As a philosopher Deleuze pursued a philosophical trajectory that subsequently sought to undermine these standardized, stereotypical models and codes by making of philosophical thinking a creative thinking. "To think is to create," Deleuze argues, "but to create is first of all to engender 'thinking' in thought."[2] This creative thinking, this "thinking" in thought, Deleuze will refer to as "nomad thought," and this thinking "lies beyond all codes of past, present, and future, [and it seeks] to transmit something that does not and will not allow itself to be codified."[3] It is through his efforts to make of philosophical thought a nomadic thinking that Deleuze sought to resolve the aesthetic problem and instill art and creativity into everyday life. Moreover, with the emphasis upon creativity in Deleuze's thought it is not surprising to find that the philosophy of Whitehead would interest Deleuze. Deleuze, in fact, will assert that Whitehead's *Process and Reality* "is one of the greatest books of modern philosophy."[4] For Whitehead, as well, the aesthetic problem takes the form of an absence of adventure, such that when one is "without adventure," Whitehead argues, then "civilization is in full decay."[5] Whether this threat to civilization comes from a routinization of thinking enforced by a "learned orthodoxy"[6] or the "prolongation of outworn forms of life,"[7] Whitehead is similarly concerned with injecting adventure into everyday life.

Of course, Deleuze and Whitehead are not the only two philosophers to be concerned with a lack of creativity in thought and culture—with what we will call the problem of cultural creativity. Nietzsche, Heidegger, Oswald Spengler, and Allan Bloom, among many others, have voiced similar concerns.[8] The affinity between Deleuze and Whitehead, however, is, as will be argued, much more profound and can be traced right to the central concepts each develops and uses in his efforts to address the problem of cultural creativity. In particular, both Deleuze and Whitehead break ranks with longstanding philosophical tradition by calling for a thought (a nomadic thought) that seeks not to begin and end with facts—whether these be empirical facts or Platonic Ideas—but rather they seek a thought that is discordant to facts, a thought that eludes easy categorization and capture. Deleuze and Whitehead, in other words, are each centrally concerned with unleashing nomadism within thought.

To understand Deleuze's efforts to develop a nomadic thought, a few key concepts need to be clarified. First, and most importantly, is the concept of immanence. This is perhaps the most important concept in all of Deleuze's work. Throughout his published writings, a philosophy of immanence is repeatedly contrasted with the philosophies of transcendence, and the philosophers Deleuze frequently returns to—Duns Scotus, Spinoza, Nietzsche, Leibniz, Bergson, and Hume—offer, as Deleuze understands them, important contributions to the philosophy of immanence. So what are these contributions and what is the philosophy of immanence? Put simply, a philosophy of immanence is an attempt to understand the emergence of identities, whether social, political, individual, ontological, or other, in a manner that does not entail a condition that transcends the conditioned. Plato, for example, would offer an explanation where the condition—the Form or Idea—does indeed transcend the conditioned. The Form (*eidos*) of justice is separate from and is a truth that transcends each and every institution of justice that might emerge and approximate this Form. A philosophy of immanence, by contrast, will speak of the condition as being in the conditioned.

A consequence of this understanding of immanence is the equality of being, or the nonhierarchical nature of reality. Deleuze is clear on this point: "From the viewpoint of immanence the distinction of essence does not exclude, but rather implies, an equality of being: it is the same being that remains in itself in the cause and in which the effect remains as in another thing."[9] In other words, unlike Plato's Forms, where the Form is the condition beyond (transcending) the conditioned, and operates as the superior model or code that the conditioned can only approximate, an immanent condition contains the conditioned within it, not as a degraded imitation, but rather as a modification of the being of the condition itself. To cite an example, capitalism is for Deleuze a system of immanent causation. In an essay detailing his affinity with Marxism, and why in fact he and Guattari "remain Marxists," Deleuze argues that it is precisely because Marx offers an "analysis of capitalism as an immanent system that continually redraws its proper limits, and that always finds itself increasing by steps, for the limit is Capital itself."[10] Whenever a new market is discovered or opened, this market becomes incorporated into the capitalist system itself, though a now-expanded system (e.g., the expansion of capitalism into China where labor and the products of labor have become commodities). These expanded limits are an effect of capitalism but are within capitalism itself as an effect in the cause. Moreover, as an immanent system, capitalism entails a fundamental equality of being in that all things are equal insofar as they are commodities—they can *all* be bought and sold on the open market.

Related to immanence and the equality of being (or what Deleuze will most often refer to as the univocity of being), is the concept of multiplicity. Deleuze defines multiplicity as what results "when the multiple is effectively treated as a substantive, 'multiplicity,' [whereby] . . . it ceases to have any relation to the One as subject or object, natural or spiritual reality, image and world."[11] In other words, for Deleuze a multiplicity is what he will call a nomadic distribution of fundamentally nonhierarchical being (univocity), a distribution that cannot be reduced to identifiable unities. Deleuze and Guattari are straightforward on this point:

> The rhizome [or multiplicity[12]] is reducible neither to the One nor the multiple. It is not the One that becomes Two or even directly three, four, five, etc. It is not a multiple derived from the One or to which One is added (n + 1). It is not composed of units but of dimensions, or rather directions in motion. It has neither beginning nor end, but always a middle [milieu] from which it grows and which it overspills.[13]

To understand a multiplicity in terms of the One or as a multiple of units (the French word used here is *unités*, which means both units and unities) would be to relate it to a privileged form of being, to a being that operates as "emanative cause" in that the things that come to be identified come to be by virtue of a One or multiple that transcends them. Socrates makes this position clear in the *Euthyphro*. It is not the diversity and multiplicity of pious actions that interests Socrates, but rather he wants "to know what is characteristic of piety which makes all pious actions pious." Whatever their apparent diversity, there is from the perspective of Plato a privileged unity that is superior to the diversity it conditions. On this point, Deleuze and Whitehead are in agreement against Plato's understanding of a privileged, superior unity. Although Whitehead will speak of God (more on this below), he nonetheless is adamant that God "is the presupposed actuality of conceptual operation, in unison of becoming with every other creative act";[14] or, to state it differently, God is an actual entity that does not transcend every other actual entity, but is "in unison of becoming" with them as their immanent cause. The problem with philosophies of transcendence for Deleuze, however, is that they fail to recognize that identities have to be constituted. Identities (*unités*) are not a preordained given but are constituted and come into being by virtue of a multiplicity of contingent factors and conditions. "A people," for example, "isn't something preexistent . . . [but] is constituted."[15] And it is with the concept of multiplicity that Deleuze begins to account for how identities come to be constituted without the need for a transcendent, emanative cause.

Before turning to Deleuze's concept of multiplicity, it should be noted at this point that Deleuze's project bears striking similarities to the work of Judith Butler. In taking on what she sees as the dominance of identity politics within, for example, the discourse surrounding feminism, among other political movements, Butler argues that the very identity and unity of "women" as a gender needs to be questioned. To that end, Butler proposes "the task of a feminist genealogy of the category of women."[16] More precisely, Butler argues that the very notion that one's sex or gender is a given, is that which is not constructed but is prior to our discursive formulations and statements regarding it, is itself an effect of a constitutive process. As with Deleuze's claim that a people "isn't something preexistent" but "is constituted," so too, for Butler, gender is constituted. As Butler puts it, her "antifoundationalist approach to coalitional politics assumes neither 'identity' as a premise nor that the shape or meaning of a coalitional assemblage can be known prior to its achievement."[17] A feminist politics, therefore, can neither begin with a presupposed "identity" that serves as the foundation for a political action and discourse, nor can a presupposed identity serve as the predetermining goal to be achieved through political action and discourse.

With this last point, Butler's feminism converges with the nomadic thought for which Deleuze calls. As an experimental thought that challenges and undermines the established identities of thinking and politics, nomadic thought is not guaranteed of success. There is no identity the attainment of which will be the mark of success. Rather, by drawing attention to the multiplicity of heterogeneous practices that are inseparable from each and every identity, Deleuze seeks to force the possibility for creative moves beyond this identity. Similarly, for Butler, she challenges the presupposition of many feminist theories of "the coherence and unity of the category of women," for this presupposition "has effectively refused the multiplicity of cultural, social, and political intersections in which the concrete array of 'women' are constructed."[18] By arguing for this multiplicity of intersections inseparable from the identity of "women," Butler concludes that "there need not be a 'doer behind the deed'"; moreover, "the 'doer,'" she argues, "is variably constructed in and through the deed."[19] There is thus no subject of nomadic thought, no subject in charge of this thought; rather, as Butler argues, the subject is "a consequence of certain rule-governed discourses that govern the intelligible invocation of identity."[20] Moreover, the subject is a consequence of the repetition of these rules, a repetition that masks their constitutive role, and thus political agency, or nomadic thought for Deleuze, consists of "the possibility of a variation on that repetition."[21] In other words, the task of feminism, for Butler, is to seek out possibilities that are made possible by these repetitive structures but are not reducible to them. In short, Butler calls for nomadic feminism, or, as she puts it:

> The critical task is, rather, to locate strategies of subversive repetition enabled by those constructions, to affirm the local possibilities of intervention through participating in precisely those practices of repetition that constitute identity and, therefore, present the immanent possibility of contesting them.[22]

Central to Butler's account, as we saw, is the notion that the identity and coherence of gender presupposes a multiplicity of practices that is inseparable from the very identity and coherence it makes possible. A similar point is made by Butler, as we will see below, in her discussion of giving an account of oneself. The self of such an account presupposes, to use Deleuze's terminology, a multiplicity that is irreducible to either the one or the multiple. The concept of multiplicity is crucial to Deleuze's philosophy, but with this concept a new problem emerges—namely, how does a multiplicity become a system, or how do the pre-individual singularities of the transcendental field (as Deleuze refers to it) come to form a unity and hence a one or multiple of ones (*unités*)?[23] How does the multiplicity of practices, etc., become a presupposed identity? The concept that comes to assist Deleuze here is that of "event," which he defines in *Logic of Sense* as follows:

> With every event, there is indeed the present moment of its actualization, the moment in which the event is embodied in a state of affairs, an individual, or a person, the moment we designate by saying "here, the moment has come." The future and the past of the event are only evaluated with respect to this definitive present. On the other hand, there is the future and past of the event, considered in itself, sidestepping each present, being free of the limitations of a state of affairs, impersonal, pre-individual, neutral.[24]

The event, in other words, is Janus-faced, and on one side it is inseparable from the actualities and unities we associate with states of affairs, and yet it has another side drawn toward that which is "free of the limitations of a state of affairs," the transcendental field of pre-individual singularities that nomadically elude capture by such states of affairs. To clarify by way of example, David Sudnow, in his book *Ways of the Hand*, details the experience he had attempting to teach himself to play improvisational jazz. The challenge in playing improvisational jazz is that it *be* improvisational, that one not follow an already written score. And yet as Sudnow sat down to play, the recurring question that surfaced as he sought "to make up melodies with the right hand, was, Where?"[25] Sudnow's teacher, when pressed, gave Sudnow a list of scalar devices (i.e., jazz-sounding scales, runs, etc.) that Sudnow then incorporated into an ever-expanding repertoire of skills, a repertoire of predetermined paths in short. This set of skills was still not improvisational jazz as Sudnow's teacher could play it, for when his teacher played, "he was not simply using the few scalar devices that I had been employing for each of the chord types. He was going many more places over the keyboard . . . (and yet he was) 'orderly.'"[26] What Sudnow's teacher was able to do was, as Deleuze would put it, to access the multiplicity of ways without predetermining this multiplicity by a predetermined unity—namely, the scalar devices, etc.—and then he actualized this multiplicity within a new improvisational performance that is irreducible to any of the predetermining paths and techniques. Sudnow himself was only successful in his efforts to play improvisational jazz when he was able to actualize the multiplicity by way of the event that is an improvisational performance (becoming), a performance that is now a state of affairs that can be used as a new source of scalar devices, etc. In short, what is at work with the event is a double articulation.[27] The creative event, such as an improvisational performance, nomadic thinking, and so on, articulates the multiplicity of pre-individual singularities such that they can become actualized within a second articulation that is the creative state of affairs itself, the state of affairs that is individual, identified, and able to be taken up within future efforts to be creative. It is this understanding of double articulation, and its ubiquity within creative processes, that leads Deleuze and Guattari to assert that "God is a Lobster, or a double pincer, a double bind."[28] God is indeed the double bind, or the double articulation that identifies and individuates the non-identifiable and pre-individual multiplicities.

At this point we can turn to compare Deleuze's efforts to develop a nomadic thought that actualizes a multiplicity of pre-individual singularities with Whitehead's efforts to understand the process whereby actual entities become. As with Deleuze's emphasis upon multiplicity, Whitehead offers a "cell-theory of actuality,"[29] and for much the same reason. In the same way that Deleuze argues for multiplicities that are inseparable from the state of affairs that actualize them—for example, the multiplicity of musical paths that are inseparable from the improvisational performances that actualize this multiplicity—so too for Whitehead "each ultimate unit of fact is a cell-complex, not analyzable into components with equivalent completeness of actuality."[30] In other words, although facts are cell-complexes, or societies of actual entities as Whitehead will also understand them, these complexes cannot be analyzed and reduced to a complex of identifiable units or facts. This would be to understand facts in terms of more ultimate facts, which is precisely the traditional move in philosophy that Whitehead rejects; as Deleuze would put it, this would reduce multiplicities to the multiple, a collection of units (*unités*). As Whitehead makes clear, in contrast to Leibniz's theory of monads where "monads change," Whitehead's cells or monads, by his theory, "merely become." That is, one cannot say of Whitehead's actual entities that they are, and hence that they change from being in one state to being in another, for once the process is complete whereby the actual entities have become an identifiable, static fact, the process of becoming associated with actual entities has ended. As Whitehead puts it, "an actual entity has perished when it is complete," that is, when it has become a fact. For Leibniz, by contrast, not only do monads change rather than become, but each monad expresses the ultimate fact that is the pre-established harmony of the universe. And thus, in the end, Leibniz forecloses any possibility for novelty, which leads Deleuze, despite his admiration for Leibniz in many other respects, to this harsh conclusion: Leibniz "assigns to philosophy the creation of new concepts provided that they do not overthrow 'established sentiments.'"[31]

As is well known among Whitehead scholars, Whitehead's account of the creative advance, of process, involves two poles—the physical and mental pole. As the actual entities become complete, they acquire what Whitehead will call an "objective immortality" in that they are objective but not in the temporal sense of actual entities that become. They are, instead, the physical or objective component of the mental pole that is able to explore for possibilities (i.e., multiplicities) that are inseparable from the completeness of the objective pole. "The mental functioning," Whitehead argues, "introduces into realization subjective forms conformal to relevant alternatives excluded from the completeness of physical realization."[32] Among "the societies of inorganic bodies," when "there is no reason to believe that in any important way the mental activities depart from the functionings which are strictly inherent in the objective datum of the first [objective] phase . . . [then] no novelty is introduced."[33] The very essence of life, for Whitehead, is the "introduction of novelty."[34] In particular, novelty occurs when there is a discord between the physical and mental poles. "Progress," Whitehead makes quite clear, "is founded upon the experience of discordant feelings," and as these discordant feelings become resolved through the attainment of perfection—namely, when the mental and physical poles conform to one another—then progress withers away unless new discordant feelings arise, prompting yet another process of attaining perfection. Whitehead refers to this process as adventure: "To sustain a civilization with the intensity of its first ardour requires more than learning. Adventure is essential, namely, the search for new perfections."[35]

Key to the adventure of ideas is the ability of the mental pole to access the nomadic, antisocial actual entities that have not been actualized within the complete physical realization of a social nexus, or, more simply, as facts. A nexus of actual entities that is complete "enjoys a history expressing its changing reactions to changing circumstances," much as Leibniz's monads change; however, "an actual occasion has no such history. It never changes. It only becomes and perishes. Its perishing is its assumption of a new metaphysical function in the creative advance of the universe."[36] And what is crucial to this creative advance is precisely that there is no pre-established harmony, no pre-determining completeness, but rather there is order and chaos, or, as Deleuze understands this point, there is a multiplicity that cannot be reduced to states of affairs and which yet allows for the possibility of creative transformations of, and moves beyond, these states of affairs. For Whitehead, then, the "societies in an environment will constitute its orderly element, and the non-social [nomadic] actual entities will constitute its element of chaos." The actual world, therefore, is neither "purely orderly" nor "purely chaotic."[37] It is, as Deleuze and Guattari have argued, a chaosmos.

We can now return to our discussion of the importance of nomadic thinking for both Deleuze and Whitehead. Deleuze, as we saw, found in Nietzsche's philosophy a thinking that "does not and will not allow itself to be codified." This nomadic thinking breaks free from the models and stereotypes that would predetermine our thought processes. It is a thinking that eludes what Deleuze and Guattari will later call the apparatus of capture—namely, the state and the thinking that is subservient to the predetermining, capturing identities of the state. Deleuze and Guattari will refer to this form of philosophy as royal philosophy, and Leibniz would be an example of such a philosophy. Whitehead, however, would not be such an example; moreover, and as we have seen, Whitehead outright calls for nomadic actual entities, for chaos, as an indispensable condition for the creative advances of thought, civilization, and so on, that were of central concern to him. Nomadic thought, however, is not simply a thought that moves beyond the actual by destroying it. Although Nietzsche indeed leaves the impression that this is precisely the philosophy he practices, and what it means to "philosophize with a hammer," Nietzsche clearly argues otherwise. In *Human, All Too Human*, for example, he claims that "He who strays from tradition becomes a sacrifice to the extraordinary; he who remains in tradition is its slave. Destruction follows in any case."[38] Similarly for Whitehead, as we saw, the universe is neither purely orderly nor purely chaotic, and what assures the successful balancing of social and nomadic actual entities, order and chaos, is God. It is in the realm where the physical and mental poles are in discord—and hence where novelty becomes possible—that Whitehead "conceive[s] of the patience of God, tenderly saving the turmoil of the intermediate world by the completion of his own nature."[39] God thus prevents chaos from gaining the upper hand and assures the successful territorializing of nomadic actual entities into societies, or, as Whitehead puts it, God "does not create the world, he saves it."[40]

Deleuze will not follow Whitehead on this point. It is not the completion of God's nature that assures the successful completion of ordering processes for Deleuze, but rather there is an "immanent principle of auto-unification through a nomadic distribution, radically distinct from fixed and sedentary distributions," including, Deleuze notes, the syntheses that unify by way of "the form of the I, or the point of view of the Self," such as, for example, the completion of the Self or subject that is God's nature.[41] For Deleuze there is no predetermining form of the I or the Self that assures the unification of a multiplicity. Despite this notable difference, Deleuze nonetheless argues, along with Whitehead, for a nomadic thought that will instill a hesitation, discord, or adventure into ideas, into what is actual and otherwise complete, that will, when actualized within a creative event, express the auto-unification immanent to multiplicities themselves; this is what we should expect since Deleuze's stated effort was to develop and practice a philosophy of immanence.

Butler will echo these points as well, though she is perhaps less sanguine than Deleuze when it comes to affirming an "immanent principle of auto-unification." In *Giving an Account of Oneself*, for instance, Butler argues that a recurring theme in the works of Adorno, Levinas, Laplanche, and Foucault, among others, is the impossibility of giving an account of oneself, of producing a narrative account that can unify the multiplicity of affects, passions, relations, etc. "The 'I,'" Butler claims, "has no story of its own that is not also the story of a relation—or set of relations—to a set of norms."[42] There is, according to Butler, "no self-making outside of the norms that orchestrate the possible forms that a subject may take."[43] Giving an account of oneself, therefore, will, for Butler, entail a "social critique"[44] for despite the fact that one cannot give a complete account—or that "Life," as Butler puts it in a Deleuzian vein, "exceeds any account we may try to give of it"[45]—we are nonetheless called to give an account and must do so by virtue of the social norms our very account may indeed challenge.

It is at this point where Butler's work converges with the nomadic thought we found in Deleuze and Whitehead. For just as Deleuze argues that an auto-unification presupposes a nomadic distribution, a distribution that assures the becoming-other of whatever comes to be unified; and just as Whitehead argued that cell-complexes and societies harbor the non-social actual entities that guarantee the continuing processes of reality; so too for Butler any account we may give of ourselves is not a simple rendition of social norms, a mirroring of the "collective we," but to the contrary it involves a social critique, or it is the nomadic singularity that cannot be subsumed without violence within a collective totality and unity, and yet may in the end transform the very social norms that make the account possible. As Butler stresses throughout her book, this social critique is only possible when one resists the ethical violence that "demands that we manifest and maintain self-identity at all times and require that others do the same."[46] And it is precisely this ethical violence that Butler inveighs against in her most recent work.

Returning to the aesthetic problem with which we began, it is now clear how the nomadic thought we find in Deleuze, Whitehead, and Butler aims to resolve it. For Deleuze, in particular, the effort is to combat the homogenizing tendencies of capitalism with its reliance upon predictable sales. The system of best-sellers, for example, where books, music, etc., quickly move up, down, and off the charts, this "fast turnover," Deleuze argues,

> necessarily means selling people what they expect: even what's "daring," "scandalous," strange and so on falls into the market's predictable forms. The conditions for literary creation, which emerge only unpredictably, with a slow turnover and progressive recognition, are fragile.[47]

A nomadic thought will thus be a fragile thought, a thought not guaranteed of success, and more importantly its success will be unpredictable—that is, it will be novel. For Whitehead as well, although he does praise commercial (capitalist) thinking for engendering the type of foresight necessary to civilization, he also notes that the very success of the commercial, capitalist economies has left us in a situation where we "must prepare individuals to face a novelty of conditions."[48]

Unlike Whitehead's distant ancestors, for whom much did not change from one generation to the next, we now live in a context where we have come to expect change and novelty. We have become desensitized to novelty. As a result we are perhaps, as was likely Whitehead's hope, more tolerant of novelty, more accepting of the discords that prompt the adventures of ideas. On the flip side, however, novelty itself has become predictable, and as a result what sells is precisely what is "daring," "scandalous," and strange. To the extent then that novelty itself has become the form of predictability itself—what we now have come to expect—it is much less likely to produce the discord Whitehead saw as essential to the adventure of ideas that is civilization. A nomadic thought that seeks to instill the aesthetic discord into everyday life will thus take seriously Nietzsche's claim that what is truly new emerges away from the marketplace.[49]

To avoid a thought that comes to be captured into one of a number of predictable forms, nomadic thought will seek, as Deleuze puts it, though in reference to historical nomads, "a sort of adventure." These nomads, Deleuze points out, do not realize a fundamental nomadism, a nomadism conceived of "as a primary state"; to the contrary, nomadism is "an adventure suddenly embarked upon by sedentary groups impelled by the attraction of movement, of what lies outside."[50] Nomadic thinking, similarly, is an adventure of thinking, an adventure that begins within a context of already established thoughts, a tradition that predetermines what one should think, the account one can give of oneself, what problems are important, and how one's thoughts should progress in resolving these problems. Although one must begin with thought, Deleuze sought to "engender 'thinking' in thought," and this thinking, for both Deleuze and Whitehead, is an adventure without a map, a thinking that cannot predict what thoughts may come to be established when the adventure ends. Whenever and however an adventure may end, Deleuze and Whitehead would certainly encourage us to become unsettled with it, and, without cause or purpose, to become nomads and suddenly embark upon an adventure of thinking.

CHAPTER 3

Transcendental Empiricism in Deleuze and Whitehead

Steven Shaviro

In one of his few direct references to the philosophy of Alfred North Whitehead, Gilles Deleuze praises "the list of empirico-ideal notions that we find in Whitehead, which makes *Process and Reality* one of the greatest books of modern philosophy."[1] Deleuze opposes Whitehead's proliferating list of categories—a list that includes "the Category of the Ultimate," together with eight "Categories of Existence," twenty-seven "Categories of Explanation," and nine "Categoreal Obligations"[2]—to the twelve fixed categories of the understanding in Kant's *Critique of Pure Reason*. Kant's categories are logical and epistemological; they "belong to the world of representation," Deleuze says, and concern the ways in which we organize—and thereby present to ourselves—the data that we receive from the senses. But Whitehead's categories do not perform any such function. They are "generic notions inevitably presupposed in our reflective experience,"[3] but they do not *represent* that experience, nor explain how it is possible for us to *know* things in experience. They cannot be *applied* to experience, because they are already located *within* experience itself. Deleuze calls them "notions which are really open and which betray an empirical and pluralist sense of Ideas.... Such notions... are conditions of real experience, and not only of possible experience."[4]

82

Kant's categories of understanding are universal and intrinsic to the mind that imposes them upon an otherwise inchoate external reality. But Whitehead's categories are not imposed by the mind. They are immanent to the "data"—the events or actual occasions—out of which they arise by a process of abstraction. "It is a complete mistake," Whitehead says, "to ask how concrete particular fact can be built up out of universals. The answer is, 'In no way.' The true philosophic question is, How can concrete fact exhibit entities abstract from itself and yet participated in by its own nature?"[5] Whitehead abstracts "empirico-ideal" categories from the events that participate in them, rather than imposing a priori categories upon phenomena that remain external to them. In analyzing events, he does not assume any priority of the subject, but rather traces its genesis alongside that of the world in which it finds itself. And he delineates the conditions of real experience, which determine concrete processes of emergence, rather than proposing apodictic conditions for all possible experience. Whitehead rejects Kant's "endeavor to balance the world upon thought—oblivious to the scanty supply of thinking." But he still agrees with Kant on the fundamental principle "that the task of the critical reason is the analysis of constructs; and 'construction' is 'process.'"[6] Whitehead is far from simply rejecting Kant; rather, he converts Kant's "transcendental idealism" into something like what Deleuze calls "transcendental empiricism."[7]

Deleuze's own "transcendental empiricism" centers on his notion of the virtual. I think that this much-disputed concept can best be understood in Kantian terms. The virtual is the transcendental condition of all experience. And Ideas in the virtual, which are always "problematic or problematizing," are Deleuze's equivalent of "regulative ideas" in Kant.[8] For Kant, as Deleuze points out, "problematic Ideas are both objective and undetermined." They cannot be presented directly, or re-presented, but their very indeterminacy "is a perfectly positive, objective structure which acts as a focus or horizon within perception." The error of metaphysical dogmatism is to use these Ideas constitutively: to take their objects as determinate, transcendent entities. This is to forget that such objects "can be neither given nor known." The correlative error of skepticism is to think that, since the Ideas are indeterminate and unrepresentable, they are thereby merely subjective, and their objects merely fictive. This is to forget that "problems have an objective value," and that "'problematic' does not mean only a particularly important species of subjective acts, but a dimension of objectivity as such which is occupied by these acts." Against both of these errors, Kant upholds the regulative and transcendental use of the Ideas. A regulative idea does not determine any particular solution in advance. But operating as a guideline, or as a frame of reference, the regulative idea works *problematically*, to establish the conditions out of which solutions, or "decisions," can emerge. In positing a process of this sort, Kant invents the notion of the transcendental realm, or of what Deleuze will call the virtual.

There are, of course, important differences between Kant's transcendental argument and Deleuze's invocation of the virtual. For one thing, Kant's stance is legislative and juridical: He seeks to distinguish legitimate from illegitimate uses of reason. Deleuze seeks rather (citing Artaud) "to have done with the judgment of God"; his criterion is constructivist rather than juridical, concerned with pushing forces to the limits of what they can do rather than with evaluating their legitimacy. Also, Kant's transcendental realm determines the necessary form—but only the form—of all possible experience. Deleuze's virtual, in contrast, is "genetic and productive" of actual experience.[9] Finally, Kant's transcendental realm has the structure of a subjectivity; at the very least, it takes on the bare form of the "I" in the "transcendental unity of apperception." But Deleuze's virtual is an "impersonal and pre-individual transcendental field";[10] it does not have the form of a consciousness. In making these corrections to Kant, Deleuze himself does what he credits Nietzsche with doing: He "stands [Kantian] critique on its feet, just as Marx does with the [Hegelian] dialectic."[11]

To convert Kant from transcendental idealism to transcendental empiricism, and from a juridico-legislative project to a constructivist one, means to move from the possible to the virtual, and from merely formal conditions of possibility to concrete conditions of actualization. Deleuze's transformation of Kant thus leads directly to his famous distinction between the virtual and the possible. For Deleuze, the possible is an empty form, defined only by the principle of noncontradiction. To say that something is possible is to say nothing more than that its concept cannot be excluded a priori, on logical grounds alone. This means that possibility is a purely negative category; it lacks any proper being of its own. Mere possibility is not generative or productive; it is not *enough* to make anything happen. This is why Deleuze says that "the possible is opposed to the real."[12] Something that is merely possible has no claim to existence, and no intrinsic mode of being. Its only positive characteristics are those that it borrows from the real that it is not. The possible "refers to the form of identity in the concept"; it "is understood as an image of the real, while the real is supposed to resemble the possible."[13] That is to say, the possible is exactly like the real, except for the contingency that it does not, in fact, exist. And the real is nothing more than the working-out of what was already prefigured and envisioned as possible. In this mirror play of resemblances, there can be nothing new or unexpected. When a possibility is realized— when it *does* come into existence—no actual creation has taken place. As Deleuze says, "it is difficult to understand what existence adds to the concept when all it does is double like with like."[14]

The virtual, on the other hand, is altogether real in its own right; it "possesses a full reality by itself."[15] It is just that this reality is not actual. The virtual is like a field of energies that have not yet been expended, or a reservoir of potentialities that have not yet been tapped. That is to say, the virtual is not composed of atoms; it doesn't have body or extension. But the potential for change that it offers is real in its own way. In the Proustian formulation so frequently used by Deleuze, the virtual is "real without being actual, ideal without being abstract."[16] One can in fact explain the virtual in entirely physicalist terms: as Gilbert Simondon did in work that greatly influenced Deleuze,[17] and as Manuel DeLanda has more recently done.[18] But Deleuze most often describes the virtual as a transcendental field or structure, conditioning and generating the actual. The virtual is a principle of emergence, or of creation. As such, it does not prefigure or predetermine the actualities that emerge from it. Rather, it is the impelling force, or the principle, that allows each actual entity to appear (to manifest itself) as something new, something without precedence or resemblance, something that has never existed in the universe in quite that way before. That is why the virtual is entirely distinct from the possible. If anything, it is closer to Nietzsche's will-to-power, or Bergson's *élan vital*. All of these must be understood, not as inner essences, but as post-Kantian "syntheses" of difference: transcendental conditions for dynamic becoming, rather than for static being.

The virtual works as a transcendental condition for the actual by providing a "sufficient reason" for whatever happens. Linear causality, of the sort that physical science traces, is always, and only, a relation among bodies. It is a matter, as Deleuze puts it in *The Logic of Sense*, of

> bodies with their tensions, physical qualities, actions and passions, and the corresponding "states of affairs." These states of affairs, actions and passions, are determined by the mixtures of bodies . . . all bodies are causes—causes in relation to each other and for each other.[19]

Everything in the world is determined by such physical causes; they constitute a necessary condition for every event—but not a sufficient one.

This linear causality, and this necessity, are what Kant seeks to guarantee against Hume's skepticism. But Kant never questions Hume's initial dubious assumption: that causality cannot be found *out there*, in the world, and that consequently it can only be located *in here*, in the mind of the perceiver. Hume appeals to habit as the basis of the mind's ascription of causality to things; Kant's transcendental argument converts this empirical generalization into an a priori necessity. But Kant still accepts what Whitehead calls the *subjectivist* and *sensationalist* principles derived from Locke and Hume.[20] In consequence, Kant's transcendental deduction remains caught within "a logic of tracing and reproduction,"[21] or "a tracing of the transcendental from the empirical."[22] Kant merely transfers the structure of causal efficacy from the world to the subject apprehending the world. The possible just doubles the real, without adding anything to it.

Deleuze converts Kant's argument from possibility to virtuality, and from the role of guaranteeing causal efficacy to one of providing sufficient reasons, by positing a different sort of transcendental logic. Alongside the actual, material "connection" of physical causes to one another, there is also a virtual relation, or a "bond," linking "effects or incorporeal events" among themselves.[23] The virtual is the realm of effects separated from their causes: "effects in the causal sense, but also sonorous, optical, or linguistic 'effects,'"[24] or what in the movies are called "special effects." Effects come after causes, of course, in the physical world of bodies. But transcendentally, these incorporeal special effects establish a strange precedence. Considered apart from their physical causes, and independently of any bodily instantiation, they are something like the generative conditions—the "meanings" and the "reasons," or what Whitehead calls the final causes—for the very processes that physically give rise to them.

Deleuze calls such generative aftereffects "quasi-causes."[25] Quasi-causality is "an unreal and ghostly causality,"[26] more an insinuation than a determination. It happens, not in the bodily density of the living present, but in an "instant without thickness and without extension, which subdivides each present into past and future."[27] The quasi-cause "is nothing outside of its effect"; but neither can it just be identified with, or reduced to, its effect. For "it haunts this effect . . . it maintains with the effect an immanent relation which turns the product, the moment that it is produced, into something productive."[28] In itself, the virtual quasi-cause partakes only of "extra-being"; it is "sterile, inefficacious, and on the surface of things."[29] But at the same time, by virtue of its infinite relations, and insofar as it "evades the present,"[30] the quasi-cause is also a principle of creativity. Looking forward, it *induces* the process of actualization; looking backward, it is an expression of that process. Deleuze's transcendental realm is thus "an aggregate of noncausal correspondences which form a system of echoes, of resumptions and resonances, a system of signs—in short, an expressive quasi-causality, and not at all a necessitating causality."[31] Only in this ghostly, paradoxical way can Deleuze posit a transcendental that neither copies the actual, nor prefigures it.

What does all this have to do with Whitehead? As far as I know, Whitehead never uses the word virtual. But as Keith Robinson notes, Whitehead's "distinction between the actual and the potential . . . resembles the Deleuzian distinction between the actual and the virtual."[32] And potentiality, for Whitehead, is always something more, and other, than mere possibility. Alongside events or actual entities, Whitehead also posits what he calls "eternal objects." These are "Pure Potentials,"[33] or "potentials for the process of becoming."[34] If actual entities are singular "occasions" of becoming, then eternal objects provide "the 'qualities' and 'relations'" that enter into, and help to define, these occasions.[35] When "the potentiality of an eternal object is realized in a particular actual entity," it is "contributing to the definiteness of that actual entity."[36] It gives it a particular character. Eternal objects thus take on something of the role that universals,[37] predicates,[38] Platonic forms,[39] and ideas[40] played in older metaphysical systems. But universals, or "things which are eternal," can and must be abstracted from "things which are temporal."[41] They cannot be conceived by themselves, in the absence of the empirical entities that they inform. Eternal objects, therefore, are neither a priori logical structures, nor Platonic essences, nor constitutive rational ideas. They are adverbial, rather than substantive; they determine and express *how* actual entities relate to one another, take one another up, and "enter into each others' constitutions."[42] Like Kantian and Deleuzian ideas, eternal objects work regulatively, or problematically.

To be more precise, Whitehead defines eternal objects as follows: "Any entity whose conceptual recognition does not involve a necessary reference to any definite actual entities of the temporal world is called an 'eternal object.'"[43] This means that eternal objects include sensory qualities, like colors (blueness or greenness) and tactile sensations (softness or roughness), conceptual abstractions like shapes (a helix, or a dodecahedron) and numbers (seven, or the square root of minus two), moral qualities (bravery or cowardice), physical fundamentals (gravitational attraction or electric charge), and much more besides. An eternal object can also be "a determinate way in which a feeling can feel . . . an emotion, or an intensity, or an adversion, or an aversion, or a pleasure, or a pain."[44]

"Sensa"—or what today are more commonly called "qualia"—are eternal objects; so are affects or emotions; and so are "contrasts, or patterns," or anything else that can "express a manner of relatedness between other eternal objects."[45] There is, in fact, "an indefinite progression of categories, as we proceed from 'contrasts' to 'contrasts of contrasts,' and on indefinitely to higher grades of contrasts."[46] The levels and complexities proliferate, without limit. But regardless of level, eternal objects are ideal abstractions that nevertheless (unlike Platonic forms) can only be encountered *within* experience, when they are "selected" and "felt" by particular actual occasions.

Eternal objects are altogether real, but they are not the same as actual entities. Like Deleuze's virtualities, they are precisely not actual. This is because, in themselves, they are not causally determined, and they cannot make anything happen. Eternal objects "involve in their own natures indecision" and "indetermination";[47] they always imply alternatives, contingencies, situations that could have been otherwise. This patch of wall is yellow, but it might have been blue. This means that their role is essentially passive. "An eternal object is always a potentiality for actual entities; but in itself, as conceptually felt, it is neutral as to the fact of its physical ingression in any particular actual entity of the temporal world."[48] You might say that yellowness "in itself," understood as a pure potentiality, is utterly indifferent to the actual yellow color of this particular patch of wall. Yellowness per se has no causal efficacy, and no influence over the "decision" by which it is admitted (or not) into any particular actual state of affairs. Eternal objects, like Deleuze's quasi-causes, are neutral, sterile, and inefficacious, as powerless as they are indifferent.

At the same time, every event, every actual occasion, involves the *actualization* of certain of these mere potentialities. Each actual entity is determined by what Whitehead calls the *ingression* of specific eternal objects into it. "The term 'ingression' refers to the particular mode in which the potentiality of an eternal object is realized in a particular actual entity, contributing to the definiteness of that actual entity."[49] Each actual entity creates itself, in a process of decision, by making a *selection* among the potentialities offered to it by eternal objects. The concrescence of each actual entity involves the rejection of some eternal objects, and the active "entertainment," or "admi[ssion] into feeling" of others.[50] And by a kind of circular process, the eternal objects thus admitted or entertained serve to define and determine the entity that selected them. That is why—or better, how—this particular patch of wall actually *is* yellow. By offering themselves for actualization, and by determining the very entities that select and actualize them, eternal objects play a transcendental, quasi-causal role in the constitution of the actual world.[51]

Whitehead also explains the difference, and the relation, between eternal objects and actual entities by noting that the former "*can* be dismissed" at any moment, while the latter always "*have* to be felt."[52] Potentialities are optional; they may or may not be fulfilled. But actualities cannot be avoided. Indeed, "an actual entity in the actual world of a subject *must* enter into the concrescence of that subject by *some* simple causal feeling, however vague, trivial, and submerged."[53] An actual entity can, in fact, be rejected or excluded, by the process of what Whitehead calls a *negative prehension*: "the definite exclusion of [a given] item from positive contribution to the subject's own real internal constitution."[54] But even this is a sort of backhanded acknowledgement, an active response to something that cannot just be ignored. Even "the negative prehension of an entity is a positive fact with its emotional subjective form."[55] An actual entity has causal efficacy, because in itself it is entirely determined; it is empirically "given," and this "givenness" means Necessity.[56] Once actual entities have completed their process, once the ingression of eternal objects into them has been fixed, they "are devoid of all indetermination. . . . They are complete and determinate . . . devoid of all indecision."[57] Every event thus culminates in a "stubborn matter of fact,"[58] a state of affairs that has no potential left, and that cannot be otherwise than it is. An event consists precisely in this movement from potentiality (and indeterminacy) into actuality (and complete determination). The process of actualization follows a trajectory from the mere, disinterested (aesthetic) "envisagement" of eternal objects to a pragmatic interest in some of these objects, and their incorporation within "stubborn fact which cannot be evaded."[59]

In the course of fully determining itself, an actual entity thus perishes, and subsists only as a "datum" for other entities to prehend in their own turn. An eternal object, on the other hand, is not exhausted by the event into which it ingresses, or which includes it; it "never loses its 'accent' of potentiality."[60] It remains available for other events, other actualizations. This is another mark of the transcendental. As Deleuze similarly says, referring both to Kantian Ideas and to his own notion of the problematic virtual, "true problems are Ideas, and . . . these Ideas do not disappear with 'their' solutions, since they are the indispensable condition without which no solution would ever exist."[61] Eternal objects and problematic Ideas never disappear. They are "indispensable conditions" that cannot be grasped outside of the actualities that they condition, and that incarnate them. But they also cannot be reduced to those actualities, and cannot be contained within them. They are not actual, but they haunt the actual. They subsist, like specters, outside of their ingressions and actualizations, and according to a different temporal logic than that of the "specious present of the percipient,"[62] the present in which things happen. This outside, this extra-being, this space without "simple location,"[63] this time in which "a future and past divide the present at every instant and subdivide it ad infinitum into past and future, in both directions at once"[64]: All this is the realm of the transcendental.

Kant's transcendental deduction serves (at least) two purposes. It has both a juridical use, and a problematic or speculative use. The juridical use is to determine the legitimate conditions of rationality: to "make reason secure in its rightful claims and ... dismiss all [its] baseless pretensions."[65] The problematic or speculative use of the deduction is to answer the three basic questions: "What can I know? What ought I to do? What may I hope?"[66] In converting Kant from transcendental idealism to transcendental empiricism, Whitehead and Deleuze refashion both of these uses. The juridical use of the transcendental deduction is displaced, as I have already suggested, from Kant's "tribunal" in which reason turns back upon and scrutinizes itself, into an evaluation according to immanent criteria.[67] And the problematic use of the transcendental deduction is transformed because Whitehead and Deleuze ask different sorts of questions than Kant does. The fundamental questions that Whitehead and Deleuze ask, and seek to answer with their transcendental arguments about eternal objects and the virtual, are these: How is it that there is always something new? How are novelty and change possible? How can we account for a future that is different from, and not merely predetermined by, the past?

The shift from Kant's questions to Whitehead's and Deleuze's questions is largely a historical one, deeply embedded in the progress (if we can still call it that) of our modernity. Kant, of course, is a great thinker of Enlightenment, which he famously defines as "man's emergence from his self-imposed immaturity" into intellectual adulthood.[68] Michel Foucault, commenting on Kant's Enlightenment text some two centuries later, remarks that "the historical event of the Enlightenment did not make us mature adults, and we have not reached that stage yet."[69] Nonetheless, he praises Kant's stance for providing "a point of departure: the outline of what one might call the attitude of modernity."[70] And he urges us today to continue Kant's reflection in the form of "an attitude, an ethos, a philosophical life in which the critique of what we are is at one and the same time the historical analysis of the limits imposed on us and an experiment with the possibility of going beyond them."[71] This is the task that lies behind Whitehead's and Deleuze's renewals of the Kantian transcendental argument. As for the shift from foundational questions about knowing, obligation, and belief to pragmatic, constructivist questions about events, potentialities, and the process of actualizing them, this is not a betrayal of Kant, but an urgent and necessary renewal of his legacy, at a time when "all that is solid melts into air," and when we are told that the grand narratives of modernity are dead, and even that "we have never been modern" in the first place. For, as Deleuze and Guattari suggest, "it may be that believing in this world, in this life, becomes our most difficult task, or the task of a mode of existence still to be discovered on our plane of immanence today."[72] It is such a task, with the aim of converting ourselves to this kind of belief, that Whitehead envisions as "the use of philosophy," which is "to maintain an active novelty of fundamental ideas illuminating the social system."[73]

CHAPTER 4

Can We Be Wolves? Intersections between Deleuze's *Difference and Repetition* and Butler's Performativity

Andrea M. Stephenson

Judith Butler and Gilles Deleuze could both be called nomads within the field of philosophy. Deleuze, for instance, rather than reading philosophers in a traditional way, saw himself "as taking an author from behind and giving him a child that would be his own offspring, yet monstrous."[1] Butler could not find herself at home within philosophy but rather gained her niche as the "Other" in which "philosophy . . . has . . . found itself outside of itself."[2] The monstrous Others created by these thinkers are perhaps just what philosophers need in order to address the current situation in which we find ourselves. With the ecological, economic, and cultural upheavals seemingly coming at us from all sides, regardless of what part of the globe we look at, we are in need of new ways of thinking and new ways of living. One of the questions with which we have to deal, as we consider philosophy, is whether philosophy has anything to say in the face of practical concerns such as healthcare in the United States, war in the Middle East, rainforest devastation in South America, and AIDS epidemics in Africa.

It is the premise of this chapter that even when we do not think explicitly about philosophy, we are always operating out of a philosophical worldview. In other words, we live and speak and act in ways that are shaped by our thoughts about ourselves, our lives, and the world around us. Our answers to the "big questions" of philosophy have an impact on the way in which we live. By intentionally putting forth a new way of thinking or speaking, we have some hope of eventually altering ways of acting. As Judith Butler writes in *Gender Trouble*, "language refers to an open system of signs by which intelligibility is insistently created and contested."[3] In other words, the meaning in our language is not pre-existent even though we act as though it is. By developing a new language for thinking about life, we can develop and encourage new ways of acting in life. Butler and Deleuze offer words and images that confront us with our multiplicity, our nonidentity, and our interrelationships in ways that persuade us to think about ourselves as part of the rhizomatic web of thought, speech, and action that forms our life on this planet.[4]

To be more specific (but not with the specificity of closure), this chapter will explore the concepts of difference and repetition and nonidentity in relation to the images of multiplicity and performativity. These are concepts to which both Deleuze and Butler give voice. Before embarking on this adventure, however, it is important to note that there is little work thus far linking Butler and Deleuze. However, in *Undoing Gender*, Butler comments that she has had people tell her she is, or that she should be, a Deleuzian.[5] While she spends some time discussing what she sees as a main difference between them, she does acknowledge points of intersection. It is with this acknowledgement that this chapter proceeds in finding that these two thinkers occupy intersecting and sometimes overlapping "planes of immanence," to use the Deleuzian phrase, and that the very nonidentity of their thoughts are shaped by one another.

Wolves in a Pack: Difference and Repetition

Who is ignorant of the fact that wolves travel in packs? . . . Every child knows it.

GILLES DELEUZE AND FELIX GUATTARI,
A Thousand Plateaus: Capitalism and Schizophrenia

Repetition—the very word brings to mind notions of sameness, routine, boredom. We speak of elderly people repeating their same old stories again and again, and we roll our eyes when our grandparents repeat their tales of past hardships or present ailments. We think of the desert as an unending repetition of drab colors, heat, and sand. The gray, rainy days of an autumn in the northeast impress upon us the depressing repetition of colorless skies and cold drops of rain. Children who get tired of hearing the same lessons repeated in school stir up trouble just to experience some difference. When I played the piano, there were times when I skipped a repeat because it did not seem as interesting to play the same thing over again.

What is not recognized in these notions of redundancy that have (unfortunately) become attached to repetition is the fact that every seeming repetition is an opportunity for novelty and difference. The stories our elders tell change over the years as the tales are colored by their memories and their present situations. As Butler explains, "the narrative authority of the 'I' must give way to the perspective and temporality of a set of norms that contest the singularity of my story."[6] The desert landscape is alive with brilliantly colored lizards, surprisingly beautiful cacti, and minutely shifting sands that can cause the entire shape of the earth to change over time. "The desert is populous."[7] Perhaps the rainy November days in the northeast would seem less monotonous if we could perceive the subtle differences made by the wind, if we could hear the difference between the drops of rain as they hit upon the pavement. Thankfully, teachers recognize that the repetition of a lesson is never the same lesson over again. Just think of the lessons that would never be learned if they were never repeated. Every repetition is, in truth, difference. Every caramel macchiato I ingest at Starbucks as I write this paper is a repetition of the same drink, but it is never the exact same drink. If I had only but played those repeats in the songs, I could have experienced nuances in the music, in the way I played it, in the emotions I experienced as I played it, that could not be realized in one unrepeated motion of fingers on keys.

Repetition is even more than the possibility of novelty. As Roland Faber notes, "to see novelty in repetition is already to understand the groundlessness of essence."[8] In other words, repetition and the novelty of difference is a means toward opening up a space for multiplicity in such a way that it becomes transformative, transgressive, or subversive. "Repetition belongs to humour and irony; it is by nature *transgression* or exception, always revealing a singularity opposed to the particulars subsumed under laws, a universal opposed to the generalities which give rise to laws."[9] How is repetition transgression? One might ask, isn't repetition just sameness, as in the examples above? Isn't it the repetition of traits that allows us to categorize people and objects and events? Aren't the categories we develop based on what we observe as repetitive characteristics or behaviors, like those physical and social characteristics that lead to being characterized as male or female? Deleuze makes an important distinction between two types of repetition. One is the repetition of the same, and the other is repetition that "includes difference."[10] For Deleuze, true repetition involves the imagination; it is the repetition that "unravels itself." The other repetition is the repetition "deployed and conserved for us in the space of representation."[11] He explains that these types of repetition are not independent of one another, as every "repetition of the Same" is a disguise for the other type of repetition, the repetition that opens up possibilities through difference and is, in fact, difference itself.[12]

In my reading of *Gender Trouble*, it seems that Butler exemplifies Deleuze's notion of the two types of repetition. She writes, for example, that even "the *action* of gender requires a *performance* that is repeated. This repetition is at once a reenactment and reexperiencing of a set of meanings already socially established; and it is the mundane and ritualized form of their legitimation."[13] This is an example of repetition that is based on the norms of society. In other words, gender, identity, and so forth, are not natural, unified categories. Rather, society creates these categories and the norms that define them. In the form of repetition that *closes off* novelty, we repeat the identities handed to us by our society. However, as I will explain, I think that Butler agrees with Deleuze that this is not the only type of repetition possible. In fact, she explains that "'agency' . . . is to be located within the possibility of a variation on that repetition. . . . [I]t is only *within* the practices of repetitive signifying that a subversion of identity becomes possible."[14] We can only act within the confines of society, but we can repeat societal norms in such a way that our actions go against the definitions and categories set by our society. It is only in this type of repetition, repetition that invites novelty, that we can subvert, or transgress, society's desire for a homogenous identity for individuals and for groups. In these subversive acts we find our voice, the voice of multiplicity.

One makes a mistake when he sees repetition without difference—when one uses the Same to categorize crowds of people, to place them in a particular realm of existence, to centralize, normalize, or marginalize them. Deleuze and Guattari comment that "wolves travel in packs."[15] The attempt, however, is constantly to make sure the wolves are "purged of their multiplicity."[16] Multiplicity is seen as an illness, as a lack of the unity of identity. Judith Butler's nonidentity of self and her encouragement of subversive performativity echo Deleuze's concern with preserving multiplicity, with allowing for the existence and even necessity of the interconnections, confusions, and chaos of the wolf pack.

"*The Wolf Is the Pack*": Nonidentity

> I become this self only through an ec-static movement, one that moves me outside of myself into a sphere in which I am dispossessed of myself and constituted as a subject at the same time.
>
> JUDITH BUTLER, *Giving an Account of Oneself*

The concept of nonidentity seems to have two main interpretations in Butler's work. First, particularly in her earlier works on gender, nonidentity could be seen as describing the plight of those who are pushed to the periphery by a society that cannot define or identify them because they do not fit the norms prescribed by society. These unidentifiable individuals attempt to subvert the norms of society by enacting identities contrary to the norms. The other interpretation of nonidentity, which emerges strongly in her later works, is the notion that all of us exist in a state of nonidentity because we cannot identify ourselves as unified, homogenous, particular entities since we are all implicated in the lives of one another in such a way that we would not be who we are without the people who surround us.[17]

Let us look at the idea of nonidentity as the inability of society to define a particular person. In her earlier work on gender, Butler explains that even our identity as male or female is constructed by the norms of our society.[18] We see a baby with a penis, and we paint its room blue and call it a boy, teach it not to cry, and train it in sports and other "masculine" efforts. Anyone who does not fit into the norms of what it means to be a man or a woman is considered odd or an outsider in the community. These individuals who find themselves at the periphery of their society seem to fall into an obvious place of nonidentity. They do not "fit" the norms, so they cannot be easily categorized or identified. This notion of nonidentity is one that reappears in Butler's later texts as well, particularly when she writes about the illusion of national sovereignty.

In *Who Sings the Nation State*, Butler and Gayatri Spivak enter deeply into the work of Hannah Arendt. Through the course of their dialogue, many issues concerning the concept of nation, state, and nation-state are brought to light. Butler, at the very beginning, states that the state "can signify the source of non-belonging, even produce that non-belonging as a quasi-permanent state."[19] She continues on to explain that the nation-state "expresses a certain national identity" in which the "nation . . . is singular and homogenous."[20] In this attempt to appear as a homogenous unit, the nation is guilty of the expulsion of those who do not "fit." To the nation's great dismay, however, these outsiders are never properly outside. They are on the periphery always, challenging the nation to define itself without them. In other words, "the state derives its legitimacy from the nation, which means that those national minorities who do not qualify for 'national belonging' are regarded as 'illegitimate' inhabitants."[21] They may be "illegitimate" but they are still "inhabitants."

Butler and Spivak describe the event of a number of "illegal residents" in California singing the national anthem in Spanish.[22] In this act of singing the national anthem in a language other than English, these people, who do not have an identity within the boundaries of the United States, enact a performance that "involves a deformation of dominant language, and reworking of power, since those who sing are without entitlement."[23] In this singing, the people take something that was used as a symbol of national homogeneity and perform it in an alien, illegitimate language, forcing the nation to realize its heterogeneity and the fact that the nation is not what it is without these marginalized people. The nation has attempted to doom these individuals to a life of nonidentity, but these individuals require the nation to acknowledge its own nonidentity (in the sense that none of us has a homogenous identity).

As we are all born into or enfolded by a society, we are unable to tell our own story, to identify ourselves, without implicating those around us who formed us, who indoctrinated us into the norms of society. "When the 'I' seeks to give an account of itself, an account that must include the conditions of its own emergence, it must, as a matter of necessity, become a social theorist."[24] As Deleuze and Guattari explain, "you can't be one wolf, you're always eight or nine or six or seven. Not even six or seven wolves all by yourself all at once, but one wolf among others."[25] We can only understand ourselves through an exploration of the society which has become a part of us, as Butler comments, "the 'I' has no story of its own that is not also the story of a relation—or set of relations—to a set of norms."[26]

Those in the center and those on the periphery, those with power and those without, those who hold tight to the illusion of homogeneity and those who remind us of heterogeneity, are all part of each other's stories and identities. When we think about our identities, we often think of terms like mother, daughter, wife, husband, teacher, scholar, and so forth. These identities only make sense in the relationship to another individual or set of individuals. For instance, I am only a wife in relation to my husband, I am only a daughter because of my mother and father, a teacher is only a teacher in relation to a class of students, and so on. Thinking again of the nation, I am only an American in relation to those who are not. Our identities change over time as relationships come to be, change, and die. The question of who I am makes no sense without asking who I am in relation to others. In Deleuze and Guattari's words:

> I know that the periphery is the only place I can be, that I would die if I let myself be drawn into the center of the fray, but just as certainly if I let go of the crowd. This is not an easy position to stay in, it is even very difficult to hold, for these beings are in constant motion and their movements are unpredictable and follow no rhythm. They swirl, go north, then suddenly east; none of the individuals in the crowd remains in the same place in relation to the others. So I too am in perpetual motion; all this demands a high level of tension, but it gives me a feeling of violent, almost vertiginous happiness.[27]

The notion of nonidentity in Butler clearly echoes similar ideas in Deleuze, and particularly resonates with Deleuze's notion of difference and repetition. Nonidentity reminds us that we cannot see ourselves or anyone else as Same. No one is self-same and no one is the same as those around her. We enfold one another in our stories such that we seem to repeat what our society passes on to us, but there is always a difference involved. My story is not the same as my best friend's story, and my own story is not even the same each time I tell it. Constantly, through one another and through society, we invent ourselves so that "I" is repeated in different ways all the time. In their discourse on individuals as wolves in a pack, Deleuze and Guattari explain, "any individual caught up in a mass has his/her own pack unconscious, which does not necessarily resemble the packs of the mass to which that individual belongs."[28] As wolves, even on the periphery we find ourselves traveling in packs, always connected to the center while not necessarily following the rules in expected ways.

Becoming-Wolf: Performativity and Multiplicity

> In becoming-wolf, the important thing is the position of the mass, and above all the position of the subject in relation to the pack or wolf-multiplicity; how the subject joins or does not join the pack, how far away it stays, how it does or does not hold to the multiplicity.
>
> GILLES DELEUZE AND FELIX GUATTARI,
> *A Thousand Plateaus: Capitalism and Schizophrenia*

As explained in the preceding section, the self is not a unified identity, and even those groups that attempt to portray themselves as homogenous actually are heterogeneous. In other words, every self, and every group, is a multiplicity. "Multiplicity tolerates no dependence on the identical in the subject or in the object."[29] Butler and Deleuze both encourage us to become comfortable with our multiplicity, to try to subvert the attempts of the powerful to create unity. For Butler, this attempt is best made through performativity. Since identity is not a fixed thing, since there is no transcendent "I" that exists outside of our culture and its laws and power structures, our identity is something that we perform. Given a particular context, we may perform a different identity than in another context. Sometimes we perform an identity that fits our context and what is expected. This notion of performativity, however, also allows us the ability to perform an identity that is outside the norm. The degree to which one's performance of identity is in the center or on the periphery depends on, as Deleuze and Guattari comment, "the position of the subject [the wolf] in relation to the pack or wolf-multiplicity."[30]

We perform our identity through repeating. As explained above, repetition is never repetition of the same. Repetition produces difference. While most of our repetitions reinstate or perpetuate some version of the norms into which we are born, there are some forms of repetition that subvert the structures. Butler indicates that there are reproductions we can perform that cause "dissonance, internal confusion,"[31] and she calls this type of repetition parody. For Butler, parody repeats those things that have been naturalized by culture and language and uses them in an unexpected way that disturbs the usual understanding and illuminates the fact that these "norms" are not natural at all. The excluded often appear to be invisible within the power structures, but in the parodic repetition of the dominant norms, the excluded multitude can become visible.

Butler reminds us constantly that there is always a danger of seemingly subversive performativity reinscribing the norm. In the example of the singing of the national anthem in Spanish, Butler explains this possible problem in their performative act. The nation is confronted with a performance that makes it uncomfortable because the anthem becomes something new and different. The beloved song becomes something unrecognizable, something that subverts the norm. At the same time, the act of singing a song that lifts up the notion of national equality and homogeneity could be seen as a reinscription of the people into the fold of the nation's identity since the nation's identity is formed in part by the marginalization of these individuals.[32] Being aware of our own multiplicity and the ways in which we perform various identities allows us to perform an identity that acknowledges the multiplicity, illuminates the power structures in which we are inscribed, and attempts to subvert those structures even though they are always part of our story. "When I tell the truth about myself, I consult not only my 'self,' but the way in which that self is produced and producible, the position from which the demand to tell the truth proceeds, the effects that telling the truth will have in consequence, as well as the price that must be paid."[33]

As we perform our identities, we are confronted with the multiplicity that exists within our society and within ourselves.

> There are no individual statements, there never are. Every statement is the product of a machinic assemblage, in other words, of collective agents of enunciation. . . . [I]t is on the contrary when the individual opens up to the multiplicities pervading him or her, at the outcome of the most severe operation of depersonalization [nonidentity], that he or she acquires his or her true proper name.[34]

Only by a performative repeating of identities do we become aware of the multiplicity that resides within us. Deleuze explains that "the individual is far from indivisible, never ceasing to divide and change its nature. It is not a Self with regard to what it expresses, for it expresses Ideas in the form of internal multiplicities, made up of differential relations."[35] In other words, our internal multiplicity, which makes up our nonidentity, is illuminated when we recognize the performativity of our acts and the way in which they adhere to or subvert—through the repetition and difference of social norms—the social structures into which we are born.

"The Wolf-Man Keeps Howling": Philosophy for Social Transformation?

> That philosophy might be divorced from life, that life might not be fully ordered by philosophy, struck me as a perilous possibility.
>
> JUDITH BUTLER, *Undoing Gender*

To return again to our beginning question: What is the use of all of this abstract theorizing and word-play? Does it matter, on a practical level, that we do not have a unified, homogenous identity? Why should we try to become-wolf by recognizing our multiplicity, the way in which we perform identities, and the fact that we are implicated in one another's self-narratives? As stated in the introduction, in agreement with Butler and Deleuze, I see language, or the way in which we talk, as a means for challenging the ways in which we think and, subsequently, act. I also agree with Butler that philosophy is nothing more than abstract pondering unless it has implications for us as actual people living together.[36]

When it seems we are merely performing academic acrobatics by throwing around terms like "multiplicities," "nonidentity," and so forth, we must remember that this language can indeed be used to "invoke, incite, and solicit a different future."[37] In considering the concepts brought forth in this chapter, "difference and repetition," "nonidentity," "multiplicities," and "performativity," we must recognize the practical possibilities within these ways of thinking and speaking. Philosophers who work in areas like feminist philosophy and environmental philosophy find a clear and direct link between their thoughts and the situation in the real world. Butler, as a thinker who has written specifically on feminist issues as well as more broad political issues, explains that she is "not a very good materialist. Every time I try to write about the body, the writing ends up being about language."[38] One cannot separate language from thought and action.

If we can begin to think about ourselves as multiplicities constructed by those around us, if we can begin to think of ourselves as not just one wolf, but many—the wolf is the pack—then perhaps we can begin to think about the ways in which we act toward one another. If my identity is formed by those around me, then those people are part of who I am on a very intimate level. "The uniqueness of the other is exposed to me, but mine is also exposed to her. This does not mean we are the same, but only that we are bound to one another by what differentiates us."[39] Even when we do not agree with one another, even when we hurt one another, we are connected. When someone acts on us in helpful or harmful ways, they act on themselves as well, and vice versa. Victim and victimizer are inextricably bound. Their stories are inseparable, their identities are formed by one another and by the way in which they treat one another. The CEO who closes his plants in America in order to save money by shipping the work overseas is implicated in the identities, in the narratives of those American workers who lose their jobs and in the narratives of those overseas workers who do not make what they should for the work they are doing. Not only is the CEO a part of their identities, but they become a part the CEO's identity when he becomes known as a smart businessman by his competitors or as a tight-fisted money-maker by his past employees. Perhaps when we begin to consider the ways in which our lives are intertwined—so intimately that those on whom we act have a direct impact on who we are—we will begin to consider acting toward one another differently.

"We are in our skins, given over, in each other's hands, at each other's mercy. This is a situation we do not choose. It forms the horizon of choice, and it grounds our responsibility. In this sense, we are not responsible for it, but it creates the conditions under which we assume responsibility. We did not create it, and therefore it is what we must heed."[40] In other words, we do not have a choice concerning how our identities are formed, who becomes a part of them, and whom we affect as a result of our thoughts, speech, and actions. This lack of choice makes it imperative for us to think about those who surround us. It gives us a responsibility to ensure that our thoughts and actions have the effect we would wish them to have on ourselves and on those around us. If our choices as consumers have an impact on the identity of those around us, even those from other countries, then these choices also have an impact on our own identity because of the link between us created by our purchasing choices. If we become aware of the fact that certain imported products have contributed to the devastation of rainforests and the subsequent ruination of the lives of the people who depend on the rainforest, we realize that our lives are connected to their lives. However, by understanding that we are already all implicated in one another's identities and lives (rather than starting with an awareness of the products we buy), then we will be more likely to take the time to examine our behavior and our choices.

Butler's explanation of nonidentity and the way in which we cannot even speak of ourselves without speaking of those around us makes this interconnection clear. My story is your story and yours is mine. This requires us not only to acknowledge these connections but also to carefully consider what type of story we are creating together. Those on the periphery of our society, those we have shunned because they do not fit our ideal of identity, have been constructed by us and we have constructed ourselves in relation to them. As Deleuze writes, "I know that the periphery is the only place I can be, that I would die if I let myself be drawn into the center of the fray, but just as certainly if I let go of the crowd."[41] Those in positions of power and those they stepped over and excluded to get there are part of each other. The powerful are still part of the identity of the marginalized, even as the marginalized attempt to subvert them; the marginalized are still part of the identity of the powerful, even as the powerful attempt to banish them. We may not think that the AIDS epidemic in Africa impacts us here in America. But a sickness in one community means a sickness in all communities because our networks of relationship extend infinitely, continuously folding and enfolding and unfolding us into one another. If my religion is responsible for encouraging African communities to eschew condoms, and I do nothing to try to change the way of thinking of my religious leaders, I am implicated in the plight of the African community, and they become a part of my identity.

In the end, the only responsible action is one of love. This is not love in the sense of sexuality or romance, which are so often bound up with the themes of power and desire to possess.[42] This is love in the sense of acting out of a recognition of our rhizomatic interdependence. It's a love that understands the dependence of the center on the periphery, and of the periphery on the center, a love that seeks to value the multiplicity and chaos inherent in our lives and to strive for justice in the acknowledgement that perhaps the "Golden Rule" is not so much a religious ideal but a way of living responsibly with and in difference. In love, we must carefully consider the choices that we are making. We may not be able to think about every identity of which we are a part, but if we can begin to change our thinking in such a way that we can acknowledge the connections and begin to make choices more carefully, we can encourage a change in speech and action.

> What does it mean to love somebody? It is always to seize that person in a mass, extract him or her from a group, however small, in which he or she participates, whether it be through the family only or through something else; then to find that person's own packs, the multiplicities he or she encloses within himself or herself which may be of an entirely different nature. To join them to mine, to make them penetrate mine, and for me to penetrate the other person's. Heavenly nuptials, multiplicities of multiplicities.[43]

The question is, can we become-wolf? Can we see ourselves not only as one wolf among many but also as a wolf who *is* the pack? The identities with which we are intertwined, the very multiplicities that construct our own identities are calling out, waiting to be heard and acknowledged. The Wolf-Man is howling.

PART TWO

Negotiating Bodies and Societies

CHAPTER 5

Butler and Whitehead on the (Social) Body
Michael Halewood

It is, perhaps, well known that the body made a late entry into the sphere of social theory and has since burgeoned into an important area of research and theorizing so that it now seems surprising that the body and bodily life received such scant attention for so long (albeit with some honorable exceptions). However, the success of this new realm of study also masks a problem. The further that research uncovers and describes the very sociality of the body, the further such analyses, both empirically and conceptually, distance themselves from the "biological" body. As a result the "natural" body is viewed more and more rigidly as either some kind of a fiction (paradoxically, a fiction created by science, yet not simply a "science fiction"), or as irrelevant to the varied levels of social and cultural meanings that are somehow attached or written upon such a body. Consequently, as Mariam Fraser has pointed out, within social science the "'naturalness' of the biological body is hardly challenged," so that the "cultural" body becomes the object of study for the social sciences and the "biological" becomes limited to the concern of the natural science.[1] As Judith Butler has pointed out, such divisions are not only unhelpful but replicate a way of thinking that itself is historical (and gendered) in that they reproduce the subject/object, active/passive binaries of modern Western thought. They are also prime examples of the legacy of what Whitehead refers to as the bifurcation of nature.[2] Such bifurcations have significant consequence with regard to the body. They leave bad post-modernists free to play in a world solely constituted in, through, and by language—thereby treating the body as either an illusion or an impossibility. As such, there is a danger that the findings of social research on the body are too easily dismissed as, at most, interesting but unreal reportings on an epiphenomenal realm that is subsequent to and less consequential than the supposedly real reality of the realm of cells, genes, blood vessels, enzymes, and so on. Of course, to suggest that social research is unaware of such problems would be to overstate the case greatly. A number of writers—for example Karen Barad, Mariam Fraser, Vicky Kirby, and Stella Sandford[3]—have all addressed the need to confront head-on the status of the biological body with regard to and within social analyses. It would thus seem that the time is right to develop a theoretical account of the complex status of the body within existence, an account that is able to describe both the materiality of the body *and* its sociality.

This chapter will attempt to suggest some first moves in this direction through an analysis of the work of Judith Butler and Alfred North Whitehead in terms of the body. It will start by reviewing the input and importance of Butler's work on materiality and the body and will then review some critiques of this work. Whitehead's approach to the body will then be discussed as a possible way of countering such criticisms, specifically through the introduction of the notion of process, and the development of a concept of the social that is not predicated on, or limited to, the human realm. The conclusion will review the possibilities offered by Butler and Whitehead to developing new ways of theorizing the body and will end by tentatively introducing how their work might be developed into producing novel conceptualizations of sexual difference.

Butler on Materiality

One of the most important and influential examples of an attempt to reconceptualize the relation between matter, the body, and subjectivity is to be found in Butler's *Bodies That Matter*. In this text, Butler distances herself from the position of social constructionist that was assigned to her after the publication of *Gender Trouble*. In this later text, Butler is firm in her critique and rejection of social constructionism with regard to "sex," gender, nature, and culture. In *Bodies That Matter*, she clarifies how such constructionism tends to see the social as acting upon a passive nature that, in terms of human sexual difference, is epitomized via the anatomical. Hence, the physical body is viewed simply as the substrate upon which the social and cultural meanings of gender are built. There are thus two kinds of bodies—man and woman, or male and female, depending on the severity of the constructionism that you adopt—yet such distinctions only gain importance through the granting to them of significance by a specific society, culture, or discourse. The latter are thereby designated as active agents, and, consequently, the physical body is reduced to a lifeless, inert receptacle. It is thereby rendered theoretically invisible (although medicine has been happy to accept such a fixed, yet invisible, body as its own). Hence, Butler argues that gender constructionism merely replicates certain masculinist notions: "Is sex to gender as feminine is to masculine?"[4]

As opposed to such accounts, Butler aims to demonstrate that "sex" has a history, as does the concept of nature. In doing so, she argues that linguistic (gender) constructionism is caught in a double bind. For, if language is a cultural phenomenon that is separate from the physical world, as would seem to be the case with the social-constructionist distinction between the physical body and its cultural meanings, then either language cannot gain access to "sex" as a site upon which it acts—thereby demonstrating the limits of constructionism—or "sex" is a prediscursive fiction that entails that everything is already, only linguistic. To put it another way, social constructionism entails that either it is impossible to get to the body through language (or any other means), or a different kind of subject must be posited elsewhere (discourse must be granted a form of subjectivity) in order to account for the social body and to create the human subject. Butler reduces the various strands of this problematic to one succinct question—in what ways is it possible to talk meaningfully about the body? Her short answer is—through a reconsideration of the materiality of matter:

> What I would propose in place of these conceptions of construction is a return to the notion of matter, not as site or surface, but as *a process of materialization that stabilizes over time to produce the effect of boundary, fixity, and surface we call matter*.[5]

The key words here are "process," "time," and "effect" as they indicate the inter-weaving of the notions of materiality and temporality in the coming-to-be of the body. However, there seem to be two types of time operating within Butler's notion of materialization, which she does not clearly indicate as separate. In the quotation given above, she forefronts time as a general, historical mode in which matter sediments within the normative requirements that induce certain forms of matter and subjectivity. This normativity makes up the environment where all further subject formations occur. In this regard, time is not just an aggregation of separate moments of time, for "the 'past' will be the accumulation and congealing of such 'moments' to the point of their indistinguishability."[6] This is a broad view of time. This is the time of discourse in its efficacy as the producer of normative effects; this is time as the macro configuration of the sedimentation of these effects and their continuing influence in materialization. But within such congealment there must also be those "acts," those moments within the process that go to make up that process.

This is a crucial point and one that points up both the value of Butler's approach and a problem in inherent in it. Butler's work is a bold attempt to account both for the general, abstract conditions that envelop and produce the individual occasions of materiality, yet is always aware of the machinations of power within both aspects: She aims to account for "performativity" as an abstracted, limiting, and enabling process *and* to describe individual separate momentary manifestations of performativity. The Whiteheadian question at this point would be: "What is the ontological status of these momentary acts?" "Are they individuated within this process or are they false entities that are merely thought of as atomizing a more general flux?" Butler recognizes this distinction but does not make it explicit within the text. "Construction not only takes place *in* time, but is itself a temporal process,"[7] whilst also maintaining that "an act is itself a repetition, a sedimentation, and congealment of the past which is precisely foreclosed in its act-like status."[8]

This tension between different apparent ontological levels is recognized by Butler in some of her later writings on the body:

> The distance between gender and its naturalized instantiations is precisely the distance between a norm and its incorporations. . . . In fact, the norm only persists as a norm to the extent that it is acted out in social practice and reidealized and reinstituted in and through the daily social rituals of bodily life. The norm has no ontological status, yet it cannot be easily reduced to its instantiations; it is itself (re)produced through its embodiment, through the acts that strive to approximate it, through the idealizations reproduced in and by those acts.[9]

Here Butler critiques Lacan and Lévi-Strauss for separating the symbolic from the social; the symbolic position of the father, they say, is not reducible to those actual fathers who populate the social world.[10] Instead, Butler inverts the level of priority and says that it is social practices and the "daily social rituals of bodily life" that produce the idealizations of the symbolic. But this emphasis on bodily life comes at the expense of the denial of ontological reality to norms. This renders problematic an account of the *process* by which norms are instantiated in the body and then return to the ideal in the re-figuring of norms; that is to say, the lack of a conceptualization of process undermines the attempt to describe the separation of the bodily from the norm, of the social from the symbolic. Furthermore, Butler's elaboration of a concept of the social is one that, whilst avoiding some of the problems of Lacan and Lévi-Strauss, tends to uncritically accept the status and effectivity of the social itself as entirely with the realm of the human or humanity. As will be discussed later on, it is possible that Whitehead's development of the body as process *and* his redeployment of the social as a concept that permeates existence and is not referable only to the human realm might help extend Butler's account and strengthen her critique.

To return to Butler's argument as set out in *Bodies That Matter*, there is a reconciliation to be made between the exterior temporal process that is exemplified in the inculcation of gendered subject positions (for example masculine, feminine), and the actual, individual renderings of these subject positions on different occasions by specific bodies and subjectivities. "The bodies produced through such a regulatory enforcement of gender are bodies in pain, bearing the marks of violence and suffering. Here the ideality of gendered morphology is quite literally incised in the flesh."[11] The detailing and confronting of such violence and suffering is clearly a major concern of Butler's oeuvre and is a thread that runs throughout her work. The need to describe, explain, and re-valorize modes of existence and kinds of bodies that have been refused and abjected is of critical importance. In doing this, Butler also points up the de-politicized character of much philosophy and the need to challenge such un-engaged approaches. "It is not a matter of a simple entry of the excluded into an established ontology, a critical opening up of the questions, What is real? Whose lives are real? How might reality be remade? Those who are unreal have, in a sense, already suffered the violence of derealization."[12]

In order to reapproach the question of lives, bodies, and ontology, Butler is clear that it is necessary to challenge the orthodoxy of a certain strand of post-structuralism that appears to grant all power and agency to the linguistic or the discursive.

Thus, there are, for the purposes of the argument being made here, five main issues that are clarified within *Bodies That Matter*. These are:

The questioning of the sex/gender binary as being able to account for the relation between the natural and the cultural, and the consequent need for a reappraisal of the status of matter.

The description of matter as a result of a process of materialization.

The importance of the concept of time (and, by implication, that of space) as part of such a process.

The need to theorize language (or the linguistic) as utterly material.

The need to engage at a philosophical level with the concepts of matter and subjectivity. For, as Butler has shown, contemporary analyses of their interrelation both rely upon and invoke a theoretical field that has its own history, stretching back to Aristotle.

Overall, Butler has raised a whole field of inquiry and debate and pointed up the need to engage at a philosophical level with the concepts of matter and subjectivity and the body. This marks an important shift in theorizing the body, and Butler's work stands as an important marker and injunction to question and develop new modes of analysis within this politically charged arena. However, her work has not been unanimously accepted. What now follows is a consideration of certain critiques that is intended not as a dismissal of Butler's ideas but as a further consolidation and focusing of the themes of the body and materiality.

Critiques of Butler

One of the most sustained analyses of both Butler's work and the ideas surrounding the notions of matter, corporeality, power, and subjectivity is to be found in Vicki Kirby's *Telling Flesh*. Like Butler, Kirby is striving to think another way through the nature/culture dichotomy with all its accompanying philosophical baggage. And Kirby is also aware of the pitfalls of overexuberant linguistic or discursive constructionism. "I am critical of an empiricism that perceives data as the raw and unmediated nature of the world. However, I am just as critical of postmodern correctives that regard the apparent evidence of nature as the actual representation of culture."[13] One of the main criticisms that Kirby makes of Butler is that, in her attempt to describe how the materiality of signification must be rethought, in order to explain the process of materialization, there is a latent rendering of the signifier solely in terms of psychoanalysis. This "reliance upon a psychoanalytic understanding of the sign, or a reading of 'the discursive' that subordinates itself to an unproblematized category of 'the social,' returns us to the very nature/culture, mind/body divisions that are so politically insidious."[14] That is to say, by focusing upon the relation of language to materiality in terms that privilege the constitution of language in terms of signification, and more specifically through the analysis of such signification in terms of the symbolic and the imaginary and the "real," Butler stays within the limits posted by psychoanalytic theory, albeit the most sophisticated and post-structuralist version thereof, wherein the symbolic is effective and regulatory but is not an ideal realm in itself, but a coalescence of social practices (and thereby alterable): "The symbolic itself is the sedimentation of social practices, and . . . radical alterations in kinship demand a rearticulation of the structuralist presuppositions of psychoanalysis, moving us, as it were toward a queer poststructuralism of the psyche."[15]

However, the symbolic realm is, in such definitions, the human realm; the realm of signification is allied to the (human) linguistic realm. Both of these constitute or are constituted by culture. On such accounts, culture is still not nature. This leads to Kirby's description of Butler's version of the social as "unproblematized." By remaining within the ambit of the psychoanalytic approach to questions of signification, Butler would seem to be constrained by the possibilities already inscribed within such analyses. That is to say, a limit to the theoretical radicality seems to be set, in that the very "nature" of nature is still regarded as either out of bounds, beyond signification, or simply impossible to talk of meaningfully. And the social tends to be rendered as that which is not natural. Whitehead's work on the status of the social will be introduced later on as a way of both problematizing this notion of the social and of moving beyond a conception of the social that is predicated on the human.

Further critiques of Butler, such as Pheng Cheah's of *Bodies That Matter* and Elizabeth Grosz's *Volatile Bodies*, point up the pressing political implications involved in contemporary discussions of matter, nature, and culture:

> [The] . . . obsessive pushing away of nature may well constitute an acknowledgement-in-disavowal that humans may be natural creatures after all. Furthermore, as a theoretical position, antinaturalism itself is produced by the polemical energy that strives to keep nature at bay. . . . Consequently, antinaturalism works with a conventional philosophical definition of nature . . . the concepts of "nature" and "the given" are, in fact, neuralgic points, the contested sites around which any theory of political transformation is organized.[16]

So, it is the refusal to take on the "natural" as a contested term, as a term that is not necessarily explainable solely in relation or opposition to the cultural, that, they argue, leads Butler ultimately to produce analyses that end up simply as restatements of an entrenched philosophical position. The aim is, hence, to provide an engagement and conceptualization of existence, of nature, and of bodies that is not predicated on any form of essentialism and that also avoids prioritizing the human.

That is to say, one notion that runs through all critiques of Butler is her ultimate reliance upon some version of human priority. "In her syncretization of Foucault/Aristotle, matter is invested with dynamism and said to be open to contestation only because the matter concerned is the product of sociohistorical forms of power, that is, *of the human realm*."[17] By identifying how Butler situates changing forms of matter only in the "human realm," Cheah, like Kirby, uncovers the anthropocentric aspect of Butler's account. This leads to an assigning of a primary dynamism to the cultural, at the expense of the depth of the materiality of matter. Thus, Butler's commentary is reduced to describing the surface of bodies rather than their "weightiness": "the materiality of the body now designates its contours of intelligibility."[18] Again, Cheah identifies this position as one ultimately *within* rather than challenging established philosophical discourse. "The specter of Kantianism returns precisely because materiality becomes present, is given body, materializes only in being named or signified in language, which cannot quite avoid the role of being an epistemic grid of sorts."[19]

There is, therefore, a recourse to the dualistic approach that is more concerned with explaining the significance of matter or nature for human subjectivity rather than asking the question of "what is the significance of matter for itself?" "What is never once posed in Butler's debate . . . is the possibility that matter could have a dynamism that is neither the negativity of the unsymbolizable nor reducible to a function of productive form."[20] Here, there is evidence of a shift from a critique of Butler to the need for a theoretical reassessment along ontological lines. "Philosophically speaking, this is why we need an account of the political agency of bodies that no longer respects the form/matter or nature/culture distinctions."[21]

This chapter aims to introduce Whitehead's approach to the body as a way of developing such lines of thought. That is to say, it has been seen how one of the recurrent themes of recent critiques of Butler's writings is that of "anthropocentrism": "It is precisely the focus on materialization (rather than on 'substance,' for example . . .) that critics argue has served to confine Butler's analysis of matter only to an account of *human* materiality."[22] (And, as will be seen, it is clear that Whitehead offers more than simply an account of *human* materiality). Returning to Fraser's statement above, it indicates two important points that will be raised (even if not answered) in this chapter:

> The need to provide an account of the process through which the items of the universe gain their materiality. This is similar to Butler's concerns as evident in her usage of the term "materialization."
>
> Given that analyses of the relations between matter and subjectivity must in some way be interested in the "human realm" and the machinations of power and language therein, is it possible to give an account of the processual character of reality that is not predicated upon the "human" as a privileged aspect of such a theory? Is it therefore possible to re-think the social and the character of society as something that is not predicated on humans?

It is in these terms that Whitehead's work can be considered as an important intervention and attempt to develop lines of thought wherein matter is considered as neither a fixed and prior universal nor as something that is limited to the human, or based upon human concerns. Any definition of humanness, if such a thing is desired, must proceed from a wider understanding of the activity of matter, and not be predicated upon the agency of humans. As E. A. Wilson provocatively puts it: "Matter (human, non-human, living, technological) does not simply *have* the capacity to convert, it *is* the capacity to convert. All matter wanders."[23]

Beyond Bodies That Matter

Most of the previous analysis of Butler, and all of the critiques of her work, have focused on the text *Bodies That Matter*. Before proceeding to a discussion of Whitehead in relation to the issues raised so far, it is worth considering the extent to which Butler's more recent works might be construed as either a rebuttal or confirmation of such approaches.

With regard to the question of anthropocentrism, Butler is clear that she is concerned with explicating the status of humans within the world (but this need not necessarily coincide with either anthropocentrism or humanism): "I may seem to be positing a new basis for humanism. This might be true, but I am prone to consider this differently. A vulnerability must be perceived and recognized . . . vulnerability is one precondition for humanization."[24] And it would surely be too blinkered to assert that theorists were disallowed from addressing the constitution or non-constitution of humans merely on the grounds that this sounded too much like old-fashioned Enlightenment humanism. With regard to the charge that Butler's work is framed in terms of psychoanalytic conceptions of human subjectivity and its concomitant notion of negativity and lack, Butler is clear that she accepts, at least in part, this charge. "My sense is that it would be right to say, as Braidotti does, that I sometimes stay within the theology of lack, that I sometimes focus on the labor of the negative."[25] Again, however, it would not seem that this, in itself could be seen as fateful to her account of materiality and subjectivity, even if it were to skew her analysis. Indeed, Butler explains further: "I confess, however, that I am not a very good materialist. Every time I try to write about the body, the writing ends up being about language. This is not because I think that the body is reducible to language; it is not. Language emerges from the body, constituting an emission of sorts."[26]

Butler clearly does not think she has solved the problem of the relation of materiality to the body, and Butler's more recent work has clarified how certain aspects of the critiques made against her have, perhaps, missed some of the force or purpose of her texts. At the same time, there are clearly aspects of her work that seem to remain open to the claims that she remains within a Foucauldian, if not a Kantian, conception of the knowability of the human condition as subject to a grid of intelligibility: "Persons are regulated by gender, and this sort of regulation operates as a condition of cultural intelligibility for any person."[27] It is in these terms that Butler would seem to instantiate either the cultural (or the social) as distinct from the natural. And it is this refusal to go beyond the conceptualization of the cultural and the natural (or the social and the natural) that is perhaps the most telling and pervasive critique of Butler's approach to the body. It is not so much that she refuses to engage with questions of the natural. But that, in her texts, the social is granted a self-explanatory (if not prioritized) form.

For example, in her refutation of the charge of humanism, as discussed above, where she talks about, rather, how "vulnerability is one precondition for humanization," the notion of vulnerability is developed in the following terms: "Each of us is constituted politically in part by virtue of the social vulnerability of our bodies."[28] And the question arises of what Butler understands by the social here. What extra work or force is assumed or dismissed by the term "social" here? What is at stake in not referring to natural vulnerability (which might smack of essentialism)? Does the term "social" here immediately invoke sympathy? This reliance upon a wide-ranging notion of the social permeates various sections of more recent Butler texts, especially in relation to her renewed conception of the body and the bodily:

> Constituted as a social phenomenon in the public sphere, my body is and is not mine. Given over from the start to the world of others, it bears their imprint, is formed within the crucible of social life; only later, and with some uncertainty, do I lay claim to my body as my own, if, in fact, I ever do.[29]

Again, this seems to grant a priority to the social-political-cultural realm that in and of itself is not explained. However, its meaning, its animus, its status, all seem to be predicated on the human, on humanity.

This may seem like a surprising criticism, to state that Butler invokes a conception of sociality that is based on a notion of the human. Is not this the point of the social? Is the social not that concept that by definition refers to and accedes to humanity? The fact that the answer is historically "yes"—that this is exactly how the social has been conceived—is only the more problematic. For surely Butler is trying to shift, challenge, deepen, widen (as opposed to simply reject) the notion of humans, humanity, and humanization. That is to say, some of Butler's assertions, perhaps, make sense too easily. For example, Butler states that the problem that sexual difference poses is "the permanent difficulty of determining where the biological, the psychic, the discursive, the social begin and end."[30] That is to say, putting the question in these terms would tend to repeat and even confirm the modes of thinking of the body, of bodies, as implicated within or without or between a set of fields and problems that have their own identity, range, and sense. For example, what exactly is meant by biology? Why is it not social? There is not time to review all these questions here, clearly. However, it should be noted that a reappraisal of their status and interrelation would seem to be an important element of that task of developing an effective politics that recognizes the sedimented character of our practices, thoughts, abstractions, actions, and bodies and yet the need to work within these to move beyond them. As Butler puts it: "If there can be a modernity without foundationalism, then it will be one in which the key terms of its operation are not fully secured in advance, one that assumes a futural form for politics."[31]

The following section will take up the challenge, specifically, of rethinking the body in relation to sociality and to process. This is certainly not intended as a rejection of Butler's important and continuingly significant work. For, as will be seen, the texts of Whitehead could be seen as lacking political engagement or significance. His thought has to be made to work for us. This chapter will use the work of Butler and the critiques thereof as the focus around which Whitehead's notion of the body can best contribute to contemporary research. In the later sections, elements of Butler's thought will be reintroduced as the notion of the social body as a process is developed. All this will be undertaken in the spirit of Butler's approach where she states that "perhaps the most important task is to think through the debates on the body, since it may or may not be true that cultural construction effaces both sexual difference and bodily process."[32]

Whitehead on the Body and the Social

For Whitehead, writing his philosophical works primarily in the 1920s and the 1930s, the distinction between nature and society did not have the political aspect that it does today. Nevertheless, there is much that is still, perhaps even more, relevant in his attempts to challenge the prevalent scientific approach that views nature as a separate entity, fixed and external to humans whose task it is to investigate, discover, or uncover the laws hidden therein. So, while Whitehead had no direct interest in questions about sexual difference or gender, he maintained that accounting for the body was one of the main tasks of philosophy.[33] Although he describes his philosophical approach as "a recurrence to pre-Kantian modes of thought,"[34] this is not to suggest some kind of a return to a premodern conception of the world. Whitehead's thought is not backward looking or nostalgic. Rather, it demands us to understand, rethink, and reconstruct some of the most trenchant of modernity's concepts in order to advance science, philosophy, society, and life. So, when Whitehead does use the term "nature" throughout his work, it is in a very specific manner: "Nature is a process"[35]; it is not an inert or objective realm. Furthermore, for Whitehead, there is no sharp division between a body and its environment: The former is a complex rendition or aspect of the latter. "Mankind [sic] is that factor *in* nature which exhibits in its most intense form the plasticity of nature."[36] It is Whitehead's attempts to situate the human body within his notion of a *plastic* nature that will be taken up in the rest of this chapter.

Within the philosophy of organism, neither the body nor the mind is to be given any privileged place. The human body is no more than an element, although a complex one, within the more general solidarity of the world considered as an extensive region constituted by the becomings of myriad actual entities. "The body is that portion of nature with which each moment of human experience intimately cooperates. There is an inflow and an outflow of factors between the bodily actuality and the human experience, so that each shares in the existence of the other."[37] As such, just like all other bodies, the human body can only exist in relation to the "external" world of which it is another element. Moreover, all bodies comprise the living and nonliving in differing combinations. Hence, Whitehead has already made an important step in avoiding the claim that he prioritizes either life or matter (or by analogy, culture or the body) by insisting upon their intermingling as constituting all "things" (everything).

For Whitehead, the status and situatedness of the body are not merely physical. Whitehead uses the term the "witness of the body" to describe how the body is always situated and operating within and in relation to its environment. And, crucially, this is not a brute, physical relation; there is always the manner of that relation. This brings in a qualitative element to the positioning and continual existence of the body. There is no gap between the body, the world, and experience. "For instance, we see the contemporary chair, but we see it *with* our eyes."[38] In order to explain how the world is presented to the body in a manner that does not reduce either of these to being a simple physical fact or a constitutive subject, Whitehead introduces one of his technical terms: "eternal objects." This notion has provided some confusion and consternation among readers of Whitehead that it will not be possible to address here. Put simply, if Whitehead is correct in his critique of those philosophical and scientific accounts that reduce existence to inert matter, separate from living subjects, humans, consciousness, etc., then he will have to invoke how potentiality, conceptuality, and mentality are neither excluded from fact nor confined to human subjectivity. "Fact includes in its own nature something that is not fact, although it constitutes a realized item within fact. This is the conceptual side of facts."[39] And one of the ways in which he does this is through the term "eternal objects" (as well as that of "Propositions").[40] The point being made here is that the body, perception, experience, the world, facticity, the past, individuality, potentiality, and conceptuality are all co-constituents of existence. A taste of Whitehead's approach to this is as follows:

> These [eternal] objects are "given" for the experience of the subject. Their givenness does not arise from the "decision" of the contemporary entities which are thus objectified. *It arises from the functioning of the antecedent physical body of the subject*; and this functioning can in its turn be analysed as representing the influence of the more remote past. . . . Thus these sense-data are eternal objects playing a complex relational role.[41]

The point here is to indicate Whitehead's thorough and on-going insistence that existence, any existence, all existence, insofar as it is genuine existence, does not simply comprise brute, isolated, physicality. Its becoming always involves what is variously referred to as mentality, conceptuality, potentiality. The core of this is established in his account of the metaphysical status of existence in terms of what he calls "actual entities"—"each actuality is essentially bipolar, physical and mental, and the physical inheritance is essentially accompanied by a novel conceptual reaction."[42]

So, this is not an attempt to develop a new theory of concepts or the conceptual and it is certainly no reassertion of the primacy of the mind through the back door of conceptuality. Rather, it is all part of Whitehead's rigorous emplacement of potentiality within the very materiality of matter. This is effected by the process of materiality and enables Whitehead to avoid the trap of having to resort to culture, discourse, or the symbolic as the primary realm wherein such matter is signified or materialized.[43] As such, conceptual feelings, in Whitehead, operate as the vector from eternal objects to the constitution of individual entities, via concepts. As such: "the eternal object . . . is the datum of the conceptual feeling."[44] And, conceptual feelings "are the particular feelings of universals, and are not feelings of other particular existents exemplifying universals."[45] But still, this notion of conceptuality is not one that is predicated on the existence of the (human) mind. Instead, thought is an outcome—"The philosophy of organism . . . conceives the thought as a constituent operation in the creation of the occasional thinker."[46]

It will be noticed that the last of these quotations moved from the abstract metaphysical level to that of a thinking (human) subject. That actual entities and eternal objects appear to be the prime metaphysical elements of Whitehead's philosophy is often discussed. However, actual entities, although they describe the general nature of existence, do not and cannot immediately explicate the complexity of the world of humans, cells, rocks, and plants. Such a world or worlds are not distinct from the realm of actual entities nor are they identical with them. Whitehead uses the term "societies" to refer to those continuing, enduring groups of actual entities that populate the world as rocks, stones, cheese-boards, etc. Didier Debaise has both clarified and emphasized the importance of recognizing the role of societies within Whitehead's work. For the argument being made here, in relation to the work of Butler, this notion of societies is crucial to a reconsideration of the social as something that is not predicated on the human. However, this recasting of the social starts, for Whitehead, at the most metaphysical level.

> Every actual entity is in its nature essentially social; and this in two ways. First, the outlines of its own character are determined by the data which its environment provides for its process of feeling. Secondly, these data are not extrinsic to the entity; they constitute that display of the universe which is inherent in the entity.[47]

Thus, the social, for Whitehead, is a way of describing how each entity is constituted by and through its environment; how each entity is a rendering of the past in the present; how that which is originally external becomes constitutive of the internality of an individual (and all this at the metaphysical level). In one sense this is echoed in Butler's statement that "individuation is an accomplishment, not a presupposition."[48] What is crucial to note in Whitehead's formulation is that there is no recourse to the "other" (or the "Other") or to negativity or lack as constitutive of being or identity. Rather, being an individual is an outcome of the combining of elements that were previously diverse. And this is what guarantees individuality and posits sociality at the core of existence. But, this is only possible exactly insofar as it is not predicated on the human as the progenitor or guarantor of sociality. This thereby distinguishes Whitehead from the attempt to describe individuality as sociality that is to be found in Butler, especially when she bases sociality on the interrelation of humans within the cultural realm. For example: "At the most intimate levels, we are social; we are comported toward a 'you'; we are outside ourselves, constituted in cultural norms that precede and exceed us, given over to a set of cultural norms and a field of power that condition us fundamentally."[49] That is to say, perhaps Whitehead's formulation of sociality as constitutive of all individuality might enable Butler to better describe the utter intimacy of the social and also to avoid positing the human cultural realm as either a prioritized mode of understanding or of being (and, hence, the charges of anthropocentrism etc. as outlined above).

As Debaise reminds us, to equate the description of metaphysical individuality with a description of the enduring bodies that populate the contemporary world (as dogs, human bodies, libraries, ants, plastic toys, etc.)

is to misunderstand Whitehead's account.[50] Such continuing existents cannot be accounted for simply in the terms of being an actual entity. Rather, they are, in Whitehead's sense of the term, "societies." A "society," in the sense in which that term is here used, is a nexus with social order; and an "enduring object," or "enduring creature," is a society whose social order has taken the special form of "personal order."[51] This social order is defined by the common manner in which the entities of that society prehend or grasp the world. In this sense they share a common characteristic, a common form. However this form is not a preexisting category, class, or Platonic form. Instead, this common characteristic refers to the shared manner in which this society constitutes itself out of, and in relation to, its milieu, its environment. As such, societies describe the common qualitative aspect of the enduring existence of a body.[52] And this applies to any body—animal body, human body, a rock, a toy.[53] This is not to suggest that there is only one society in an enduring object such as a human. Whitehead deploys the term "structured society" to account for such creatures.[54] Hence, the human body is a structured society in that it includes various subordinate societies yet has a level of individuality. More specifically, Whitehead maintains that the eyes, hands, ears, etc., atomize the body in that they can be seen as structured societies in their own right. Thus, the body itself is both atomized and yet exhibits some form of "community"; it holds together not simply in a physical way but through the communality of its experience of both the physical and the conceptual. The organs of the body are no more and no less than that which both gain their individuality from the "external" world and amplify the fact that they are composed of the external through their interrelation with the rest of the body: "The human body is to be conceived of as a complex 'amplifier.'"[55] But once again, this is not simply a physical relation; indeed, it cannot be (given the role of eternal objects), nor is it limited to those eternal objects associated with sense-perception. "Our bodies are largely contrivances whereby some central actual occasion may inherit these basic experiences of its antecedent parts. . . . In a sense, the difference between a living organism and the inorganic environment is only a question of degree."[56]

Thus, the body provides the immediate environment within which sense-data (the contemporary relationship with eternal objects) are felt; the contemporary body manifests the history of a specific set of becomings, and this history influences but does not determine the contemporary body. Eternal objects must always ingress in a particular way and the body will play an important role in influencing this. For instance, an angry person will smell coffee in a different manner than a calm person; the contemporary body is the temporary site of this anger (it arises from the past) and thereby affects the contemporary ingression of eternal objects (how the smell of the coffee is, literally, in-corporated). In a sense, the body repeats itself but only insofar as it is always different. Whitehead's work is, therefore, not necessarily a dismissal of Butler but suggests a way of thinking the active repetition of the body within a specific environment and in regard to a specific and traceable historical milieu (in the sense that the past is implicated) but without needing to reduce this to a cultural intelligible or explanatory realm.

> Our dominant inheritance from our immediately past occasion is broken into by innumerable inheritances through other avenues. Sensitive nerves, the functionings of our viscera, disturbances in the composition of our blood, break in upon the dominant line of inheritance. In this way, emotions, hopes, fears, inhibitions, sense-perceptions arise, which physiologists confidently ascribe to bodily functionings . . . physiologists, who are apt to see more body than soul in human beings.[57]

Hence, the task of philosophy, of theory, of sociology is not to ignore the physicality of the body nor is it to focus solely on the meaningful realm of emotions, hopes, and fears. Both of these approaches simply replicate the bifurcation of nature. Instead, the complex task is to account for manner in which real material bodies come to be. This will involve an account of the manner in which they emerge, that which they repeat, that which they include, and that which they exclude. And, while this is not to suggest that we need to give an account of the soul per se, this quotation from Whitehead does indicate the need to include in our analyses every thing and every factor that is relevant to the constitution of bodies, of all bodies, of human bodies, of gendered bodies, of sexed bodies, of sexual bodies.

Conclusion

The first part of this chapter was taken up with an analysis of Butler's work on materiality and the body and then proceeded to present a range of critiques of her work that focused on her recourse to a theory of signification that remained within a psychoanalytic framework and was thereby ultimately limited to explanation of and within a human realm. The subsequent reading of Whitehead was then offered as a way of avoiding such problems and indeed of broadening our understanding and analysis of bodies. This analysis was intended to reappraise the status of the body and the ability of social theory to account for it, in all its materiality and physicality, and not simply its metaphorical or significatory properties. However, it should be noted that such a return to the materiality of the body is *not* a return to socio-biology or some form of essentialism. Quite the opposite, one of the great aspects of the work of Whitehead is the opportunity that it offers social theory to address fully the material body without falling back into static, fixed, essentialist philosophical or scientific categories.

For example, it may enable social theorists to reapproach one of the most thorny problems with regard to human physicality, namely that of sexual difference. Within recent years and especially within feminist thought, the important question as to the status and consequences of conceiving and describing the body in terms of sexual difference have been explored in various ways. One possible position suggests that sexual difference is itself a fiction. Another solution might be to suggest that there are as many sexes as there are humans, thereby getting over the problem of sexual dimorphism but lacking the critical purchase required to explain ongoing gender and sexual inequality. Between, or beyond these poles, Butler's position is as follows:

> To the extent that the "I" is secured by its sexed position, this "I" and its "position" can be secured only by being *repeatedly* assumed, whereby "assumption" is not a singular act or event, but, rather, an iterable practice. . . . This suggests that 'sexed positions are not localities but, rather, citational practices instituted within a juridical domain.[58]

This returns us to the important distinction made at the beginning of this piece between the wider process of materialization and those individual moments or acts of congealing. With regard to sexual difference, this would seem to suggest the intriguing possibility of developing a position whereby sexual difference comes to be, but comes to be physically. This would seem to be what Butler wants to say but she is unable to do so in that she is hampered by the theoretical framework she has adopted. Hence, when Butler states that "'sexed positions' are not localities," this limits the analysis. It remains at the level of citation, the iterable, at the level of the symbolic and thus, as discussed earlier in this piece, by remaining within the system of psycho-analytic terms and theory is, ultimately, unable to account for the material materiality of such sexed positions. While there is not space to develop the implications of Whitehead's work for conceptions of sexual difference, it would seem clear that Whitehead would disagree with Butler and insist that each sexed position is indeed a locality—a social-physical, enduring, yet temporary, locality. Again, it must be emphasized that this is not an attempt to indulge in a naming or re-naming of the sexes. This is not a re-assertion of the "genuine nature" of sexual difference. Rather, it is to suggest that, following Whitehead's account of the becoming to be of the body—a coming to be that includes both physicality and potentiality—it might be possible to describe sexed positions as localities, remembering that, according to Whitehead such localities, while always actual (material) are also temporal. They come to be but they pass and are gone beyond. One has to keep becoming, to keep being made, to keep making oneself a man (for example) and the manner, place, and situations whereby this is achieved will vary. What it is most important to note is that the possession (or non-possession) of a penis does not subtend or define or create the materiality of the sexed position of a man, though its materiality may well be a crucial element within that sexed position. As Butler puts it: "There may be ways that masculinity emerges in women, and that feminine and masculine do not belong to differently sexed bodies."[59] So, instead of isolating masculine and feminine within the symbolic or significatory realm (as opposed to the physical realm of the body), the task would be to reconceptualize masculine and feminine as qualitative aspects of existence as expressed by Whitehead's notion of eternal objects. It is through the ingression of such potentialities that matter comes to be and that bodies become individualized. Such individualizations are neither determined nor determining but they can become crucial elements of the contemporary renditions of power, matter, and the body. Whitehead gives us a framework for thinking in this way. Butler provides an account of the conditions and consequences of the valuations of specific and different bodies in the present world. So, while the conclusions of this chapter are intended to be tentative, they do point to the importance of Butler and Whitehead in enabling us to rethink the materiality of the body. Butler's work points to how social theory might build on Whitehead so that it is able to fully describe the processes and effects that produce and are produced by the limited sexed positions that are recognized in our society: "We cannot represent ourselves as merely bounded beings, for the primary others who are past for me not only live on in the fiber of the boundary that contains me (one meaning of 'incorporation'), but they also haunt the way I am."[60]

This chapter has argued that, under Whitehead's influence, any such re-consideration of the relationship of individuality to boundedness must involve a dispersal of current notions of the social so that they are not limited to or predicated on the human. This might then enable social theory to analyze and account for the limited localities and becomings that populate the contemporary world, with all the consequences, effects, and rendering of power that that entails. The notion of process thereby becomes key to explain how, when, and where the establishment of such actual but temporary sexed positions occurs and what and "who" is excluded from these. The point is not to fix the sexed body as the guarantor of identity but to investigate the methods by which the repetitions of bodily materiality are linked to profound and continuing social inequalities.

CHAPTER 6

Conflict

Isabella Palin

> A strong disinclination to obey is often accompanied by an equally strong disinclination to dominate and command.
>
> HANNAH ARENDT, *On Violence*

The purpose of this chapter is to show how selected elements of Judith Butler's recent work, of Gilles Deleuze's reading of Nietzsche, and of Alfred North Whitehead's mature philosophy together contribute to constructing an alternative rationale for action in situations of "conflict" in the widest sense, an alternative rationale with respect to one that is often seen operating in various spheres of human affairs, and that involves the use of various kinds of violence against a perceived enemy. These three authors have been chosen for their common appreciation of conflict as being not only an inevitable feature of human life but also an essential, vitalizing factor in the construction of "better" conditions of life with respect to prevailing social structures. The chapter also raises the question of how institutions that organize political decision-making might become infected by this alternative mode of thought. It is not the purpose of the chapter to review practices of diplomacy, conflict-management, etc., or, with respect to the question that will be raised at the end, to argue the virtues of types of political institutions—that is to say, it is not the purpose to intervene in current discussions of practice, but to treat the problem of conflict conceptually, with the hope that it may provide some propositions of use in such discussions. By "propositions" I mean speculative ideas thrown up in the mode of possibility ("perhaps . . .") that are susceptible of providing agency in the work of solving problems, without having the power of defining concrete solutions or making normative claims.[1]

The problem we shall be addressing concerns situations where incompatible positions are locked in conflict in a way that seems non-negotiable, and that tends to constitute the rivaling positions as "evil" with respect to each other, requiring recourse to some form of violence for resolution. The problem concerns, therefore, situations where no common ground can be assumed for communication and where the opposition embodied in the conflict seems to necessitate the elimination of one or several of the terms involved. This "elimination" can take various forms in the concrete; for example, it may have the effect of perpetuating a cycle of violence when, as Butler points out, retribution or self-defense is invoked to justify it;[2] or it may take the form of stigmatism, when others are branded, according to one's point of view, as "inhuman" or "sick," as "infidels," as "unpatriotic" or "undemocratic," as "fascists," "terrorists," etc., with the effect of disqualifying their voices from the scene of possible negotiations and debate;[3] or elimination may present itself as a salvation and a boon when conversion to their own point of view (which will be the correct, rational, authoritative one, etc.) structures the method of communication. There are doubtless many other ways of eliminating the opponent, but whether the violence involves ostracism and psychological terrorism, conversion to a right opinion, killing, torture and humiliation, or other methods, the rationale of violence at work in attempting to resolve conflict through the destruction of any of the voices involved may be described as corresponding to a certain traditional conception of power that relies on the "command-obedience" relationship discussed by Hannah Arendt.[4] Arendt, however, also describes a variant tradition, in which the notion of power does not rely on this relationship, and which can be discerned, according to her analysis, in the Athenian notion of isonomy, the Roman notion of *civitas*, and the thought of the eighteenth-century French revolutionaries. This tradition does "not identify power and rule or law and command," but understands the power of the law as citizens' "*support* of the laws to which [they have given their] consent."[5] She concludes from her discussion of these distinct conceptions of power and their relationship to violence:

> Power and violence are opposites; where the one rules absolutely, the other is absent. Violence appears where power is in jeopardy, but left to its own course it ends in power's disappearance. This implies that it is not correct to think of the opposite of violence as nonviolence; to speak of nonviolent

power is actually redundant. Violence can destroy power; it is utterly incapable of creating it.[6]

What is this power that is the opposite of violence? This question will become pertinent at the end of the chapter, after we have seen what elements our three authors might provide towards producing a conception of conflict that might be able to participate in this tradition.

Grounds for Dialogue and Scenes of Address

The problem is that we sometimes find ourselves in situations embodying a fundamental conflict of values such that there is no common ground, no site for the negotiation of positions to find a solution that might accommodate the concerns of the different parties—and that *it nevertheless happens* that we recoil at the violence implied in the rationale of dominance and submission (even when we are not the immediate victims of it and however sympathetic we may be to the concerns and fears behind the reasons invoked to justify it). The problem consists, to paraphrase Butler, in the question of *what it might mean to refuse* this rationale;[7] or, in the spirit of Herman Melville's Bartleby, of what it might mean *to prefer not to* follow it: If nonviolence does not, perhaps, have to mean capitulation to the other's demands, what does it mean—rather, what might it mean? What might it come to mean?

It is not enough to call for goodwill, for an effort to enter into dialogue, however repulsive the prospect. For a start, both the appeal and the refusal to enter into dialogue can be made from the vantage of a claimed moral high ground or can constitute a strategy for imposing one's own will on the other, and dialogue itself can embody various forms of violence if it is structured according to the morality of dominance and submission. Furthermore, goodwill may simply not be forthcoming, especially in situations where dialogue itself is likely to be interpreted as constituting a form of "collusion with the enemy" or relinquishing of one's position. How far, in effect, does our idea of dialogue embrace the notion not only of a clash of *interests* upon some common ground, even the minimal common ground of goodwill, but also of a fundamental difference of what I shall call *values*? There is more than interest at stake in such conflict. Consider, for example, a point Butler makes about gay marriage in *Undoing Gender*: She asks whether campaigning for the right to marry does not serve to consolidate dominant norms (values) in the sense that it is acceptance and recognition within those norms for which one is asking in this circumstance.[8] The exclusion of alternatives to the norm of marriage from the field of recognizable concerns is not questioned (marriage brings with it certain rights denied to those who are not married, for instance). The problem of violence and its possible refusal concerns situations where there is no such framework of mutually accepted values within which to negotiate. Values, in this sense (in contrast to interests), escape negotiation in that they are what provide the very ground, the site, for dialogue: In dialogue, we rely on a shared sense of the importance and legitimacy of the issues argued.

In *Giving an Account of Oneself*, Butler describes Michel Foucault's analysis of how a social "regime of truth" structures the arena in which subjects come to recognize each other as partners in communication.[9] It provides the norms according to which the act of recognition operates, and delineates "who"—what type of "body" (in the widest sense), or "form of being"—qualifies as a subject of recognition in that space.

> In Foucault's view, there is always a relation to this regime, a mode of self-crafting that takes place in the context of the norms at issue and, specifically, negotiates an answer to the question of who the "I" will be in relation to these norms. In this sense, we are not deterministically decided by norms, although they do provide the framework and the point of reference. . . . [I]t is in relation to this framework that recognition takes place or the norms that govern recognition are challenged and transformed.[10]

As Butler points out, the framework is not always rigid; ways may be found to challenge and alter it in places, as, for example, her figure of the melancholic drag queen illustrates in *Bodies that Matter*.[11] Such critique is not easy, as it involves "putting oneself at risk, imperiling the very possibility of being recognized by others, since to question the norms of recognition that govern what I might be, to ask what they leave out, what they might be compelled to accommodate, is, in relation to the present regime, to risk unrecognizability as a subject."[12] Nevertheless, the implication is that regimes of truth can be challenged only by subjects establishing themselves subversively in relationship to those norms: that, like the drag queen, they use and act out elements of the normative framework in such a way as to reconfigure it performatively—"from within." The possibility of subjects recognizing each other in their various relationships to the norms in sway then depends on them being established in some way through the regime:

If the "I" and the "you" must first come into being, and if a normative frame is necessary for this emergence and encounter, then norms work not only to direct my conduct but to condition the possible emergence of an encounter between myself and the other.[13]

There would seem to be some normative framework, some common ground, necessary for mutual recognition to take place, however subversive. In pointing to this condition, Butler raises the question that is relevant to our problem of violence, the question of how an "encounter," instead of a disqualification, might take place between bodies "foreign" to each other to the extent that they do not exist for each other as possibly recognizable subjects, embodying possibly debatable issues. Examples of such oppositions include the *cordon sanitaire* erected by "mainstream" parties in Belgium against the Flemish far right (branded "undemocratic") to exclude it from political negotiations in the country's multi-party system, regardless of how many votes it gets; the *New York Times* describing "Arundhati Roy's critique of U.S. imperialism as anti-U.S., implying that any position that seeks to critically reevaluate US foreign policy in light of September 11 and the ensuing war is anti-U.S. or, indeed, complicitous with the enemy";[14] the media invisibility in the West of the 200,000 children killed in Iraq in and after the Gulf War;[15] etc. There are thus various ways in which social norms distribute the validity for recognition, or affective power, of perceptions, concerns, and lives (and one may be sympathetic to some and not to others, or one may wish to question their strategic efficacy while supporting the violence they imply, etc.). But in the light of the problem concerning us, this cannot be the whole story. The odd preference *not to* disqualify and eliminate, which on occasion does arise, must be accounted for, and in such a way that it does not become reduced to a mere call—to a call for dialogue, or for "tolerance," "openness," "humility and generosity," or, correlatively, "courage" in the face of non-recognition—for such calls do not address the issue of the structures of thought that might come into play, of "what it might mean to prefer not to" follow a logic of dominance and submission.[16] In what way, by what channels, by what logic might, for instance, critiques such as Arundhati Roy's possibly become "heard" (recognized, even if not agreed with) by those who decide about policy, if those people are not like Arundhati Roy?

In response to this question of how an encounter might take place where it seems impossible, Butler describes Levinas's concept of the *presubjective* scene that arises as soon as one is "addressed" by another.[17] A nascent subject arises as a "me" in a situation of address that puts it in the accusative, calling it to account. The account it manages to give of itself (even if it is a refusal to answer the convocation) constitutes the taking shape of the "I" in relationship to the address, through the exhibition of the modes of thought it employs. On this pre-subjective scene, which arises time and again in the interstices of one's various normative frameworks as one is addressed by or addresses another (or more precisely, which has no time and place, being the conceptual moment in which the structure of communication is exhibited), it is not that the normative environment in which one finds oneself is eclipsed, or that the account one gives of oneself or that one is offered by the other is constituted without reference to established practices, but that the interpretations and evaluations that normally—normatively—provide a reference framework for the recognition of perceptions and concerns are rendered subject to questioning.

The pre-subjective scene of address is therefore not specific to special moments where it is impossible, according to the norms in sway, to receive or to give recognition to another; what it does is exhibit the fault line of any determinate regime of truth—a moment of indetermination, where responsibility for the way in which one claims reasons for one's practice and evaluates that of the other cannot be referred to "the norm": for it is "the norm," or one's mode of thought, that is being given an account of in the account one gives of oneself. This exhibition of oneself, which Butler likens to the Greek practice of *parrhesia* discussed by Foucault in *Fearless Speech*,[18] consists in the presentation of one's concerns *without one being able to take for granted* the interpretations and evaluations that are constructed around them. The rationality, or *logos*, logic, in which one's perceptions and concerns are cast is revealed through the type of questioning that operates in address: What are the presuppositions of your practice; what are the conditions that enable your practice to do what it does and that it can't do without; what is important to you . . . ? The challenge of such questioning consists in finding a way of presenting one's concerns—of presenting the issues that are of importance to one and that subtend one's practice's interpretation of facts and the values it distributes—that also might *gain* meaning for the other. Such presentation cannot take for granted that the other will agree with the value and meaning one normally confers oneself to one's practice.

This contrast between scenes of address and grounds for dialogue is designed to ensure that the concept of conflict that it is the purpose of this chapter to describe is able to account for the preference not to use violence without assimilating it either to a call for courageous persistence or to a call for humility and tolerance: Accounting for the "preference not to" in terms of either of these would risk violating its "neither . . . nor . . ." imperative (neither command or victory, nor obedience or capitulation). In other words, the concept should be able to indicate an escape route from the logic of violence that proceeds according to the alternative "submit or vanquish," by resisting the assimilation of the "preference not to" to either of these imperatives.

Responsibility for Norms of Thought: Just Deserts?

What the notion of the scene of address exhibits is that our thought is responsible for the norms it uses to think. When we, for example, blame ourselves for the violence we suffer as being a consequence of our actions or justify the violence we inflict on others as a consequence of their actions, we are using a particular normative framework for the determination of what is to count as a cause and what is to count as an effect, one that embraces violence as a normal response to conflict, justified by facts and circumstances. But while on normative grounds we are responsible *to* norms and accountable *to* facts in this way, on the pre-subjective scene of address our responsibility *for* the norms we use is revealed: We are brought to account *for* the facts we normally use to *justify* action, through our presentation of their *presuppositions*, or "conditions":

> When . . . Arundhati Roy claims that bin Laden has been "sculpted from the spare rib of a world laid waste by America's foreign policy," something less than a strictly causal explanation is being offered. [She is] pointing to conditions, not causes. . . . Conditions do not "act" in the way that individual agents do, but no agent acts without them. They are presupposed in what we do, but it would be a mistake to personify them as if they acted in the place of us.[19]

The way in which the presentation of one's concerns in terms of presuppositions and "conditions" exposes them to a type of questioning not afforded by their use as justification is addressed by Deleuze in *Nietzsche et la philosophie*. Nietzsche's genealogical question (Is the genealogy of this thing joyous and affirmative or resentful and negative?) concerns the way values and interpretations are produced. Taking values "at face value" (in their rivalry and opposition), then, *separates* them from their genesis, that is, from the presuppositions and concerns they embody, while finding their genealogy involves exposing these presuppositions and concerns and asking what type of logic, or rationale, they are made to enter into. In the tracing of their genealogy, values therefore undergo questioning regarding the logic that produces them out of the concerns to which they respond.

In this way, Nietzsche's process of evaluation "regenerates" values through the test of its questioning ("evaluation is creation").[20] This means that the genealogical question is not a question that *we* can ask, but a question addressed *to us*. It is not a question that "we," in the nominative, with our constituted values representing a particular "position," address to things (to practices), lending them an unquestioned interpretation in accordance with which we act (making our action a function of fact), but a question addressed "to us," in the accusative, on the pre-subjective scene where the way in which our action relates to what we feel is important is rendered indeterminate and open to question. It is a question of how *we* behave in regard to issues that concern us, of how we have them affect us, of how we, with the values and meanings we give them, make them into reasons for our actions.[21]

> There is no truth that, before being a truth, is not the effectuation of a meaning or the realization of a value.... It all depends on the value and the meaning of what we think. We always get the truths we deserve according to the meaning of what we conceive of and the value of what we believe.[22]

Through our evaluations and interpretations, therefore, we create the norms and means for recognition of concerns, or for what lives are "livable." These norms are created: The way things *appear*, or rather are, is different from the *way* they appear, or become.

Trusting to Possibilities of Thought: A Celebration of Conflict?

Implied in this responsibility of thought for the regimes of truth it produces is a trust to the possibility of creating new values and interpretations. It is a trust that conflicting values are not doomed to be acted on at face value, and that, as a consequence of the type of questioning involved in genealogy, of the exhibition of the presuppositions and concerns that subtend them, they may be regenerated in a way that does not require the suppression of, or render unrecognizable, any of these concerns.

This trust does not depend on a judgment as to the likelihood of such a solution to a conflict of values, for the roles that the concerns exhibited will play (their affective power) become defined in the solution. It is, in this sense, an unjustifiable confidence, one that cannot be assimilated to the notion of trust *in* any particular regime of truth or *in* the goodwill of an interlocutor on a scene of dialogue.[23] The way in which a possible solution may be said to succeed or fail depends, then, on no principle external to the process, but on the "I" and the "you" being able to recognize themselves in, or lend their support to, the identities they acquire in the value system produced.

Conflict is therefore, on this account, a real fact for which there is no ready solution or for which finding a solution is not a matter of "drawing the consequences" according to principles, but which involves the "interpretation and evaluation" of concerns and presuppositions. In Whitehead's words "The interpretation to be achieved is a reconciliation of seeming incompatibilities. But these incompatibilities are not hypothetical. They are there on the stage of history, undoubted and claiming interpretation."[24] And the interpretation given will be a particular solution, valid nowhere but in that particular associative situation, engaged on the stage of history with the particular concerns it interprets. As Whitehead explains, no novel value, because of its finitude—because of its genesis in relation to local matters of unjustifiable concern—is capable of neutralizing further conflict.[25]

In this way, in contrast to placing trust *in* a regime of truth, trusting *to* the possibility of creating new values implies a rejection of the notion of universal values that would put an end to conflict. Deleuze emphasizes, in *Nietzsche et la philosophie*, that the petrification and rivalry of values—their mutually destructive opposition—results necessarily from the genealogical, creative movement of value-production and, similarly, in *Différence et Répétition*, that "illusion" is inevitable, that "abstract effects" are the necessary travesty of their creative conditions (that values only exist at face value), etc. This serves to prevent the trust in the possibility of creating solutions respecting the concerns that raise themselves on a scene of address from becoming assimilated with a universalizing ideal that would differ only in degree, and not in nature, from the urge for dominance that the "preference not to" is supposed to resist. Whatever regime of truth is produced, it will sooner or later be confronted with what it excludes (with possibilities for life it cannot recognize), as it will always be a particular, situated regime, answering to particular, situated concerns. The successful solution of a conflict, such that those involved recognize themselves in the measures taken and the regime produced, where before they opposed one another in non-recognition of each other's concerns, will never be a "higher synthesis," a wider, more universal norm. The criticism of regimes of truth on the scene of address does not proceed according to higher values, as we have seen, for norms are precisely what are rendered indeterminate and criticized on such a scene, along their own particular fault lines, as they come to be challenged by questioning in the light of new concerns.

So if there will always be exclusion of one kind or another, why bother about questioning regimes, about finding "better" ones? There can be no final justification for such a preference. Where there is a felt conflict of values, it is the "livability" of lives that is at stake, to use Butler's excellent term. Not of lives in general, but of lives here and now, in the unjustifiability of what they deem important for their own existence. In Deleuze's Nietzschean terms, this means conquering, becoming worthy of, our masks, our illusions, our travesty (our values), creating them in their relevance to the specific forms of life that come to affect each other: critique as action, not reaction.[26] Deleuze's portrayal of the actual (of actual values produced) as something negative in itself therefore serves to make the point that to take up arms, to take sides among values, is to go against the striving for a "better" life, which exceeds the urge for the preservation of existence or of established values. (In Whitehead's words, "the art of persistence is to be dead": We desire not only to live, or even to live well, but to live "better" than any bets on probabilities of success based on present facts may warrant.)[27]

The concept of conflict is released from its attachment to judgment and violence ("We are democratic, they are undemocratic, so let's make war," to take a recent example), to become attached instead to the *possibility* for constructive engagement with the live concerns that challenge our modes of thought. (Which is not to say that it can bring about such engagement.) What the celebration of conflict that our authors embrace effects, therefore, is the opposite of a celebration of violence: It blocks the automatic assimilation of the notion of trust to trust *in* an authority (moral, religious, or whatever), or *in* the rightness of a position.

Acceptance of Risks of Thought

The trust "to" the possibility of finding a livable solution to the conflict of values, unable as it is to guarantee success, demands that thought accept the risk of failure. That is to say, one's account of oneself must undergo the test of its effects on the other in generating a solution in which one's concerns may, *or may not*, be recognized. Failure, in this context, spells violence undergone (and is susceptible, if we accept Hannah Arendt's analysis and Butler's discussion of "conditions" and "breeding grounds" for violence, of provoking violent reaction as one's power to act wanes through its disqualification from recognized practice).[28] The demand placed on thought to undergo this test of the effects produced on the other by its translation of concerns on a scene of address is very different from any calls for courage to stand firm in one's position in the face of overwhelming resistance on the scene of debate. The parrhesiastic test requires something different from the courage that can be obtained from a firm conviction in one's position: Failure in this case cannot be attributed to "the antagonisms of our fellow men."[29] Correlatively, the demand placed on thought to accept the challenge of being questioned on a scene of address, of having to reveal its intimate presuppositions, is also very different from calls for sympathy with the other's position or for tolerance of other values.

As mentioned earlier, and as Butler points out, the refusal to answer an address already constitutes a response. If calls for courage or for tolerance do not always succeed in inspiring willingness to enter into negotiations, the test of one's modes of thought is *already* being undergone as soon as one is questioned by another. The pre-subjective scene of address is always present in the interstices of normative frameworks: There are no final calls to be made before the play can begin. One figures on the scene of address whether one accepts the part or not. And in that case, it may perhaps in some circumstances be wiser to attempt a translation of oneself instead of leaving the interpretation and evaluation of one's acts entirely up to the other.

This type of acceptance of the challenge therefore requires no special courage, integrity, or goodwill as a precondition. One's thought is not safer or more protected from the risk of failing to bring about a livable solution for one by refusing to answer the address. One is returned to face one's responsibility for one's mode of thought through its effects on others, whether one raises one's concerns and tries to give an account of oneself or not.

This said, it is difficult to prefer not to resort to violence. If calls for bravery and persistence or for tolerance and humility require superhuman efforts to be made in order to "make oneself heard by" or to "hear" the other in situations where normative frameworks are in conflict, and if, according to our three authors' analyses of human affairs, such frameworks inevitably tend to conflict with each other, the question arises whether the active engagement with the risks involved in attempting a translation of one's concerns on a scene of address might be able to be encouraged in some way—or are we doomed to confront, whatever our regime of thought, equally large hurdles every time, in the form of the "natural" tendency to act according to consolidated values?

Power

This question of encouraging an active "acceptance" by thought of the risks involved in undergoing questioning is a practical question and lies beyond the scope of this chapter. Here I wish only to raise the question by indicating a possible "bridge" between the concept of conflict sketched out above (which should indicate how the "preference not to" resort to violence can be understood without assimilating it either to the desire for imposing values that would suppress conflict, or to mere acceptance of the other) and Hannah Arendt's formulation of power as being the opposite of violence.

I have tried to show "what it might mean to prefer not to" embrace the logic of violence by articulating three component notions:

> the notion of thought being responsible *for* the meanings and values it confers on presuppositions and concerns, in contrast to its being responsible *to* norms or *to* facts as they present themselves within an unquestioned regime of truth;
> the notion of thought trusting *to* the possibility of regenerating values in the face of conflict in a way that recognizes the concerns involved, in contrast to its placing trust *in* particular values; and
> the notion of thought accepting the risk of undergoing questioning by the other on a scene of address, in contrast to its either persisting in its convictions or submitting to another's.

These three components of what it might mean to prefer not to resort to violence in the face of conflict each correspond to a problematization of categories of thought that we use very often. The responsibility for creating social conditions for livable lives responds to the problem of values as something to be created in an encounter, rather something adhered to come what may; similarly, trusting to the possibility of respecting the concerns expressed by voices in conflict responds to the problem of the local production of "better" regimes of truth that, in order to be "better," do not require an appeal to "higher" values or "wider" universals; and thirdly, the acceptance of the risks involved in testing the consequences of our modes of thought in response to questioning from outside responds to the problem of how the preference for nonviolence might be dislodged from its associations with superhuman efforts to go against what one may presume to be a natural tendency for values to oppose each other destructively.

Now, how might the concept of conflict relate to practical power?

The type of practical "freedom" for creating conditions for "more livable lives" lies with Butler, Arendt, and Whitehead in a similar idea, the idea of "concerted" or "corporate" action (Arendt and Whitehead), or of non-state-centered forms of alliance (Butler), which do not presuppose a "collective subject," or identitarian position or project.[30] In Whitehead's words:

> The new epoch in the formation of social institutions unfolded itself very gradually. *It is not yet understood in its full importance.* . . . The novelty consists in the deliberate formation of institutions, embodying purposes of special groups, and unconcerned with the general purposes of any political state, or of any embodiment of tribal unity playing the part of a state.[31]

The idea implies that the freedom to challenge norms and institutionalized practice, to regenerate them in regard for concerns for "better" lives, may be able to be given institutional support. For freedom is nothing without the means to exercise it, socially and collectively, in the context within which one lives:

> When we think of freedom, we are apt to confine ourselves to freedom of thought, freedom of the press, freedom for religious opinions. Then the limitations to freedom are conceived as wholly arising from the antagonisms of our fellow men. This is a thorough mistake. . . . The essence of freedom is practicability of purpose.[32]

Similarly, for Butler, the practice of translating one's concerns or of actively undergoing the challenge of address may be able to be promoted:

> The only possible unity will not be the synthesis of a set of conflicts, but will be a mode of sustaining conflict in politically productive ways, practice of contestation that demands that these movements articulate their goals under the pressure of each other without therefore exactly becoming each other.[33]

How might public culture be transformed so as not to make violence and reactive aggression norms of political life?[34]

> [Cultural criticism might prompt us] to create a sense of the public in which oppositional voices are not feared, degraded or dismissed, but valued for the instigation to a sensate democracy they occasionally perform.[35]

Butler and Whitehead share the idea that a practice of contestation may be able to be cultivated, that social conditions may be able to be created that encourage an active response to concerns for "better" lives, rather than resist them.

In this context, it is of note that there exists today a growing movement for "direct democracy," that is to say, for the introduction of systems of binding referenda on popular initiative, the aim of which is to make our present representative systems more accountable to the living *support* that is supposed to legitimize legislation, in Arendt's sense:[36]

> It is the people's support that lends power to the institutions of a country. . . . Under conditions of representative government the people are supposed to rule those who govern them. All political institutions are manifestations and materializations of power; they petrify and decay as soon as the living power of the people ceases to uphold them.[37]

The institutional *promotion* of this type of power may therefore constitute a real possibility relevant to our present society. As mentioned, it is not the purpose of this chapter to provide a discussion of issues of practice, but a few questions can be raised to illustrate the topic.

The most common objection to it is that people would make bad decisions under conditions of "direct" democracy. What, or who, makes good decisions? And how?

How are policies lent support? What might be the consequences of having the possibility of deciding to vote on an issue *and* delegating representatives rather than voting only for representatives?

Who governs whom, and how?

Who draws up an election list? Who initiates a "popular initiative"?

Is the professional a better decision-maker than the concerned crowd?[38] Where is trust placed? And by whom?

Another common objection to direct democracy is that minority interests would be suppressed by the majority. Who is a minority? What, or who, defines an identity? And how? And how is it used? How might it be used? How does an identity become prescriptive of action?

Who is afraid of dissent?

Who can take part in debate? Who can raise an issue of concern?

Who, or where, is the "unrepresentable"?

Who is interested in politics? Politicians today often lament that "people" are not.

What is the power of a vote? What is the power of a vote for a representative? And on an issue of concern?

Where does power lie? Who wants power?[39] And what is the power of questioning?

Butler: "[A certain agonism and contestation] must be in play for politics to become democratic."[40]

Might we, through some sort of practice designed to promote the practicability of contestation, envisage the cultivation of conflict? Might we envisage cultivating conflict as a means of resisting violence? In the words of Hannah Arendt, the support lent to institutions established through power as opposed to violence "is never unquestioning:" "as far as reliability is concerned it cannot match the indeed 'unquestioning obedience' that an act of violence can exact."[41] The opposition of some of our present practices and political institutions to the promotion of this type of power is certainly great, and some institutions present themselves as the most "reliable" authorities. But is there perhaps a difference between reliance and confidence?

Power does not, as Arendt notes, provide a guarantee against violence, but perhaps the concept of conflict sketched out in this chapter can contribute to undoing the connection between nonviolence and loss of power supposed in the understanding of political life as the "domination of man over man by means of violence."[42] The concept of conflict does not have the power of justifying the conclusion that it is wrong to quash dissent, to kill, to fight opposition with violence, and to seek to spread the dominance of one's own, untransformed modes of thought and life. But perhaps it has the power of suggesting what it might mean to prefer not to.

CHAPTER 7

Becoming through Multiplicity: Staying in the Middle of Whitehead's and Deleuze-Guattari's Philosophies of Life

Luke B. Higgins

> It's not easy to see things from the middle, rather than looking down on them from above or up at them from below, or from left to right or right to left: try it, you'll see that everything changes.
>
> GILLES DELEUZE AND FELIX GUATTARI,
> *A Thousand Plateaus: Capitalism and Schizophrenia*

> Life lurks in the interstices of each living cell, and in the interstices of the brain.
>
> ALFRED NORTH WHITEHEAD, *Process and Reality: Corrected Edition*

What would it mean to *begin always from the middle*? To experiment with renouncing that lure of mastery with which definitive beginnings and endings seduce thought? Might this renunciation be one way of characterizing the basic commitment of postmodern thought? For staying in the middle would mean abstaining from that very old Western philosophical and theological craving for perfect unities—ultimate forms that gather and order the world's pluriform reality. It would mean approaching multiplicities not as mere multiples of the one but as unique individuals or haecceities unto themselves. It is a practice for which no small amount of courage would be necessary—for staying *within* multiplicities rather than trying to gather them from their ends or from above commits one to an adventure of becoming. Perhaps this refusal to abandon the irreducible "middles" of multiplicities is also one of the most important steps toward a deeper ecological consciousness. The latter, I would submit, begins with this basic principle of life: that we always find ourselves in the middle or the between of some given multiplicity. And by multiplicity I refer to not just *external* multiplicity but *internal* multiplicity as well—indeed, the boundary between these inevitably blurs in the context of life's constant exchanges and flows. One of the most remarkable aspects of theologian Catherine Keller's engagement with creation and eschatology is her insistence that these ultimate beginnings and endings are not absolute brackets but rather ongoing processes whose most significant meanings unfold right here, in the middle of things—in the ever-concrescing now that belongs to, yet can never be reduced to, its future or its past.[1] Staying in the middle would then refer to a mode of negotiating both temporal and spatial multiplicities—one that would stay productively suspended *between* future and past, inner self and outer world. It not only would describe the very condition for life's emergence but also may chart a path beyond the modern preoccupation with transcendence and control over our constitutive material reality—a preoccupation that is proving deadly to our living biosphere.

Both Gilles Deleuze and Felix Guattari (to whom I will refer, from here on, as Deleuze-Guattari, in the "rhizomatic" spirit of their partnership) and Alfred North Whitehead develop innovative strategies for resisting that stubborn impulse in Western philosophy and theology to derive all multiplicity from a transcendent unity. In the words of Roland Faber, "Deleuze deeply honored Whitehead . . . [for] his profound love for this impermanent world that exceeds any abstract reconstruction, the appreciation of the unconquerable wildness of open-ended becoming over against any systematic derivation of multiplicity from hierarchical unity."[2] Both Whitehead and Deleuze-Guattari can be considered philosophers of *becoming* whose normative ideals avoid those static, unitary states of perfection that are so omnipresent in the Western tradition. In both Whitehead's and Deleuze-Guattari's systems, the larger aim is not a *perfection of being* so much as an *intensity of becoming*—intensity measured not by proximity to some static form or pure line of filiation but simply by what can be made to pass between various singularities coming into play in any given moment. My examination of these thinkers will issue in a proposal that the most creative and ecologically life-giving path presents itself when we *stay with* our constitutive multiplicities, inside their betweenness or interstitiality, rather than attempting to command them from a dimension superior to the ones already in play.

Part of my objective in bringing post-structuralist thinkers such as Deleuze-Guattari into close conversation with Whitehead is to advance a more "immanental" interpretation of process thought. That is to say, I will suggest that it is more fruitful to think of our source of value—in theological terms; the aim God offers for our becoming—as that which emerges precisely in and through a deep awareness of the relational fields that we occupy, rather than something that orders those fields from "above." While I believe this reading is upheld well by Whitehead's texts, it may be perceived as departing from certain traditional approaches to process thought. The latter has tended to emphasize Whitehead's assertion of a *universal* locus of value—the feature of his thought perceived as being most resistant to postmodernism's overly "dissolute," relativizing tendencies. According to this logic, postmodernism's (supposed) refusal to recognize any source of value transcendent to the changing whims and fluxes of the present moment can only threaten process thought's advancement of its progressive social, cultural and environmental agenda.

In the case of the environmental crisis, for example, some process theologians may find it more important than ever to counter an "anything goes" attitude in relation to the earth with an assertion of God's real, transcendent hope or aim for the world (if one is not theologically inclined, one may articulate it as a transcendent locus of truth or value). This can lead to the postulation of some perfect ecological "blueprint" or "mold" existing transcendently in the mind of God, which it is our job to simply access and then realize in our actions. While perhaps motivated by legitimate concerns, I suggest this approach risks selling short some of Whitehead's most original and important insights—namely, that divine value is dynamically contextual and that creation itself *is* a radically opened-ended process of creative transformation. Part of the goal of this paper, then, is to demonstrate how a more postmodern/post-structuralist thought-orientation (such as that represented by Deleuze-Guattari) may not threaten process thought so much as keep it truer to its roots and more effective in its politics.

Instead of conceptualizing the divine aim as that which arrives from above to organize the material web of relationships that sustains us, I would suggest that it is better understood as a certain crystallization *of* that web, one that occurs from within its "middle" or from its deep interstices. In perhaps a paradoxical way, I want to propose that the ecological balance and stability of which our biosphere is in such desperate need might be best attained, not by submitting its relational flows to a transcendent schema of order, but precisely by keeping ourselves *within* the changing immediacies of its demands. Letting go of our need to possess some ultimate, once-and-for-all knowledge of our constitutive ecological multiplicity actually may be the first and most important step towards releasing the very creative possibilities that will enable us to balance and harmonize our collective life. An analogy to a certain Buddhist understanding of spiritual practice might be apropos here: Precisely by resisting the fear-driven urge to control and submit to a transcendent schema the complex, dynamic flow of our awareness, we find ourselves in the only real place of peace and stability that is possible—a centerless center that remains in the *middle* of the world's living flows. In short, I believe that bringing post-structuralist thinkers such as Deleuze-Guattari into close dialogue with Whitehead may actually help safeguard process thought against a more closed, absolutized understanding of meaning and value that could inhibit its spiritual and political (ecological or otherwise) efficacy.

The first part of my analysis will contrast the ways Whitehead and Deleuze-Guattari theorize multiplicity and becoming—Deleuze-Guattari in the analysis of the "rhizome"[3] and Whitehead in his explication of the "actual occasion."[4] Rhizomes create novel assemblages held together not by some external, unifying point but by immanent flows or "surveys" moving at infinite speeds across all their constitutive lines.[5] While there are significant disparities between this conceptualization and Whitehead's actual occasion, parallels also present themselves, particularly when one takes into account the absence of any linear chain of causation within the actual occasion. Next, I will move to Whitehead's more macrocosmic understanding of structured societies—in particular, his assertion that higher grade "living occasions" require the specialized environment of the body's interstitial spaces in order to subsist. It is these empty yet complexly shaped spaces of betweenness that allow higher-grade occasions to negotiate dense relational fields with novelty and spontaneity. I will discuss some interesting parallels between these *interstitial* becomings and the "intermezzos" from which Deleuze-Guattari's rhizomatic "lines of flight" and "Bodies without Organs" emerge. Both Whitehead and Deleuze-Guattari seem to be locating the most dynamic, intensive "events" of becoming *within* complex matrices of materiality—both that of the body and the ecosystem.[6] Both thinkers seem to suggest that it is precisely by inhabiting, with a deep awareness, the interstices of our complexly layered, material reality that we release our most creative and life-giving capacities.

In short, this discussion will aim at advancing a certain norm for philosophy and theology: that we keep ourselves in the *middle of things*. That we stay *with* the permutations and possibilities emerging in the interstitiality of the world's multiplicities instead of negating them with statically ordered lines of social transmission (in Whitehead's terms) or reverting to a plane of transcendence (in Deleuze-Guattari's terms). This project will advance modes of philosophical and theological construction that honor rather than deny the inter-flowing ecological multiplicities upon which life on this planet depends. Although I will not address environmentalism in any substantive way in this chapter, I believe these philosophical-theological reflections can be put in the service of both political and spiritual forms of ecological activism.

Multiplicity and Intensity in the Rhizome and the Actual Occasion

> A rhizome has no beginning or end; it is always in the middle, between things, interbeing, intermezzo. . . . The middle is by no means an average; on the contrary it is where things pick up speed.
>
> GILLES DELEUZE AND FELIX GUATTARI,
> *A Thousand Plateaus: Capitalism and Schizophrenia*

In *A Thousand Plateaus* Deleuze-Guattari employ the metaphor of a plant "rhizome" to describe their particular approach towards multiplicity and becoming. The defining characteristic of a rhizome, as opposed to that of a tree, is that its coherence is not attributable to any central unifying point or set of points. The multiplicity of a rhizome is a substantive unto itself, ceasing "to have any relation to the One as subject or object, natural or spiritual reality, image and world."[7] Any point within a rhizome can be connected to any other point; in this sense, a rhizome has no definitive beginning or ending—*every* point within it, occupies a kind of *middle space*. But rhizomes are actually better described not as sets of points but as converging lines of movement or transversal vectors. "[The rhizome] is composed not of units but of dimensions, or rather directions in motion. It has neither beginning nor end but always a middle from which it grows and overspills."[8] What holds together the multiplicity of a rhizome is a kind of conjunction or consistency among its flows such that an infinite movement can traverse at once every line or dimension that composes it. Rhizomes are described as laid out on "flat planes" because they assemble themselves from the middle of the dimensions they themselves actually fill—not from an empty one, "supplementary to that of the system considered."[9] The becoming of a rhizome, then, does not move or progress along a linear path of development from beginning to end—rather, it is always moving, growing, and spreading from its middle.

As mentioned, rhizomes are only definable by the lines of movement or flows they make possible and thus cannot be compared by their forms but only by their relative *intensities*. In Deleuze-Guattari's words, "This is our hypothesis: a multiplicity is defined not by the elements that compose it in extension, nor by the characteristics that compose it in comprehension, but by the lines and dimensions it encompasses in 'intension.'"[10] Although intensity is not necessarily quantifiable—there are no hierarchies of rhizomes—Deleuze-Guattari do seem to correlate a rhizome's intensity with the complexity it is able to traverse or the chaos it is able to render consistent. Maximum intensity is achieved when a new assemblage brings into continuity multiplicities that are maximally heterogeneous to one another in other respects—in process language, those that are the most highly contrasted.

Although Whitehead's handling of multiplicity appears quite different from that of Deleuze-Guattari, some unexpectedly strong parallels do emerge. The first and most obvious point of comparison is that an actual occasion is constructed by a multiplicity of prehensions, also referred to as vectors of feeling, whose convergent flows make up the very substance of that occasion. In other words, there is no preexistent vessel or substance to which these feelings are secondary or subordinate—the reality of the occasion *is* the togetherness of that particular multiplicity. The second observable parallel is that the larger value towards which the actual occasion strives (conditioned as it is by God's aim for the universe as a whole) is *intensity*. Higher grades of actual occasions are able to positively integrate a greater diversity of physical feelings by means of more complex conceptual contrasts, thereby achieving greater intensities of satisfaction in their concrescence. Whitehead and Deleuze-Guattari then seem to share this aim at an intensity derived from the novel interrelationship of contrasting terms.

Perhaps it is the atomic structure of becoming in Whitehead's schema that is most inconsistent with Deleuze-Guattari's conceptual mappings. The idea that multiplicity could achieve "satisfaction" and thus a kind of atomic unity—however temporary—seems very much at odds with Deleuze-Guattari's notion of the plane or plateau, "whose development avoids any orientation toward a culmination point or external end."[11] Two considerations might temper the severity of this contrast: First of all, we have to remember that the microcosmic level of Whitehead's analysis (his explication of the actual occasion) is not intended to describe the "experience" of real living beings, who are not in themselves actual occasions, but rather "societies" of occasions. On a comparative level, then, Deleuze-Guattari's descriptions may actually map more effectively onto the macrocosmic dimension of Whitehead's analysis—something I will take up in the next section of this paper.[12] Secondly, I would assert that Whitehead's notion of an occasion's subjective aim—perhaps the most telos-driven, transcendent component of his micro-cosmic analysis—should not be understood as possessing an independent existence external to the actual occasion that it enables to concresce.

This reading of the subjective aim not as a transcendent organizational form so much as an event of crystallization immanent to the multiplicity in question—one that enables a certain strategic alignment of its "forces"—is well supported by Whitehead's unique understanding of the temporality of the actual occasion. Although, for analytic purposes, Whitehead genetically maps an occasion into its successive phases, concrescence itself occupies only a single, indivisible quantum of time. The integration of concrescence, then, happens either all at once or not at all. In Whitehead's words, "the genetic process is not a temporal succession. . . . Each phase in the genetic process presupposes the entire quantum, and so does each feeling in each phase."[13] In other words, technically there exists no linear chain of causation whereby physical prehensions are progressively "corralled into submission" by the subjective aim. Like the rhizome, concrescence cannot be traced through from a definitive beginning to a definitive ending; rather, all points inter-cohere with all other points in a single moment of time. In other words, the actual occasion becomes all at once—from its own middle.

From this perspective, might not we use the language of Deleuze-Guattari to describe prehensions as emerging and inter-cohering at *infinite speed* in the actual occasion? The subjective aim, then, might be conceived less as a transcendent organizing principle than a state of *survey* immanently traversing its prehensions at infinite speed.[14] Concrescence would be more a matter of spontaneous, immanent "emergence" than submission to a reigning plan or form provided by the subjective aim. This perspective would encourage us to see the occasion not as a more or less "correct" assembly of puzzle pieces (a more teleological understanding of becoming) so much as a convergence of flows or vibrating strings whose reciprocal alignment allows them to *resonate* together with more or less intensity—intensity measured by the depth and complexity of this harmonic resonance. This more "flow-based" description of the actual occasion and the subjective aim may shift the way we understand our relation to value: Instead of searching for that "right" mode of abstraction with which to "capture" our pluriform reality, we would instead recognize the need to remain deeply embedded *within* that reality, seeking creative openings and crystallizations on the very plane of multiplicity rather than over or above it.

Life's Interstices and Intermezzos: Becoming in the Middle

> Life is a characteristic of "empty space" and not of space "occupied" by any corpuscular society.
>
> ALFRED NORTH WHITEHEAD, *Process and Reality*

Some distinctly interesting parallels between Deleuze-Guattari and Whitehead come into focus as we move into the macrocosmic dimensions of Whitehead's analysis. God's larger aim or value for the universe is, of course, to increase the intensity of satisfaction among its members, and one of the key strategies for bringing this about is the emergence of "societies" of occasions. Layers of "structured societies" nesting within each other provide the more specialized environments required for higher-grade occasions—the highest, of course, being "living societies" of occasions, which can only subsist in the particular environment of the body.[15] The ecosystem and the body together constitute the complexly ordered matrix—woven from both inorganic and organic societies—which alone can sustain the threads of living occasions that Whitehead calls "living persons."[16] In this way, no definitive line can be drawn between ecosystem and body insofar as they function together as the complex sets of "filters," "amplifiers," and "feedback loops" that constitute the particular conditions necessary for life.

Whitehead's explication of the "entirely living nexus" is perhaps the key component of his unique understanding of life.[17] For Whitehead, life cannot be defined as some consistent set of characteristics transmitted faithfully from one moment—or set of occasions—to the next. This definition would be better applied to an inorganic society of occasions whose "strategy" of becoming is to repetitively transmit a certain pattern of self-ordering by massively ignoring (negatively prehending) diverse and changing aspects of its environment.[18] Life, on the other hand, functions by constructively drawing these diverse prehensions into complex contrasts that issue in novel modes of becoming: "The primary meaning of 'life' is the origination of conceptual novelty—novelty of appetition."[19] This understanding of life leads Whitehead to assert that groups of living occasions cannot, strictly speaking, be identified as "societies" at all because societies are defined by their commonalities whereas life is defined by its originalities. Groups of living occasions are thus given the more general descriptor of "nexus" or "entirely living nexus."

> The characteristic of a living society is that a complex structure of inorganic societies is woven together for the production of a non-social nexus characterized by the intense physical experience of its members. But such an experience [of intense satisfaction] is derivate from the complex order of the material animal body and not from the simple "personal order" of past occasions with analogous experience. There is intense experience without the shackle of reiteration from the past.[20]

The living nexus's unique capacity for intensity and complex originality is, thus, not derived from some special essence—spiritual or otherwise—bestowed upon it from above, but rather has to do with the particular way it situates itself vis-à-vis its wider environmental matrix. The distinctive characteristic of the entirely living nexus is its capacity to stay in the deep interstices, *the middle*, of the flows that make up its body and ecosystem. This is the basis for Whitehead's striking claim that life is characteristic of "empty space."[21]

These interstitial spaces upon which the entirely living nexus depends bring non-sociality and complex sociality together in a unique configuration: On the one hand, they function as a space of freedom that keeps living occasions from having to slavishly reproduce any particular chain of transmission (as they would in an inorganic society). On the other hand, their complex spatiality is also precisely what allows living occasions to access such a rich variety of influences from the ecosystem and body, which are then constructively integrated into novel superjects of becoming. Within these middle spaces, at the open junctures of a vast array of data, living occasions are able to cut across their prehensions at dimensions that did not exist before that moment. Their becoming is, in this way, marked by higher degrees of both novelty and relational complexity—in a word, *intensity*. Of course, this flow of influence does not move in only one direction—the decisions and actions of "regnant" living occasions flow back into the environmental matrix with both predictable and unpredictable consequences.

Might Whitehead's description of this interstitial milieu offer insight into the conditions necessary for the "lines of flight" and "rhizomatic becomings" that Deleuze-Guattari so innovatively conceptualize? To address this question, it may be fruitful to compare Whitehead's entirely living nexus with Deleuze-Guattari's notion of the "Body without Organs." The "BwO" (as they abbreviate it) conceptually overlaps with the rhizome in most respects—it too constitutes a novel space of between-ness that gives rise to new becomings. The distinctive aspects of the BwO are best understood in contrast to a more standard understanding of the body as a "stratified organism."[22] While the latter regulates, channels, and compartmentalizes the body's various flows, organizing them into separate functions, the BwO seeks novel conjunctions between these flows, making it possible for you to "walk on your head, sing with your sinuses, see through your skin, breathe with your belly."[23]

Unlike the organism, the BwO does not contain intensities but rather is the very plane on which they travel, cross thresholds, and conjugate energies. "The BwO is . . . necessarily a Place, necessarily a Plane, necessarily a Collectivity (assembling elements, things, plants, animals, tools, people, powers, and fragments of all of these; for it is not 'my' body without organs, instead the 'me' [*moi*] is on it, or what remains of me, unalterable and changing in form, crossing thresholds)."[24] Instead of gathering and releasing intensity along established points, the BwO keeps it circulating—it stays in the middle of its flows so to speak—and in so doing opens new possibilities for becoming. (Taoist principles of sex without the release of orgasm are invoked here.) Thus, in both the BwO and the entirely living nexus, static patterns of organization in the body are thwarted precisely by *staying in the middle* of the body's flows rather than capturing them within pre-established parameters. In both cases, our complex material matrix is not something to be transcended or controlled but strategically inhabited in such a way that its energies can be made to flow, connect, and create.

The objection may be raised that this Deleuze-Guattarian reading of Whitehead overprivileges the more chaotic, indeterminate aspects of becoming, attenuating the important stabilization that Whitehead's emphasis on a universal "center" of value offers. Indeed, a certain contrast here between Whitehead and Deleuze-Guattari is inevitable: Whereas Whitehead calls his thought system a "philosophy of organism," Deleuze-Guattari align themselves with Antonin Artaud in explicitly condemning any notion of "organism." On the face of it, Deleuze-Guattari seem to be interested primarily in subverting any stabilized strategy of organization in the body—a far cry from Whitehead's explicit appreciation of the body's stabilized, structured processes that generate intensity precisely by "canalizing" mental originality and "coordinating" spontaneity.[25] Insofar as the role of the body and ecosystem significantly overlap here, ecological concerns may cause us to be especially wary of Deleuze-Guattari's more radically open-ended approach to becoming. We might even find ourselves asking if Deleuze-Guattari's more "chaosmic" mapping of bodies—human and otherwise—can ultimately be allied with the quest for a more balanced, stabilized ecosystem. In short, would we *want* a body, or an ecosystem, that had no organs?

Upon closer reading, however, Deleuze-Guattari's war upon the "organism" doesn't necessarily extend to organs—or "strata": "We come to the gradual realization that the BwO is not at all the opposite of the organs. The organs are not its enemies. The enemy is . . . that organization of the organs called the organism."[26] In other words, stabilized structures are not the problem for Deleuze-Guattari—only the illusion of some single, reigning plan that designates *particular* structural configurations as universal and inevitable. Deleuze-Guattari are very much aware of the dangers that overly subversive or chaotic becomings can present to the process of creative construction. "Deterritorializing" too rapidly from organizational strata can result in a "botched" BwO—one on which no intensities can pass. For Deleuze-Guattari, the goal is not to *overcome* structures of stratification but, rather, to occupy these strata strategically with an eye towards their openings, gaps, and fissures, not to leap off strata but to inhabit their interstitial spaces with the "craft of a surveyor."[27]

> It is through a meticulous relation with the strata that one succeeds in freeing lines of flight, causing conjugated flows to pass and escape and bringing forth continuous intensities for a BwO. . . . We are still in a social formation, first see how it is stratified for us and at the place where we are; then descend from the strata to the deeper assemblage within which we are held; gently tip the assemblage, making it pass over to the side of the plane of consistency. It is only there that the BwO reveals itself for what it is: connection of desires, conjunction of flows, continuum of intensities.[28]

Like Whitehead, Deleuze-Guattari have in mind a kind of creative becoming that doesn't merely try to overthrow its inherited orders but rather works within them, in their interstices, to bring forth something new *from* them. The structured patterns of our material existence are not so much subverted as *strategically inhabited* such that the continuum of influences that come into play is broadened. One might even say that the very condition for the creation of a BwO or a line of flight is a kind of deep inhabitation of the material interstices of the body and ecosystem. In short, both Deleuze-Guattari and Whitehead seem to be suggesting that creative insight and awareness can only emerge when we stay in the middle of our always inter-flowing bodily and ecological systems.

Eco-Wisdom in the Deep Interstices

This reading does not aim to collapse the distinctive thought-systems of Whitehead and Deleuze-Guattari but rather to highlight certain continuities between them that push us to think about materiality and ecology in a new way. Both thinkers see the vast, complex plurality of our material existence not as something to be overcome or organized from above but as the very source of our most dynamic and creative capacities. Hopefully, this reading will dispel any doubts that the thought of Deleuze-Guattari is necessarily hostile to the development of an ecological ethic. On the contrary, I believe that—right beside Whitehead—Deleuze-Guattari's conceptualization of a radically open-ended and unpredictably creative strategy of becoming can be placed in the service of an ecological activism that is both spiritual and political. This assertion rests on the belief that genuine care for life on this planet must be based in a strategy of creative alliance-building between humans and nonhumans—one that refuses to foreclose in advance what our various bodily and ecological "organs" are capable of.[29]

In terms of the larger orientation of process thought, I hope to have shown how a more immanental interpretation of value or aim is not—as some might worry—debilitative to its political efficacy in the arena of ecology. On the contrary, I believe the metaphor of staying in the middle or the deep interstices of our bodily and ecological matrix can help us negotiate the challenging ecological situation our species faces by nurturing new kinds of respect, flexibility, and an awareness that is always contextually grounded. It is only in letting go of the belief that some single transcendent organization scheme, divine or otherwise, will save us from ecological doom that we can give ourselves over to an unfolding process of discerning the healthiest courses of action given our actual—and always changing—relational configurations.

In summary, this intertextual reading of Whitehead and Deleuze-Guattari may help to chart a certain normative course for our becomings: In Whiteheadian terms, if the milieu that makes possible more intense concrescence is the empty, interstitial spaces of our body, might it be possible to intentionally invoke a certain "spaciousness" in our becomings? In theological terms, perhaps the divine operates not by giving us transcendent instructions for how to integrate our prehensions (sometimes called the "post-it" theory of the initial aim) but by luring us more deeply into the folds and interstices of our living body where novel possibilities open up and lines of flight emerge. This may not be so different from Deleuze-Guattari's call to create a BwO by descending "from the strata into the deeper assemblages within which we are held."[30] Creating a BwO similarly seems to require us to inhabit deeply the between-spaces or energy channels that connect local assemblages to the larger planes on which they flow. Life's unique intensities pick up their momentum precisely at those open junctures where internal and external multiplicities come into continuity. In short, our ability to originate novelty directly depends upon our capacity to occupy the middle or the deep interstices of our complex, constitutive multiplicity.

Together, Whitehead and Deleuze encourage us to nurture a particular kind of post-modern discipline in our thinking and becoming—one that might not be so far away from a certain *spiritual* discipline. To enter the milieu of each moment knowing that there are no past criteria that can guide us perfectly through its dangers. To resist that ever-present impulse to trump with some inherited formation or some transcendent projection the multiplicity that has arrived. Instead, to inhabit deeply this multiplicity's between-spaces and in so doing allow its own immanent forms of complexity to emerge. By releasing ourselves to the flows that bring inside and outside, future and past into continuity, we open a kind of "centerless center," an "eye of the storm," from which novel paths for negotiating our complex, shifting relationality can crystallize. Might this allow life, in the words of Meister Eckhart, to live "out of its own ground" and spring "from its own source"?[31] This approach would find the greatest depth and intensity of feeling not in any definitive beginning or ending points, but always in the harmonics of becoming resonating from the *middle* of our interflowing multiplicities.

PART THREE

Negotiating Immanence and Divinity

CHAPTER 8

Surrationality and Chaosmos: For a More Deleuzian Whitehead (with a Butlerian Intervention)

Roland Faber

Hybrid Exchange

With Jacques Derrida's *différance* we face the problem of "the representation of a presence," which has "been constituted in a system (thought or language) governed by and moving toward presence."[1] It is the gesture of such a "metaphysics of presence"—or is it metaphysics as such?—to substantiate the ego, or even the male ego (the logo/phallocentric ego) that is in its thought-movements presupposed to encompass the world in a presence that pleases *him* by the illusion of being *his* "creation of the world"—"presence" as autoerotic game in which all objects of enjoyment are playmates *ex nihilo*.[2]

What *seem* to be "reason" and "freedom" are staged on the "presentation" of an autoerotic unification that, in reality, exercises the power of self-love, *this* kind of self-love (which some found so obvious in Hegel) that loves everything only because of *himself*, "everything" being only the medium of *his* self-enjoyment, being a mere "construct" of his power to *act* (but not acted upon) on behalf of himself. The freedom gained by this "rationality" only allows for *the self-assurance of the self-presence of an immortal ego*, one is tempted to say, the "*transcendental* ego." In this form (Kant may excuse) it is not just a subjective exertion of self-erecting power but the petrification of this power in being the *essence* of being substantial, *being* a "subject."[3]

In being the *hypokeimenon*, the subjective act generalizes itself into a self-same substrate that erases otherness, strangeness, the foolishness to wander outside. The "transcendental self," the stronghold of rationality and its imperative equation with freedom, is the secular form of the creator *ex nihilo*, who, if we believe the biblical reconstruction, had his career of "reconstructing the world as self-construct" by convincing us (and himself) that he never had to erase the chaos of the beginnings in the first place in order to become the sole king of nothingness.[4] The world is *his* presence and obviously his *accomplice*—but not ours.[5]

Consider the alternative: For Whitehead and Deleuze, in a way, we are all "multiplicities"—"neither a One nor a Many."[6] We are all hybrids, shifting identities, combinations, complexities, multiples; or *infinite* contrasts of indissoluble opposites[7] "select[ing] the whispering voices" and "gather[ing] the tribes and secret idioms" from which is extracted what we call "my Self (*Moi*)."[8] We are "entirely living nexūs,"[9] not defined by structure and persistence, but by originality and life.[10] We are the "Pink Panther," a "rhizome [that] doesn't begin and doesn't end, but is always in the middle, between things, interbeing, *intermezzo*."[11]

In being in-between, we live the world as "Chaosmos"; not as a world of "*accomplice*ment" (as creation of our interests), but of "bifurcations, divergences, incompossibilities, and discord."[12] There is no *final* unification, there is only unification as multiplication when the "many become one and are increased by one."[13] The world is not a stratosphere of unifications from the small to the large, from the microorganism to God; it is always bound back into infinite divergences whereby unity is always a "virtual gift" for a multiplicity of paths of diversifications. In such a view, even God becomes "a process that . . . affirms incompossibilities and passes through them,"[14] always "seeking physical multiplicity."[15]

In this alternative world, unity, the I (Self), and identity are only gifts of *un-forming virtuality*: not of systems, rather of *khora*, the dispersed "medium of intercommunication"[16] without pre-given structure, the unlimited "Omnitudo,"[17] the open movement of wholeness that cannot be united by any rational account. We find ourselves in a "motley world that can no longer be included in expressive units, but only made or undone according to prehensive units."[18] *Prehension*! Like Derrida's *différance*, this is Whitehead's anti-concept of unification *as* multiplication; and it calls upon us: "Be . . . multiplicities!"

There is no *one* reason, no *one* structure, no *one* system of thought, no *one* unity that could possibly "represent" this world of multiplication. Only in the view of the big brother's "presence," the "Phall/Logos" reigns, preaching (and demanding) self-satisfying identity and erecting a power-structure of universal applicability, seducing us to seek an Archimedean kingdom of clarity, simplicity, and precision. But of course, although we are thought to believe the contrary, this desire is not reigned over by the Logos, but by the Eros. And when Whitehead and Deleuze deconstruct this world, it is seen as not being a representation of a logical kingdom, but as a thrust for the erotic of intensity, a culturally disguised (auto)erotic self-justification of power, persuading us to seek the underlying *orgiastic* as *objective* condition of its perverse exclusion. Be multiplicities! Mistrust the longing for logical exemplification! Strive for Life beyond reason! There is no logic, only an erotic of existence.

Few have gone further than Judith Butler to explore the erotic intricacies of the hybrid fluency of identities and their phallogocentric suppressions. In deconstructing the substantialist paradigm of fixed "personal identities" as complicated exclusions of raw multiplicity of erotic powers guarded by regulative mechanisms of a phallogocentric Law (its own matrix of intelligibility), which then advertises itself as eternal Logos,[19] she leads us to understand the "universal capacity of reason"[20] as precisely this substitution of Eros by Logos. The fluent persona, on the other hand, although always in peril of substantializing itself as utopian aim, is rather the hybrid exchange of an infinite process of becoming. As she notes—very much in sync with Deleuze and almost in repetition of Whitehead—in relation to Nietzsche: Identity is "performatively constituted by the very 'expressions' that are said to be its result."[21]

Whitehead and Deleuze—as does Butler—had this intuition from yet another subversive figure of the philosophical underground, Henri Bergson, whose commitment to the *élan vital* brought him to believe in the strangeness of unity as always being a *mouvement*, always being a *fugue*, always being "on the run," fleeing structure and the rational embrace of the systematic octopus.[22] For the Deleuzian Bergson, "wholeness" is not a structural "set," but rather expresses what *negates* structure for radical openness.[23] This "All-One" is a "moving whole"[24] of "relations of movement and rest."[25] And Whitehead's Bergson supports the

> charge that the human intellect . . . tends to ignore the fluency, and to analyse the world in terms of static categories . . . [creating] a clear-cut philosophy [and] . . . result[ing in] . . . the subordination of fluency. This

subordination is to be found in . . . Plato's vision of heavenly perfection, in Aristotle's logical concepts, and in Descartes' mathematical mentality.[26]

For some time, we accepted that Whitehead never had such a pluralistic trait (although Deleuze has taken him as such) and that Deleuze never related to an ontology of wholeness (although Alain Badiou has demonstrated this).[27] We came to think of Whitehead as a *rationalist*, and as Deleuze an *anti-intellectualist*—an insult that Whitehead sensed to have been launched already against Bergson.[28] However, we should not forget that Whitehead was quite at ease with Bergson's "anti-*rationalism*" as based on the "ultimacy of fluency," but he tried to avoid "anti-*intellectualism*" (which Whitehead thought Bergson might have shared with Nietzsche)—the view that structures per se be only "erroneous fictions."[29] And we should not forget that Deleuze never thought of *every* structural unification as "erroneous," but rather only clear-cut organizations against which he set his rhizomatic connectivity of an "orgiastic" wholeness of a "chaotic world [in which] divergent series are endlessly tracing bifurcating paths."[30]

Pharmacology of Imperfection

Here is a short history of Whitehead's refutation of "rationalism" in nine chapters:

1. With Bergson, Whitehead held a "spatialization" of the moving whole of the world to be an abstractive construction disregarding the *event* of becoming. Any clear-cut system is, if it is understood as "re-presentation" of reality, nothing but an example of "misplaced concreteness" taking abstractions (systems) as concrete (Life).[31] This is a "light-bearer" for Derrida's critique of metaphysical "presence."

2. Against Descartes, Whitehead held the bifurcation of nature in *extension* and *cognition* as well as its presupposed substantialism to be the condition for a "rationalism" that believes that all knowledge can be grounded in a *self-reflective act* of the mind, independent from any empirical, or better, organic or ecological connectivity.

3. Against Hume, Whitehead attacked the conviction that we can only *perceive* clear-cut ideas as "representations" of the unknown, hence, *universals*. Instead, he insisted that although we might "*conceive* in terms of universals," we "*feel* particular existents"[32] that, in turn, can *never* be understood to be merely examples of general patterns.[33]

4. Against Kant, Whitehead did not understand knowledge to be the product of the self-reflective structure of the mind and, as intellectual activity of the subject, a mere production from logic and mathematics. This paradigmatic "rationalism," based on the Neoplatonic *nous*, does not need any world to prove itself as true.[34] For Whitehead, on the contrary, "Metaphysics never reaches the complete generality associated with logical necessity."[35] No "rational representation" is devoid of being embedded in becoming.

5. Whitehead's self-understanding of his "conceptual scheme,"[36] which is widely held to be the pinnacle of his rationalism, reveals that it is far from being self-explanatory. Not only is the number and division of kinds of categories elaborately deliberate, but Whitehead is well aware that if "we consider any scheme of philosophic categories as one complex assertion, and apply to it the logician's alternative, true or false, the answer must be that the scheme is false."[37]

6. Whitehead's own most basic principle is self-defeating regarding its supposed rationalism: If the "ultimate [principle] behind all forms," namely "creativity," is "inexplicable by forms,"[38] no rationalism can produce any necessities that would not be true only in the context of Life. As a universal network of becoming relations[39] "[n]o reason, internal to [this] history can be assigned why that flux of forms, rather than another flux, should have been illustrated."[40] With Deleuze it is always "contingent, excessive, and mystical essentially."[41]

7. Whitehead not only acknowledges a fundamental "irrationality" of the flux of things, which he calls "principle of empiricism,"[42] but he doubted the sheer *possibility* of metaphysical knowledge in the sense of rationalist necessities: If, he says, the "metaphysical characteristics . . . —in the proper sense of 'metaphysics'—should be those which apply to all actual entities," then "it may be doubted whether such metaphysical concepts have ever been formulated in their strict purity—even taking into account the most general principles of logic and of mathematics."[43]

8. With Plato, Whitehead mistrusted any system as just a betrayal of the "variousness of the universe, not to be fathomed by our intellects," so that he follows Plato who "in his Seventh Epistle . . . expressly disclaims the possibility of an adequate philosophic system."[44]

9. With Nietzsche's conviction that "there is no 'being' behind doing, effecting, becoming,"[45] Whitehead followed a rule that he called "principle of process" indicating that "'being' is constituted by its 'becoming.'"[46]

If there is a *trust* in "rationality" in Whitehead's thought, it is a highly qualified attempt to seek the "essence of the universe" as a *relational complex of ever-becoming*[47] for which, to be truthful to it, he submitted himself to a highly paradoxical contrast of two opposites: on the one hand, that, in order to allow for most general (metaphysical) relationships, every appearance must be understood in terms of a connectedness of which it then is an example;[48] but, on the other hand, that *no* concrete reality can be reconstructed from these relations when they are taken to be universal abstractions of the concrete interrelations in their creative and unique togetherness in a singular happening.[49]

If rationalism is the urge for the possibility of, and the belief in, self-explicative arguments that would enlighten the universe beyond mystery, and to which to stand up against would be tantamount with irrational self-defeat and ridicule, Whitehead was *not* a rationalist.[50] On the contrary, in believing in the "rationalization of [the] mysticism" of a Creative Future of an Open Whole that cannot be "explained away,"[51] Whitehead was a *sur*rationalist, meaning that he always trusted an infinite reality *beyond* any rationalistic simplifications. *Understanding* the "depths as yet unspoken"[52] is to approach it by—"hope"! In a testimony of his "surrationality," Whitehead writes that, while we seek "to apprehend the rationality of things," we might, due to the "imperfection of all metaphysical systems,"

> lose hope at the exact point where we find ourselves. The preservation of such faith must depend on an ultimate moral intuition into the nature of intellectual action—that it should embody the adventure of hope. Such an intuition marks the point where metaphysics . . . gains assurance from religion and passes over into religion.[53]

Whitehead's account for metaphysical conceptualization has always this surrational flavor of an "ultimate ideal," but, at the same time, always is "but a hopeless quest."[54] This is not a lack, however, but a deeper contact with the Eros of becoming and its essential *Imperfection*: "there is no perfection which is the infinitude of all perfections"; the beauty of the whole always exists only as "Discord."[55] Surrationality appeals to this Discord and Imperfection not as defects of missed "totality," but as a hope for infinite intensities to come in an unending process of the "Harmony of harmonies"[56]—or dare we say: "polyphony of polyphonies"?[57]

When Deleuze counter-conceptualizes his "transcendental empiricism,"[58] its surrationality despises all pre-given possibilities pre-forming actuality, but demands every happening to actualize virtuality in yet *undefined land*—the open space, the formless *khora*, a late echo of the Platonic "sieve"[59] that Whitehead recalls as the "fostermother of all becoming,"[60] the Void that harbors the Eros of unpredictable novelty and incommensurable diversity.[61] Surrationality seeks this Eros, desires her coming and always longs for her satisfaction, which is multiplication, differentiation, plurivocity.[62]

The real enemy of surrationality is a rationalism that seeks the disappearance of diversity in its desire for totality. While the Eros of surrationality is the love for multiplicity, the Logos of rationalism presses for inescapability. While surrationality is "polyphilia"—the love of and for manifoldness—rationalism urges for an oppressive unification in the name of the self-same.[63] For Whitehead, there is no self-same system; there is only a "discordance of comprehensive philosophical systems" as "a factor essential for progress" without "triumphs of finality."[64] And in the voice of Deleuze, we might rephrase: There is no *monadic*, pre-established harmony; there is only a "desert" of *nomadic* interconnections.[65] The proper realm of rationality is the *Void*—always *beyond* itself, always *sur*rational, always becoming.[66]

The real enemy—*totalizing* rationalism—presents itself in the disguise of "persuasion," but this is just the wolf musing as sheep, and as is its nature, it will finally *eat* the sheep![67] The wolf tends to appear in the form of "necessary first principles," which fittingly seem to "explain" the whole universe (away); or it disguises itself as "transcendental argument," forcing us to accept necessities or be otherwise incoherent.[68] Because of obvious reasons, I have called it the "Transylvanian argument"—it sucks all Life out of any living whole.[69] Robert Nozick describes this "coercive philosophy" as a rationalist wolf asking Transylvanian questions:

> Wouldn't it be better if philosophical arguments left the person no possible answer at all, reducing him to impotent silence? Even then we might sit there silently, smiling, Buddhalike. Perhaps philosophers need arguments so powerful they set up reverberations in the brain: if the person refuses to accept the conclusions, he *dies*. How's that for a powerful argument? . . . A perfect philosophical argument would leave no choice.[70]

"Persuasion," for Whitehead, *cannot* be disguised, it can only (want to) appear as—and *be*—a (philosophical) sheep, rigorously exercising the "duty of tolerance," which is "our finite homage to the abundance of inexhaustible novelty which is awaiting the future, and to the complexity of accomplished fact which exceeds our stretch of insight."[71] Indeed, for Whitehead, the "creation of the world—that is to say, the world of civilized order—is the victory of persuasion over force"[72] and *this* "persuasion" is a *rebellion* against rationalist reduction.

Whitehead's and Deleuze's surrationalism is their shared gift, their remedy against the poisoning rationalism: In Deleuze's words on Bergson:

For, if the living being is a whole and, therefore comparable to the whole of the universe, this is not because it is a microcosm as closed as the whole is assumed to be, but, on the contrary, because it is open upon a world, and the world, the universe, is itself the Open. . . . If one had to define the whole, it would be by Relation.[73]

When Charles Hartshorne calls this relational Whole "Surrelativism," I sense "Surrationality."[74] It is *that* "rationality" that is only given by a *relationality* that has no "beyond"—only the irrational.[75] But it is *always* "beyond" itself or the Self-Same or the Logos, always *only* embodied in the *event* of relationality. Relation *as* event—Whitehead calls it *prehension*—is "the Open"—in the *khoric place*.[76] Opening immanence *infinitely* cuts through chaos, surrationally erupting not in the "respectable, rational, or reasonable," but rather in "dreams, pathological processes, esoteric experiences, drunkenness, and excess."[77]

This surrationality is inscribed in Whitehead's "ontological principle"—that the only *reason(s)* for events of becoming *is* (*are*) always *itself* an event of becoming.[78] *This* "rationality" is per se *sur*rational—without origin or end; without foundation or totality; neither inscribed by a "fiat" of, nor being itself, an eternal *being*; ever hovering over the "aboriginal chaos";[79] swimming in the Infinite, the Void.[80] Surrationality "circumscribes" order and its rationality as they are the inscription of/in creativity, harbored by beauty, and overturned by harmonies of the unspoken.[81] The surrational unleashes the beyond-within like the "flying dart, of which Lucretius speaks, hurled beyond the bonds of the world."[82]

Nevertheless, there *is* "rationality." But while for any rationalism Chaos and Life always triggers a deep *fear* of uncertainty, irrationality, and death, for the "surrational mind"—*dwelling* in Chaos, Life, and Uncertainty—it is a sheer *wonder* that the world allows for any rationality, reason, and Logos at all. The surrational mind never trusts rationality but fosters it for its marvels; nourishes it for its ability to fight irrational powers of destruction, manipulation, and reduction; and harbors it for its fragilities.[83] Surrationalism does not despise rationality, but—in her rich silence[84]—cares about it like "the foster-mother of all becoming"[85] for her child.[86]

Destiny's Child

Deleuze's and Whitehead's discoveries and explorations of the surrational can only cautiously be understood as "theories of liberation."[87] While Butler's earlier impulse to de-substantialize fixed identities and pre-given structures to the extent that their performability becomes visible ponders the political will to liberate from a phallogocentric Law[88] that erases its own *khoric* substrate, Whitehead's, Deleuze's, and the later Butler's exploration of the nature of the *khoric* harboring of structure, reason and system (be it biological or philosophical) has more the flavor of acts of enlightenment: to *live with* their harmonies as discordant, polyphone, diverging and converging, limiting and delimiting, vibrant and tragic. The *khoric* externality of systems is permeated with the taste of *moira*, of *anangke*, necessity, destiny, and fate.

Butler's earlier account of rationality is nourished by the phallogocentric thesis of the instantiation of the Law—be it the Law of Substantialism, selling the effects of becoming *as* ground, or be it the Law of suppressed Eros, of the multiple layers of exclusion and negation of complex desires and fluent identities, expressed in the condemnation of homosexuality on top of the negation of the female. For Butler (in her magical fusion of Lacan and Foucault), exclusion creates reason as the regulating mechanism of the reign of the Phallus. Rationality, in this view, is always itself irrationally based on the negation of multiplicity. But since this pre-rational multiplicity cannot be *liberated*, because there is *no outside* to the Law, any surrational account of the rational would be nothing but another irrational (suppressive) instantiation of the Law itself.[89]

For the earlier Butler, because of her Foucaultian credo, the Law seems to be an *inescapable fate*—only to be attacked from within by irony, citation, and subversive masquerade.[90] Her (and for that matter Foucault's) all-pervasive Phallogos becomes the irrational Law of a new kind of necessity, "irrational rationalism" that hinders surrationality.[91] For Whitehead and Deleuze, on the other hand, Necessity is neither rational nor a prison of irrationality. The Law is never all-pervasive; there is always a *within-beyond*, a *khoric* or creative drive undermining any static dichotomy between cosmos and chaos. But then, destiny is not a sign of the Logos either, but of Eros. This Necessity is thought to be the condition for genuine novelty.

It is only in the newer work of Butler, especially in *Giving an Account of Oneself*, that she revisits the necessities of "Foucaultian Subjects"[92] to be bound by the Law in a more Whiteheadian (and Deleuzian) mode, that is, by understanding them not only as expressions of a repressive Law, but *in* the sedimentation that this Law instantiates, being the expression of the *inescapability* of the *social* constitution of subjectivity that is not per se repressive but necessarily binding. It is precisely in the *failure* to constitute a perfect self-presence of a socially begotten subject that the fate of the

Law in its repressiveness now begins also to appear as the ground of *virtue* (and, hence, an ethics of performativity), namely to live *with* this fate in such a way that the opaque subject constitutes a reservoir of *indeterminateness* that allows for novelty to appear in the midst of the unavoidable porosity of the social inheritances, the inconsistencies of which can only incompletely be "closed" as all-determining Law.[93]

In Deleuze's surrational understanding, this amounts to an emphatic affirmation of Spinoza and Nietzsche—their rule of immanence and difference as rule of necessity.[94] While Hegel's dialectic follows the logic of the Same, Spinoza's substance and Nietzsche's Eternal Return prioritize the Different.[95] Deleuze reinterprets the necessity of Spinoza's substance "itself [to] be said *of* the modes and only *of* the modes . . . satisfied only at the price of a more general categorical reversal according to which being is said of becoming, identity of that which is different, the one of the multiple."[96] And Deleuze reinterprets the *amor fati* of Nietzsche's Eternal Return, which is often held to indicate "the return of the Identical," as novelty that "does not bring back 'the same,'" but conversely "constitutes only the Same of that which becomes," being "the becoming-identical of becoming itself."[97] Without pre-given identity, "eternal return is the power of (formless) Being, [and] the simulacrum is the true character or form—the 'being'—of that which is. When the identity of things dissolves, being escapes to attain univocity, and begins to revolve around the different."[98] When becoming constitutes being, the Being of becoming is difference *in itself*. Its (eternal) return is the fate that is the condition for unprecedented novelty that creates the chaosmic lattice of rhizomatic structures and systems.[99]

If the earlier Butler's subject is already the product of the excluding Law and if the later Butler's "opaque subject" only tentatively gains the ability to reinsert Novelty in its indeterminate constitution, it is because of her shift from Nietzsche to Foucault.[100] A clear indication of why Butler is not following Deleuze's interpretation of Nietzsche's Eternal Return as return solely of Novelty[101] can be found in her acceptance of Foucault's understanding of the constitution of the subject by the Law, which is not, as in Nietzsche, the outcome of "the force of punishment to be instrumental to the internalization" of the Law (which could be changed, at least, in principle) but by inscribed "codes of conduct" that "do not rely always on violence of prohibition and its internalizing effects"[102] but function as the constitution of the subject per se. Nevertheless, since we cannot, in our social constitution, give an account of ourselves, the ignorance of how "I" emerged, only present in an infinite "narrative reconstruction" of myself, is a limit of self-knowledge that not only takes us "in a fictional direction"[103] (Lacan) but, in so doing, opens a door to a surrationality of the subject that might begin to mirror Whitehead's and Deleuze's account of novelty that does not overturn necessity, but is its expression.[104]

In Whitehead's surrational understanding, the *khoric* nexus of becoming that harbors the (ingredient) patterns is—ontologically and epistemologically—governed by necessity of relationality, whereby "there is an essence to the universe which forbids relationships beyond itself, as a violation of its rationality. Speculative philosophy seeks that essence."[105] While rationality is given by relationality, this relationality, however, is understood as that of *prehensions*, of folds or waves of vector-intensities in ever-new compositions, ever new becomings of structures, an infinite process of a creatively "living Whole."

Nevertheless, as in the later Butler, Whitehead's *account* of this *khoric* nexus must necessarily be *fiction*. On the same level as the undisclosed subject in the later Butler, in its account of itself, it becomes ironic insofar as "in the moment of when we narrate we become speculative philosophers or fictional writers,"[106] Whitehead's "speculative philosophy" is, indeed, a *surrational* "imaginative experiment"[107] of the universal as a "likely story"[108] of relational (or social) interplay "within a local plastic environment" that, rather than be a rational description is a "creative power, making possible its own approach to realization."[109]

This *surrational* Necessity, in Whitehead, plays the dual role of expressing the harboring process of patterning the mother-nexus of aboriginal chaos while securing the novelty of an ever-pulsating, self-renewing, different-repeating universe.[110] In pondering over the irrational preexistence of a "given" and its character as "gift" of Necessity, Whitehead quotes A. E. Taylor's summary of the *Timaeus*:

> In the real world there is always, over and above "law," a factor of the "simply given" or "brute fact," not accounted for and to be accepted simply as given. It is the business of science never to acquiesce in the merely given, to seek to "explain" it as the consequence, in virtue of rational law, of some simpler initial "given." But, however far science may carry this procedure, it is always forced to retain *some* element of brute fact, the merely given, in its account of things. It is the presence in nature of this element of the given, this surd or irrational as it has sometimes been called, which Timaeus appears to be personifying in his language about Necessity.[111]

But again, in Whitehead's interpretation, this *pre*-rational element of Necessity is really *sur*-rational, because this "element of 'givenness' in things implies some activity procuring limitation," which Whitehead famously expresses with the word "decision," not implying "conscious judgment," but in its "root sense of a 'cutting off,'" expressing

> the relation of the actual thing, *for which* a decision is made, to an actual thing by *which* that decision is made. But "decision" cannot be construed as a casual adjunct of an actual entity. It constitutes the very meaning of actuality.[112]

It is activity *qua* decision qua limitation that, for Whitehead, consequently indicates a *necessary* element of the "metaphysical situation" that "provides the limitation for which no reason can be given: for all reason flows from it."[113] In what is one of the clearest confessions of surrationality, Whitehead states that:

> We have come to the limit of rationality. For there is a categorical limitation which does not spring from any metaphysical reason. There is a metaphysical need for a principle of determination, but there can be no metaphysical reason for what is determined. If there were such a reason, there would be no need for any further principle: for metaphysics would already have provided the determination. The general principle of empiricism depends upon the doctrine that there is a principle of concretion which is not discoverable by abstract reason.[114]

In Deleuzian terms, this surrational limitation is not the expression of a pre-fixed, structured Logos, which has to be fought—as in the earlier Butler—but its *"orgiastic* representation: it discovers within itself the limits of the organized; tumult, restlessness and passion underneath apparent calm. It rediscovers monstrosity."[115] This limitation points to the "unique 'total' moment, simultaneously the moment of evanescence and production of difference, of disappearance and appearance."[116] It is in this context that Deleuze's comment that philosophy should be good "science fiction"[117] becomes substantiated as surrationality that, in the interplay of necessity and novelty, might not only mirror Whitehead's "speculative philosophy" as "imagination" but maybe connects to Butler's later account of the fictional account of the subject as a possible reservoir of novelty.

It is with a forthright Nietzschean move that Whitehead then traces the roots of rationality back to the Greek concept of fate, which, of course, in being the mother of rationality, is itself *not* rational, but *sur*rational and the tragedy from which the Law flows.

> The effect of Greek dramatic literature was many-sided. . . . The pilgrim fathers of the scientific imagination as it exists today are the great tragedians of ancient Athens, Aeschylus, Sophocles, Euripides. Their vision of

fate, remorseless and indifferent, urging a tragic incident to its inevitable issue, is the vision possessed by science. Fate in Greek Tragedy becomes the order of nature in modern thought . . . Let me here remind you that the essence of dramatic tragedy is not unhappiness. It resides in the solemnity of the remorseless working of things. This inevitableness of destiny can only be illustrated in terms of human life by incidents which in fact involve unhappiness. For it is only by them that the futility of escape can be made evident in the drama. This remorseless inevitableness is what pervades scientific thought. The laws of physics are the decrees of fate.[118]

In all three thinkers, finally, rationality and freedom seem to be related through necessity and novelty, i.e., both cannot be totalized. There is no all-reigning Law of a Logos, but there is no Liberation to Anarchy either (and even the liberation to equality is, as Butler has shown so convincingly, already the expression of the Law of suppression of inequalities out of, and comparisons from, the privileged perspective of a Rule of exclusion). Against the tantalization of reason (rationalism) and freedom (liberation), we face the hyper-rational (not reasoned) and hyper-free (not willed) *surreality* of necessity and novelty.[119]

Musicology of Discordance

For rationalism, surrationality is indistinctly irrational; for Whitehead, Deleuze, and Butler, on the other hand, rationalism is irrational.[120] But, while for the earlier Butler any surrational *affirmation* of rationality, reason, Logos, and system must itself already be the expression of the Irrational, i.e., of the suppression of desire (of presence) or execution of power,[121] for Whitehead and Deleuze, it is the paradoxical affirmation of the "Chaosmos." Where do they diverge, and where maybe, with the later Butler, do they converge? Maybe the shortest way to state their hiatus is this: Whitehead's and Deleuze's surrationality is not a *negation of reason*, but a *rejection of negation*.

Indeed, in a rather hidden, but nevertheless revealing remark, Butler makes the point that she "opposed Deleuze," because she found "no registration of the negative in his work"[122] and a rejection of *negation* as a creative (constructive) force in Deleuze's appropriation of Nietzsche's affirmation of the Eternal Return. Based on Butler's experience of her Jewish identity after the Holocaust—there is nothing to affirm!—she cannot resonate with Deleuze's view on the positivity of negation, and her affinities fall in line with "the labor of the negative in the Hegelian sense," instead.[123] Considering Deleuze's and Whitehead's affirmation of "system"[124] and their rejection of Hegel as the basis for their understanding of system,[125] the divergence between Butler, on the one hand, and Whitehead/Deleuze, on the other, occurs exactly in their stance toward negation, especially in the guise of the Hegelian *dialectic* of negation.

For Deleuze, dialectic negation is the implementation of the "original sin" of philosophy, from which all errors follow, namely the *negation of immanence*, the opening of the gap of *transcendence*.[126] But while others would interpret this affirmation of immanence (in the sense of Nietzsche's Eternal Return) as glorification of nihilism, for Deleuze, the affirmation of immanence is the affirmation of novelty: Only the *singular* becomes universal; only *novelty* returns.[127] Hegel's dialectic, however, *utilizes* (the gap of) negation, i.e., transcendence and disconnection, to *rationalize* the irrational—thereby rendering the surrational irrational. Hegel's dialectic, in Deleuze's eyes, becomes a *totalizing* move of the System (Spirit/Self) that includes the irrational as a *rational* moment and as a created *product* of own omnipotent reign.

Although, other than in Deleuze, there are important functions of negation in Whitehead,[128] Deleuze, in his important (and relatively unknown) lecture from March 10, 1987, on Whitehead, makes the bold and ultimately adequate claim that Whitehead's "cry for the event" (all is event!) begins with the *sheer affirmation of relation* and of inter-relationality as *the event of vibrations of relations*.[129] No negation in the mythos of creation undermines this universal affirmation of relationality, which Deleuze calls "the Open . . . by Relation"[130] and Whitehead the "necessity in universality," in which "what does not so communicate is unknowable, and the unknowable is unknown" so that only "this universality defined by 'communication' can suffice."[131] Deleuze is right: Everything begins with vibration! Everything in Whitehead's universe "seems to be wasting itself in the production of the vibrations."[132] The primordial relation that Whitehead calls *prehension* is nothing but a "vector-feeling," a "vector transmission of primitive feeling" in which "the primitive provision of width for contrast is secured by pulses of emotion, which in the coordinate division of occasions . . . appear as . . . vibrations."[133]

For the divergence of Whitehead (Deleuze) from Hegel (Butler), the event as building "Contrasts, or Modes of Synthesis of Entities in one Prehension, or Patterned Entities"[134] is crucial. There is a point in which Whitehead describes this event as "nothing else than the Hegelian development of an idea."[135] But the difference is that the triadic structure of the Hegelian Ideas, as mediated through negation, and negation of negation, is an activity that produces its own process of negation (out of the One, the Self, the I), while Whitehead's triad—prehensions, initial aim, satisfaction—creates a *contrast out of opposites*, which are not dialectic negations of one another, but divergent, even incoherent moments in a process of compositional transformation, that is, a multiplicity that cannot be reduced to a mediated "One."[136] For Whitehead, "'becoming' is the transformation of incoherence into coherence."[137] Contrast originates from the *affirmation* of abysmal opposites; the heterogeneous hiatus of opposition and impossible difference is never bridged by any homogeneous dialectic. To the contrary, oppositions-turned-contrasts produce an infinite *différance*, "proceed[ing] from 'contrasts' to 'contrasts of contrasts,' and on indefinitely to higher grades of contrasts."[138] It is not through negation, therefore, but "is due to the origination of reversions in the mental pole" that novel contrasts *as* "vibration and rhythm"[139] appear. As Deleuze observes, Whitehead's universe of affirmative reversions creates series of divergent and convergent vibes, folds, warps, and waves, interrelated in networks of chaosmic polyphonies, discordant harmonies of the unending becoming of structures out of vibratory, contrasting novelty. The creation of systems of vibration is the "exemplification of composition."[140]

As the *"function of Reason"* for Whitehead is always *"to promote the art of life,"*[141] for Deleuze, the Chaosmos is the sheer affirmation of structures *harbored and nourished* in the "Open" that is Relation in Chaos. Paradoxically, the more these vibrant structures complicate themselves, the more they begin to express the chaos out of which they emerged. Life is the "the production of a non-social nexus ... in the interstices"[142] of structures that treasure this "entirely living nexus," which "is not properly a society [in Whitehead's sense] at all, since 'life' cannot be a defining characteristic. It is the name for originality, and not for tradition."[143] Although Life needs for its emergence a "complex inorganic system of interaction ... built up for [its] protection,"[144] it is essentially the expression of "non-social nexus" that "answers to the notion of 'chaos.'"[145]

While for Whitehead "life is a characteristic of 'empty space' and not of space 'occupied' by any corpuscular society,"[146] for Butler, as noted earlier, this empty space of chaos, which is pre-rational, is always already occupied by structured societies, the Law of suppression, desire, exclusion, and negativity.[147] Following Lacan and Foucault, for her, "the law might be understood to produce or generate"[148] the effect that is said to be its "before" or "outside." While for Whitehead the chaotically vibrating discords are not dialectically, i.e., *rationally explained*, but *surrationally transformed* into a convergent contrast that *affirms* the differences; and while for Deleuze the event of the togetherness of these divergences is the "*inseparatibility of a finite number of heterogeneous components traversed by a point of absolute survey at infinite speed*;"[149] for Butler, the dialectic form of "occupation" includes already the excluded as part of its own activity: negation functions as *production of the excluded* so that its *rationalization* is in peril of repeating the seamless synthesis of the Idea. Consequently—and although even the early Butler is well aware of the profound problematic of any totalizing universalization (even that of patriarchalism or phallogocentrism)[150]—with her dialectic of negation of any "prejudicial" imagination,[151] at least the early Butler is in danger of erecting the very totalizing rationalism in which a force of negativity is *rationalized* into the inescapability of the Law.

Regarding this Hegelian background, Whitehead's and Deleuze's Chaosmos lives from an entirely different account of diversity: the *mutual immanence* of *khora* and its harbored vibrating structures. Surrationality is nothing but the affirmation of this *mutual immanence* in which rationality, reason, structure, and system are co-created without negation. The only "system of all things"[152] is the *event* of their ever-new composition.[153] Born out of Chaos or Void or *Khora*, reason, structure, and system can never totally take over, but will—as its vibrant expression—always fall back onto (and conversely, harbor) this chaotic, *khoric*, surrational Life. In this surrational affirmation of a creative universe, "there is an ultimate which is [only] actual in virtue of its accidents."[154] Logos never reigns absolutely, but is the child of creativity, which itself is—nothing (for it-Self).

The early Butler's *homogeneous* rationalization of the irrational haunts her right to the core of her thought, the deconstruction of the Law. This materializes especially in Butler's criticism of Julia Kristeva and her *khoric* undermining of rationality as based in the Symbolic Law.[155] While Kristeva contests "Lacan's equation of the Symbolic with all linguistic meaning,"[156] for Butler, she falls prey to Foucault's rule that there is no prediscursive reality. Moreover, Kristeva "fails to understand the paternal mechanisms by which affectivity itself is generated,"[157] so that the "very law might well be the cause of the very desire it is said to repress."[158] In stating that any utopian striving for an "outside" of the Law is not just fictitious, but even *produced* by the very Law that represses the commitment of its own deposition by the utopian alternatives, Butler immunizes the Law, which now braces to become the omnipotent ruler of its own conditions, imagined alternatives, and underlying contingencies.[159]

Seen from the perspective of Whitehead's and Deleuze's *heterogeneous* affirmation as the alternative to Hegelian dialectic of negation, Butler's move must appear as the totalizing mechanism of dialectic.[160] While Butler's reconstruction of the Law through de-substantialized performativity wants to challenge the phallogocentric omnipotence of the Logos, it now turns out to be another instantiation of the omnipotent Law insofar as it creates its exclusions and thereby integrates them as part of his rationality. Foucault's and Lacan's negation of the pre-discursive nature of the *khora*, which is emphatically affirmed by Whitehead and Kristeva, generates another totalizing rationalism. Instead of this *unilateral* Law (of Self-Identity), which is the production of its own causes (as its effects), Whitehead's and Deleuze's surrational approach affirms the *mutual* immanence of system and *khora*, whereby they can be said to be *effects of one another*.[161]

With the treatment of Hegel in Butler's *Giving an Account of Oneself*, however, we might gather a different picture, one that is ostensive because it obviously becomes porous to the Whiteheadian/Deleuzian modes of affirmation, and, hence, of the affirmation of surrationality beyond the prevalence of negativity. Two elements make all the difference: First, now she takes Hegel's dialectic in a different direction (although one that in her own judgment also will fail), namely that of the *affirmation* of transparency (instead of its all-pervasive force of negativity).[162] This leads her to the second element: While denying the totalizing claim of Hegel's dialectic of transparency in favor of the opaqueness of subjectivity that in its social, bodily, and regulatory inscriptions can never become self-present and, hence, never become self-transparent, Butler now *affirms* the limitation of this opaqueness not as lack, but as virtue of responsible existence (and, hence as ground of an ethics).[163]

Meta-Khoric *Magic?*

If there is a difference between Whitehead's and Deleuze's surrational account of mutual immanence—and there is indeed a profound one—then it is based on their divergence of what *constitutes* genuine necessity-as-novelty in the Chaosmos. While both thinkers derive the Chaosmos through "passive genesis"[164] or the "remorseless working of things,"[165] for Deleuze, this uncontrolled, pre-individual, and non-personal process is based in the vibrating self-organization of the *passive* virtual;[166] for Whitehead, however, it is based on the *activity of a field of decisions*, which is facilitated by a principle of intensity and harmony we do not find in Deleuze. This is where Whitehead infamously suggests that the surrational necessity-as-novelty is primordially symbolized by a Divine dimension of the Chaosmos. Insofar as the "function of God is analogous to the remorseless working of things in Greek and in Buddhist thought,"[167] the vibratory universe "is rooted in the nature of God"[168]—being "the organ of novelty" and "aiming at intensification."[169] This "God," however, is interpreted as the principle of limitation/concretion, the surrational element in the "metaphysical situation" whereby there is "ultimate limitation."[170] Hence, "no reason can be given" for this "ultimate irrationality," which is "the nature of God, because that nature is the ground of rationality."[171]

To be sure, it would be false to claim that because of the "categorical space" Whitehead assigns to this Divine perspective, his "universe remains, in principle, only semi-open,"[172] while Deleuze's Chaosmos, in avoiding such a move, would be *truly* open. It can be demonstrated that through Deleuze's and Whitehead's common commitment to the mutual immanence of the *khoric* realm with its vibrations and polyphone harmonies of vibrations *both* philosophies arrive "at the magic formula we all seek—PLURALISM = MONISM."[173]

First, both philosophers find the magic formula by de-substantializing Spinoza: Deleuze by removing the remaining independence of the (Divine) substance from their dependent modes[174] in *Difference and Repetition* and recreating this difference as an infinite multiplicity of planes of immanence intersecting in Chaos in *What is Philosophy?*;[175] Whitehead by deconstructing the "substantial activity" of *Science and the Modern World*[176] as "creativity" in *Process and Reality* and as *khora* of *Adventures of Ideas*.[177]

Second, *none* of Whitehead's "formative elements"[178]—multiplicity of actualities (the World), multiplicity of eternal objects (Forms), creativity (*khora*), and God—are excluded from being the *effect of their mutual immanence*:[179] the multiplicity of actualities has no pre-forming principle of activation,[180] and creativity is nothing beyond its instantiations and formlessness beyond all forms;[181] the multiplicity of forms has no ruling rationality[182] and God is not in command of these multiplicities, neither creating them nor restricting their diversity,[183] God itself being conceptualized as multiplicity.[184]

Third, Whitehead's Divine surrationality is the most subtle *effect* of this mutual immanence, which it, at the same time, instantiates.[185] In the same sense that "the characters of the relevant things in nature are the outcome of their interconnections, and their interconnections are the outcome of their characters"[186] is the Divine nature the *effect* of the *actual process* they permeate (as is true for the mutual immanence of the primordial and the consequent aspect of God's nature). Nowhere, hence, does the Divine nature equate to a Divine individual or person[187] or subjective consciousness. Far from such a subjective "synthesis of unification," which is never "without the form of the I, or the point of view of a Self,"[188] Whitehead *repudiated* God-as-Self as a "metaphysical sublimation" of oppressive states of affairs into a "general concept of the Deity" that closes totality in itself.[189] The primordial nature is a pre-individual harmony of the "infinite conceptual realization" of potentials; the consequent nature is a trans-subjective "unity of the multiplicity of actual fact with the primordial conceptual fact,"[190] a post-individual multiplicity contrasting transformation of opposites, loss, and tragedy.[191] As primordial instantiation(s) and characterization(s) of *creativity*,[192] the Divine natures are affirmative, non-exclusive, and without any "private I (Eye)" or investigative, biased gaze. God is not a Super-Ego, but the most anti-subjectivist way to articulate cosmic intensity and harmony.[193]

Hence, in following the *strict* rule of mutual immanence Whitehead's Divine dimension of the Chaosmos does *not* externally direct the universe, but *facilitates* its openness.[194] Hence, it does *not* act as "transcendence," or "vertical Being," as an "imperial state in the sky or on earth," but implements "immanence."[195] We could say that Deleuze's surrational account of the mutual immanence of chaos-*khora* and patterns-vibrations is not in need of such a Divine perspective and, consequently, does not exhibit a philosophical and chaosmic "space" for it. Whitehead's surrational account of the mutual immanence of chaos-*khora*-creativity and pattern-vibrations, however, demands a principle of concretion-limitation-intensification-harmonization and, therefore, exhibits a philosophical and chaosmic "space" for it.

Where does this "need" come from? Two reasons can be given for such a demand: First, against ultimate rationalism that imposes a "harmony of logic . . . upon the universe as an iron necessity," Whitehead introduces the Divine surrationality as "aesthetic harmony" that "stands before it as a living ideal moulding the general flux in its broken progress towards finer, subtler issues."[196] It is the *harvest of tragedy*, the expression of the "remorseless working of things" as contrast of discordance. Second, this *subversion* of the Law *saves the uniqueness of the multiplicity transformed*. Here, Whitehead directly transcends the *khora* as "medium of communication" or, as in Deleuze, as "sieve"[197] and "paradoxical element,"[198] the "Event in which all events communicate and are distributed."[199] While the

> Platonic Receptacle is void, abstract from all individual occasions, . . . [t]he Unity of Adventure includes among its components all individual realities,

each with the importance of the personal or social fact to which it belongs ..., each claiming its due share of attention. This Appearance, thus enjoyed, is the final Beauty with which the Universe achieves its justification.[200]

The Divine perspective does not mold anything into a certain (closed) teleology; because its "purpose" is mere "intensity, and not preservation,"[201] its aim (or, rather, aimlessness) is formless, like the *khora*. Where Deleuze envisions the *"quasi-cause assuring full autonomy to the effect"*[202] to be "an immanent principle of auto-unification,"[203] Whitehead establishes (beyond that, but uncontested!) another immanent principle of quasi-causal *importance* of the singular, which is not identical with auto-creation (subjectivity), but is an element of the disinterested harmonization of intensities (objective immortality). Beyond Deleuze's still Heideggerian duality of the (ontological) difference of events and the Event, Whitehead opts for a *multiplicity of immanent principles*, none of which "resembles" (pre-forms, "realizes") their actualizations. And because of *all* of their "mutual immanence,"[204] Whitehead's meta-*khoric*, Divine principle, which is in *itself* a multiplicity (of "tragic Beauty," "initial Eros," "Supreme Adventure," "Final Fact," and "Harmony of harmonies"[205]), does *not* establish a pre-formative harmony guaranteeing a pre-ordained goal (as in Leibniz)[206]—which Whitehead understood merely as "an extreme example of the doctrine of imposition."[207] As the *quasi causal effect* of the chaosmic vibrations in their intercommunication, i.e., the effect of their stubborn importance beyond, and inexhaustible resistance against, any unification under the Law, it indicates a (disinterested, non-possessive, and non-subjective) Beauty that, for Whitehead, is the only "justification" of existence.

The point of divergence of the surrationality of Whitehead and Deleuze, therefore, is not that Whitehead reintroduces Being, and it is not that Deleuze despises of the teleology of quasi-causal effects, but it is about *how* these effects are constructed in their *transcendental* importance, i.e., *how* they are conditions of genuine novelty. For Deleuze, (teleological) effects are *virtualities*, a *passive* multiplicity-field of singularities that is *actualized* in events;[208] for Whitehead, however, these (teleological) effects are *valuations*, an *active* (though *receptive*) multiplicity-field of singularities that is created in *decisions* of events.[209] Although both notions of actualities/singularities must be understood as intersection and creation,[210] for Deleuze's virtual-events their mutual immanence is more a question of *surrational folding* (by infinite speed); for Whitehead's value-events, however, their mutual immanence is a matter of *surrational irruption*. We could say it this way: Deleuze finds the process of auto-unification transcendentally conditioned by *two* modes of "*passive* genesis"—of the events (pre-individual singularities) and the Event (communication) of which "nobody" is in control.[211] Whitehead finds them transcendentally conditioned by *multiple* modes of *decisive* genesis—of events (decisive actualities), creativity (decisive activity), potentials (decisive disposition), *khora* (decisive space), and God (decisive effect/quasi-cause)—of which nobody is in control either.[212]

Both philosophies are compositions of the polyphony of the Chaosmos, but both diverge in what exactly facilitates their compositional intensity. Regarding the "magic formula we all seek," Deleuze might have been more the monist, always searching for a continuity of becoming, while Whitehead was, the later the more, a pluralist, always seeking the "becoming of continuity, but no[t the] continuity of becoming."[213] This may be the reason that Deleuze championed "Spinoza [as] the Christ of philosophers"[214] of mutual immanence, while Whitehead could refer to "Christ as revelation"[215] of this very mutual immanence.

CHAPTER 9

Divine Possibilities: Becoming an Order without Law

Alan R. Van Wyk

From a number of differing traditions, political theory has again taken up a certain interest in the religious, such that it is becoming difficult to distinguish political theory from political theology.[1] This interest is, in part, necessitated by the realization that, in the West at least, politics and the political have already been determined by the theological. Within this realization, a number of diverse traditions are uneasily coming together to require both attention to the religious in order to understand politics and the political, and a turn to the religious in order to move beyond the theological determination of politics and the political. Within this theoretical necessity, Judith Butler's political thought has recently taken up an interest in the religious. Specifically in the essays "Precarious Life," and "Critique, Coercion, and Sacred Life in Benjamin's 'Critique of Violence,'" Butler has taken up a religious discourse that is inaugurated by an experience of the divine command "Thou shalt not kill."[2] In these recent works, the taking up of religious discourse becomes an occasion for theorizing the ontological rupture of an already theologically determined law. Here Butler argues that the divine command functions in ways other than as law, such that an encounter with the divine command functions to undo the binds of law: The divine command ruptures, as a divine violence, the linear temporality of a theologically determined law whereby subjects are

Divine Possibilities

bound to their own subjugation within the law itself. Divine violence, enacted through an encounter within the divine command, becomes a violence against the violence of law and thereby frees the subject to a possibility for life beyond the law. In this, Butler's recent turn to religious discourse is a way to think the limits of subjugation within a theological law, which is also a way to think the limits of law itself and the possibility that can arise at these limits when the law is ruptured.

If these recent reflections are a continuation of Butler's reflections on the law, they also create a space within which to begin a critical comparison between Butler and Alfred North Whitehead, and thereby to bring Whitehead's process ontology into a critical conversation with Butler's political ontology and the theoretical necessity of thinking politics and the political with the religious. Although Whitehead himself was always concerned with the political within the determination of subjects—the organic ontology is always an ontology whereby subjects become within societies—his own speculative metaphysics arises within a certain tranquility and distance from the historical that, as Isabelle Stengers has expressed it, appears as discontinuous with the radicality of the event ontology he proposes.[3] To bring Whitehead into this space with Butler is then to force a confrontation with the political radicality of an event ontology, the religious dimensions of this political ontology, and the possible limits of this politics in the determination and rupture of the law.

Although it is beyond the scope of the present chapter to fully explore the religious dimensions of Whitehead's ontology, political or otherwise, a beginning can be made with the recognition that, first, Whitehead's own constructive determination of God takes place within a demand for the secularization of God;[4] and second, that central to Whitehead's process ontology is the determination of God as the ground of possibility and the absolute future of each occasion. For Whitehead, the encounter with this divine possibility disrupts the preservative repetitions of history; as Whitehead argues: "God is indifferent alike to preservation and novelty. . . . [God's] aim [for an occasion] is depth of satisfaction."[5] The encounter with the divine becomes, then, an encounter with a possible satisfaction that transcends and also ruptures the repetitions of history, creating the possibility for a deeper satisfaction for the subject. Within the historical-social structures within which any occasion becomes, structures that are concerned with a becoming of subjects that maintains society itself, the encounter with the divine opens a range of possibility for the subject, a set of radical possibility that may fundamentally disrupt the social structure itself.

In this space of critical encounter, two sets of questions come to the fore. First, what are the political effects of Whitehead's call for the secularization of God? What does it mean to propose secularized political theology? And second, what sort of possibility is being opened in the political here? Within a secularized political theology, is an order without law possible? Under these questions, the distance between these two ontologies becomes clear. For Butler, the divine disruption of law cannot itself instate a new law; it can only open a struggle, a wrestling, that verges on the anarchic. The law will always precede its divine rupture, such that the law will remain, after its rupture, as the only ground of order. For Whitehead, though, another order is possible; an aesthetic order of intensity without law becomes possible within an encounter with the divine precisely as that which precedes the law itself. If it is not possible here to offer a full determination of this possibility, an opening will have been made for thinking again the rupture of the law of the possibility of the future.

In both "Precarious Life" and "Benjamin's 'Critique of Violence,'" the religious discourse that is taken up arises out of a religious experience: an encounter with the divine command "Thou shalt not kill." In "Precarious Life," it is not a direct encounter with the divine interdiction that is in question, but rather, drawing on Emmanuel Levinas, Butler explores this divine interdiction as it is "spoken" through the unspeaking face of the Other. Through Levinas, Butler is able to return to the key problematic of much of her earlier work: the assumptive force of law in the determination of subjects.[6] Continuing to advance an understanding of this assumptive logic, in "Precarious Life" the divine command takes place in and through the approach of the Other, so that the citational practice by which this command is assumed is always already a relational citation. Although there is, in the "Preface" to *Precarious Life*, an attempted distancing from the theorization of this relational interdependence,[7] the political ontology that is developed through this reading of the Levinasian reading of the divine command is already a relational ontology.

With a particular scriptural seriousness, Butler draws from the Biblical narrative of God's giving of the law to Moses that "the face [of the Other] makes various utterances at once: it bespeaks an agony, an injurability, at the same time that it bespeaks a divine prohibition against killing."[8] In inaugurating a relationally citational practice—in citing the divine interdiction as the already spoken ground of one's being in the presence of an Other—the encounter with the face of the Other through which the divine interdiction is announced becomes the generative occasion of a struggle, a tensed struggle that resides "at the heart of ethics."[9] This tensed struggle is created through the approach of the Other, a drawing near that creates both a fright—the experience of having one's own precarious life put into question by the Other—and an anxiety—the possible necessity of harming the Other in self-defense.[10] As Butler argues, within this Levinasian reading of the divine command, if the approach of the other creates both a fright and an anxiety, this is because the encounter with the Other within the strictures of the divine command presents both the limits of one's being as well as the limits of one's relation to the Other. The approach of the face exposes the self as a being that can be killed, while also encountering this Other as one who can be killed, but whose killing is already prohibited by the divine command. The being of the self and the Other remain always in this irreducible and threatening tension of encountering a protected threat, being always exposed to that which is approaching. This relation with the Other can never be resolved into a simple reciprocity of pure being with the Other. The assumption into the relational command does not and cannot function to produce a secure or stable subjectivity, producing instead a tensed encounter with the Other as well as a tensed experience of the precariousness of life itself.

In "Benjamin's 'Critique of Violence,'" it is no longer a relationally citational practice that is at issue, for the divine command itself can be met in itself and for the subject itself. As Butler argues, Benjamin "invokes the commandment as mandating only that an individual struggle with the ethical edict communicated by the imperative,"[11] such that it is the divine command itself with which "each individual must wrestle without the model of any other."[12] Even though, as Butler notes, the divine command is understood by Benjamin in relation to the general strike, the divine command itself is always presented as being addressed to an individual, so that it is within the inner life of the subject that the divine command is effective.

Within this individual encounter, the divine command itself can only be met with struggle, for the divine command is precisely not a law, being without the means for enforcing a singular acquiescence to itself.[13] When met within a subjugation to a law that has already enforced its own authority to bind, the divine command that leaves open the possibility of its own application opens a space for possibility within this other-than-law itself. It is the opening of possibility, of struggle, of wrestling with the command that becomes the possibility for a political subjectivity that undoes the binds of law already subjugating the subject. Although leaving behind the possibility of a relational subjectivity, "Benjamin's 'Critique of Violence'" advances beyond the tensed struggle occasioned within the face of the command in "Precarious Life," such that now the struggle occasioned by the divine command is that which shakes free a subjectivity captured in a law that allows for no struggle, a law that disavows any struggle as already necessarily being a struggle in violation of the law. To the extent that Butler, following Benjamin, understands the binding law as enacting a violence, the divine command acts against the violent binding of the law. In this violence against violence, the commandment, as Butler argues, "establishes a point of view on law that leads to the destruction of law as coercively binding."[14]

If we will risk designating a religious turn in Butler's thought at this point, this can only be understood as a turn to religion and the theological discourses arising from the religious as necessitated by the already theological determination of the law.[15] A religious turn, it seems, becomes the only possibility for unbinding an already religiously determined law. In this, Butler does not abandon her previously articulated critique of theology. In this difficult sense, the religious is turned against itself within a determination of the divine command as opposed to the law. The law that has been grounded in theology is seen to be undone in and by a divine command that is not law. The failure of the theological law, which has always been central in Butler's thought for grounding the possibility of another (un)lawful existence, is now seen to arise from a confrontation with a divine command that is not law and which thereby opens a positive possibility. Within this critical theological discourse, arising out of the religious experience of another non-law, it is the nonbinding divine command that frees the subject into another temporality and another causation. In attempting to think a political subjectivity that can undo the binds of a theological law, Butler is drawn to a religious subjectivity that is able to enact a rupture within the subjugating functionality of law itself.[16]

The encounter with the divine command becomes the fundamental failure of the law to be binding. If in her previous critique of theology, theology designated the determination of the law as perfectly binding, the religious now designates a command that will always fail as law—that functions as a command in providing the instance for a failure of law. This failure, in opening a certain perspective on the law, does so by opening into an experience of the conditions of law itself. Although in the opening of "Benjamin's 'Critique of Violence'" Butler strictly announces Benjamin's distinctions between mythic violence and divine violence, within the rhythm of the messianic that is opened to by divine violence, this distinction is blurred. The destruction that follows from divine violence provides

Divine Possibilities

an opening to an originary rhythm, a destructiveness, which is the "constantly recurring condition" of both positive law and legal violence.[17]

On the one hand, it seems, the divine violence opens to the precariousness of life already articulated in "Precarious Life," though now that precariousness is understood in terms of a rhythm of perpetual downfall. On the other hand, in "Benjamin's 'Critique of Violence,'" this rhythmic destructiveness itself designates the sacredness of life, installing at the heart of life both a sacredness and a transience.[18] Transience itself then becomes the continual downfall and suffering of all life, which is also the condition of both mere life and sacred life. In this sense, positive law, the violence of law, is the violence of transforming this continual downfall into a binding guilt by which the transient suffering subject is deemed responsible and guilty for a suffering that is its own sacred condition for being.[19] Acting against this binding, the divine command enacts a violence that provides an expiatory opening into the suffering and transience of life. Through this violence against violence, mere life is understood as being transformed into sacred life.[20] In reading "Precarious Life" and "Benjamin's 'Critique of Violence'" together, the experience of the divine command, in inaugurating a tensed realization of the precariousness of life, an experience of the transience of life "functions as the ground for the apprehension of life's value."[21]

The value of life is designated, here, as the sacredness of life, so that it is within the tensed encounter with the divine command that the subject is freed into an experience of the sacredness of life.[22] Yet this experience of the sacredness of life will always, for Butler, remain as the outside of any positive law or order. In "Precarious Life," the experience that arises from an encounter with the divine command is not yet designated as an experience of the sacredness of life, yet the experience of the divine command already attains a position as the troubling outside of any political order. It is in this sense that Butler problematizes Levinas's claim that the divine command is what should be heard in the meaning of Europe.[23] For Butler, to insist on hearing this command as the meaning of Europe is to insist that there is no recognizable Europe in this meaning precisely because the divine command can give rise to no positive civilization. If a Europe is to arise from this command, it is precisely and only within the psychic circuitry of the tension that arises as the experience of the divine command. Whatever possible civilization may arise from this tension is itself grounded in the negative overcoming of the psychic displacement of accounting for the guilt arising from a forbidden desire.

In "Benjamin's 'Critique of Violence,'" Butler is more insistent that the divine command itself cannot give rise to any positive law. First, the divine command is itself understood in terms of being a command, and not a law. Any translation of this command into law will itself undo the command as a command, rendering as impossible the struggle that the command inaugurates. More fundamentally, the divine command cannot itself ground any positive law to the extent that the divine command is only announced once the law has already been effective.[24] The commandment then only functions as disruptive, as breaking the binds of law, but this is itself a breaking that has no possibility of opening to a life of what is broken. This life that is opened becomes, then, "an omission, a failure to show, to comply, to endorse . . . [a] refusal to act."[25] What, we are left to ask, is this negative existence?

Within his speculative metaphysics, Whitehead's encounters with God are far from singular or complete so that a final interpretation of his determination of God and the relation between God and order will not be possible here,[26] just as Butler's own nascent struggles with a religious discourse forbid any claims to finality. As Lewis Ford has argued, a double trajectory can be traced in the development of Whitehead's speculative metaphysic.[27] On the one hand, there is the movement that will eventuate in an ontology of actual occasions as concrescent activity of becoming in the midst of multiplicity. With the achievements reached in the ontological development of actual occasions, Whitehead is able to develop a conception of God that eventuates in the determination of God as dipolar becoming. This doubled development is not only a struggle to determine the ontology of actual occasions and God, or the relation between actual occasions and God, but is directly, for Whitehead, a question of order and possibility. It is, as Whitehead continually insists, that God is a necessary element of his metaphysic to account for both order and possibility as arising within this order.

Given that Whitehead's reception in America has most often been filtered through process theology, it is often difficult to remember that Whitehead himself proposes the necessity of a secularization of God.[28] The necessity of secularization requires that the determination of God is itself preceded by a two-fold critique of religious determinations of God. First, Whitehead proposes a metaphysical critique of determinations of God. Any metaphysical determination of God, Whitehead argues, must satisfy the ecological requirements of that metaphysic. God cannot, in other words, "be treated as an exception to all metaphysical principles, invoked to save their collapse."[29] More importantly, though, Whitehead also proposes a theological critique of determinations of God. In *Process and Reality*, Whitehead argues that theological determinations of God produce "the doctrine of an aboriginal, eminently real, transcendent creator, at whose fiat the world came into being, and whose imposed will it obeys.... When the Western world accepted Christianity, Caesar conquered; and the received text of Western theology was edited by its lawyers."[30] Whitehead's theological critique is itself, then, also a political critique. Within the "Western world," a designation that requires a further elaboration to be accurate, God has become a legislator, functioning through law in the absolute determination of that which is to be. This determination itself is read as following from God's will, although it is, Whitehead argues, the will of an imperial domination that is being enacted. In this way, the will of God comes to justify the will of Caesar whose own desire has supplanted that of God.

This political-theological critique of the determination of God begins Whitehead's own constructive determination of God, and it is only after the effect of this critique has been registered that Whitehead proposes a threefold determination of God as "the outcome of creativity, the foundation of order, and as the goad towards novelty."[31] In this threefold determination, God is not creativity itself, but rather the first accident of creativity, the accident of creativity that allows creativity to become actuality.[32] As that which presents creativity to become actual, God is both the foundation of order and the percipient occasion for creativity to arise as novelty and not simply as repetition. Yet as both foundation and goad toward novelty God is determined by a singular purpose: the seeking of intensity within actual occasions.[33] With this determination of God's purpose as evocative of intensity, the evocation of societies becomes a "purely subsidiary" desire.[34] Although God is the foundation of order, this is precisely in order to produce intensity, just as societies, Whitehead argues, are necessary as that out of which intensity arises.[35] With this, Whitehead's entire metaphysic becomes an articulation of the conditions for the ontological production of occasions of intensity.[36]

Intensity is, for Whitehead, the structural production through which the relation between order, the subject, and the divine are related. It might appear, at this point, that a certain agreement arises between Whitehead and Butler. It may be argued that the intense inner struggle that Butler argues arises from an encounter with the divine command can be understood in relation to the divine desire for intensity in the becoming of occasions. It would then be possible to move directly, within Whitehead, from a determination of God as desiring of intensity to the divine rupture of order and law as being the means for intensity to be actualized, deploying in this move the conceptual and theoretical apparatus Butler has developed. Yet Whitehead proposes a third figure for encountering the divine that radically shifts the relation between law and order. In distinction from the position articulated in "Precarious Life," God is, for Whitehead, the ground of the becoming of each actual occasion in its own becoming as providing its own subjective aim. God is not, for Whitehead, mediated from outside through a relationality, but is within the relationality of all becoming itself. By figuring God as within an already metaphysical relationality, Whitehead is able to theorize relationality itself without determining God as the cause or ground nor as the total outside of relationality.[37]

In distinction from the position articulated in both "Precarious Life" and "Benjamin's 'Critique of Violence,'" Whitehead determines God not as a giver of law, nor even giver of command, but as the Principle of Concretion,[38] as foundation of order not by law or divine fiat, but as valuator of possibility.[39] This is, then, to fully register the effect of Whitehead's theological critique of the determination of God. For Whitehead, to understand God principally in terms of the giver of law is to already determine God as Caesar. This is also to already determine the world as obeying the divine fiat of will. When all order is given over to the will of law, God and the world appear as already determined to an economy of political and law bound will. For Whitehead, the secularization of God entails the necessity for a secularization of metaphysics itself. And this metaphysical secularization proposes not simply the failure of the law, but the abandonment of the law as the ground of being and possibility. Within Whitehead, it is not the failure of the law that opens up possibility but a rejection of the lawful as the determination of both God and the world that undoes the law of Caesar itself.

In determining God as the Principle of Concrescence and the ground of possibility, God not only does not dictate the world through law, but neither does God order the world by judgment. God is rather the primordial decision through which, as Whitehead argues, "the barren inefficient disjunction of abstract potentialities obtains primordially the efficient conjunction of ideal realization."[40] As Steven Shaviro argues, situating Whitehead in relation to both Kant and Deleuze, God functions as both the limitative and inclusive disjunctive synthesis: performing the primordial decision from which all other decisions can occur, while also providing, in this primordial decision, a wider scope of possibility in distributing a new composition of possibility itself.[41] It is as primordial decision that God becomes the primordial occasion of novelty, grounding all becoming through decision and proposing what might be to that which arises from what has been. It is in this divine decision that novelty becomes not only possible, but conceivable.[42]

It is also in this sense that God is, for Whitehead, primordial irrationality. For this divine decision from which all other decisions flow is itself the ground of decisive rationality. It is from this decision that rationality itself can be determined. God is therefore, Whitehead argues, "the ultimate limitation, and His existence is the ultimate irrationality."[43] It would seem that God is, for Whitehead, determined within what is for Butler, in her reading of Benjamin, the mythic. Here then, God would be performing the primordial instance of formative violence, a formative violence that does not answer to any previous law or rationality, but is itself the ground for law and rationality.[44] God would be, if not Caesar, then the enactor of a primordial violence of law, whereby violence would become the final ground of all becoming and being. The production of being out of the flux of becoming would be nothing more than and inseparable from this primordial violence.

Whitehead does not shy away from the realization that God, as the Principle of Concrescence, performs a primordial decision that is a primordial limitation. There is, Whitehead acknowledges, a certain "ruthlessness of God" as the Principle of Concrescence; a ruthlessness that is "inexorable in God."[45] This ruthlessness is the ruthlessness of any decision, where decision refers not first to consciousness, but to "cutting off."[46] Even so, it is difficult to render this ruthlessness as simply a violence against life, as an arresting of life.[47] On the one hand, Whitehead argues that this is a necessary ruthlessness, a ruthless decision that must be performed in order for any becoming, or novelty itself, to be possible. Without this primordial decision, the continual process could not become a process of becoming. Decision is, Whitehead argues, the very meaning of actuality.[48] The primordial ruthlessness, then, is not itself against life, but is a necessary valuation for the possibility of any becoming; it is a "valuation as an aim towards 'order'; and 'order' means 'society permissive of actualities with patterned intensity of feeling arising from adjusted contrasts.'"[49] With this, Whitehead seems to be acknowledging the same thing that Butler has always insisted on: All becoming can only arise out of what is given, and that which is given is only given through limitation, a decisive cutting off.

If it is necessary, though, in following Whitehead, to continue to speak of this primordial decision as a primordial limitation, this is neither the enactment of a totalizing order nor a fundamental foreclosure. Rather, the valuative order that is enacted in this primordial decision is only a partial determination of that which is given, the given out of which actuality arises. Disorder is, Whitehead argues, the correlative of order, and only together do they constitute what is given.[50] The ordering that is enacted in the primordial decision is the ordering of that which is given, but not in its totality. It is rather a primordial decision that creates the condition for a further decision, the decision of an actual occasion in its own becoming. As Whitehead argues, "An actual entity arises from decisions *for* it, and by its very existence provides decisions *for* other actual entities which supersede it."[51] Thus, actuality is constituted as a successive series of decisions, decisions within what is given as ordered, thereby providing an ordered given to what is to come. Yet this series of decisions are not, in themselves, complete determinations of the decisions to come. Rather, decisions are made *for* actual occasions only so that they, in their own singularity, may make their own decisions, and so attain their own actuality. Decision, the decision to enact and how to enact prior decision, is then both the ground and responsibility for each actual occasion, determining itself amidst a continuing flux of prior decisions.[52]

In positing the successive arising of actuality as a series of decisions, as a series of limitations, Whitehead finally enacts the fundamental secularization not only of God but of creativity itself.[53] For it is in this sense, Whitehead argues, "that God can be termed the creator of each temporal actual entity. But this phrase is apt to be misleading by its suggestion that the ultimate creativity of the universe is to be ascribed to God's volition. The true metaphysical position is that God is the aboriginal instance of this creativity, and is therefore the aboriginal condition which qualifies its action."[54] With this rejection of the *creatio ex nihilo*, the final effect of the secularization of God is felt.[55] On the one hand, creativity is designated as the "universal of universals characterizing ultimate matter of fact"[56] and is no longer determined solely as the will of God. On the other hand, the decisive limitation of order is not itself a totalizing enactment of that which is given, but is rather the ground of creativity amidst a given that is both order and disorder.

A strict distance arises, for Whitehead, between a primordial decision that, in its insistent repetitions, aims toward a decisive limitative ordering for the sake of intensity and a primordial violence that, in its constant reiteration, enacts a constant totalized capture of being. For Whitehead, this latter full determination of order, the determination of "one ideal order necessary for all actual occasions," only arises from a "disastrous overmoralization of thought under the influence of fanaticism, or pedantry."[57] In a derivative sense of order, where order is a designation of societal order,[58] this overmoralizing fanaticism is itself the social insistence that the given can be determined solely by and as order. This insistence is contrasted by Whitehead with the metaphysical determination of social order as a series of elicitations,[59] coupled to the contrast, announced in *Adventures of Ideas*, between a civilization grounded in force and a civilization of persuasion. It is the civilization of force that compels a final conformity to a totalized order as an overmoralization of the order of society itself.

It is precisely against this overmoralization that God functions, within Whitehead, as the ground of possibility, the future possibility of the becoming of all actuality. Within the inclusive disjunctive synthesis, God's envisagement of possibility transforms what appears as given incompatible disorder into intensive contrast, such that the given inheritance of order is "accompanied by a conceptual reaction partly conformed to it, and partly introductory of a relevant novel contrast, but always introducing emphasis, valuation, and purpose."[60] This introduction of relevant novelty is itself the ground of a decision that will become the background of the given from which further decisions will be made. The introduction of relevant novel contrasts opens a possibility for an order of intensity within each occasion that works against any totalized order as a complete determination of what is given. The introduction of this novelty then becomes the given for future occasions in their own becoming. If this novelty, in inaugurating a serial order of that which is given, seems to open to a determination of that which is given, a determination that itself installs a determined order, Whitehead will still insist that God, as the ground of this novelty, is "seeking intensity, and not preservation."[61] Whatever novel possibility is inaugurated here is inaugurated not to establish another order, but rather, the order that is established is itself for intensity, for an intensity of becoming. It is, as always, for Whitehead, order for intensity, and not primarily an order of intensity.

Within this space, where an encounter with God becomes an encounter with that which provides an opening to possibility, two figures of order appear. Reminiscent of the final figure of Antigone proposed in *Antigone's Claim*, a figure of one who acts through mourning and burial, mourning and burying both the living and the dead,[62] Butler turns, in the concluding passage of "Benjamin's 'Critique of Violence,'" to the frozen figure of Niobe. Within the form of petrified rock, petrified as the performative instantiation of the law of Artemis and Apollo, Niobe's expiation is imagined as a time of mourning where through the tears of mourning "the rock would dissolve into water, and . . . her guilt would give way to tears."[63] Here, mourning is installed in the opening produced by a divine violence, transforming the petrifying guilt of the law into erosive tears. Yet it is precisely this activity, the activity of tearing the law, that is finally read by Butler as a refusal to act, a "prompting" to "withhold action."[64] Linked to the sacred in life and enacted in the name of the living, it is precisely a withdrawal from activity, a refusal to act that is the enactment of the rupture of the law. If there is a freedom of life, it seems to be the freedom of withdrawal, of refusal. The struggle occasioned by the encounter with the divine command is the struggle that allows the possibility of this withdrawal, a withdrawal that is a refusing of the forced teleological temporality of law. In these final moments, then, Butler proposes a divine temporality of refusal, a temporality of life marked by mourning and tears, that is a withdrawal from the teleological temporality itself of the law.[65]

Whitehead, of course, will always insist on the possibility of a teleological temporality. It is, for Whitehead, the process of that which is possible becoming actual that constitutes the teleological movement of becoming itself.[66] As has been seen, though, this movement is not itself a movement into an already prescribed final nor full determination of that which becomes. There is no already determined nor totalizing singular ideal to be achieved by this teleological temporality. Yet it is also, for Whitehead, precisely this teleological temporality of becoming that is announced in the name of life. "Life is," Whitehead bluntly claims, "a bid for freedom."[67] It is this bid for freedom, a freedom "lurking in the interstices of each living cell,"[68] that grounds the figure of a teleological actuality moving into the novelty of life. Within this figure of actuality, the teleological determination of actuality becomes the actualization of possibility. If order is, for Whitehead, order for the intensity of possibility, it is an order for life as the bid into what may be.

Around these two figures two political possibilities emerge. One, a politics of perpetual critique, giving rise to a perpetual refusal of the law. The other, a politics of peace, founded on the recognition of tragedy, of what has not been opening to the possibility of what might be.[69] At stake, it seems, in these determinations of God, law, order, and possibility is not, as it first appears, a determination of the political in relation to a primary sociality. Rather, what is at stake is the determination of life itself. If there is to be an order without law, it will only arise as the possibility of a temporality of life disconnected from the teleological temporality of finality.

CHAPTER 10

"God Is a Lobster": Whitehead's Receptacle Meets the Deleuzian Sieve

Sigridur Gudmarsdottir

How can one express the reality of God in a cultural context permeated by the critique of ontology? Roland Faber raises the problem of ontology for contemporary theology in "De-Ontologizing God: Levinas, Deleuze, and Whitehead." Faber states that theology can no longer uncritically refer to Being as God. He sets out to discover new expressions of the divine reality—by "de-ontologizing" God, and thus transforming the concept of God "as an ontological reality to God as an aesthetic, in/different, and eschatological reality."[1] For Faber, the method of de-ontologization does not reject ontology as such, but rather opens up horizons of language that traditionally have fallen outside the scope of ontology. De-ontologizing God moves the discourse to the whole range of ontological tradition, to discourses of the univocity, equivocity, and eminence of Being.[2] Faber argues that the method of de-ontologization brings together the unlikely partners of figures of negative ontology such as Pseudo-Dionysius and Nicholas of Cusa with figures of positive, univocal ontology such as Duns Scotus, Baruch Spinoza, and even Gilles Deleuze.[3] For Faber, this theophilosophical intensity at the interstices of the negative and positive offers a great opportunity for de-ontologization, for the method of de-ontologization has the capacity of introducing difference and multiplicity into ontology as well as deconstructing ontological projections of unity.

Faber finds in the process philosophy of Alfred North Whitehead an ontological perspective that moves both in negative and positive directions. For Faber, Whitehead offers a point of view where *via univoca* and *via negativa* meet. If Faber's method brings together the apophatic and the univocal traditions in disruption of ontology and the de-ontologization of God, my intention in this chapter is to amplify such work at the edge of the univocal and the apophatic. I want to concentrate on a discourse that appears both in Deleuze and Whitehead on the Platonic *khora*. By "de-ontologizing" a *khoric* space in the Deleuzian cosmology, or even a "lobster space," to use a reminiscent image from Deleuze and Guattari's *A Thousand Plateaus*, I hope to give at least a partial answer to my own question, namely, how one can express the reality of God in a context where the principles of ontology can no longer be taken for granted.

Plato's *khora* in the *Timaeus* has, through the centuries of Western thought, served as the cosmological fabric of Being. Plato writes: "We must always refer to it by the same term, for it does not depart from its own character in any way. Not only does it always receive all things, it has never in any way whatever taken on any characteristics similar to any of the things that enter it."[4] Receiving everything, yet not taking any form, *khora* has also served as the apophatic escape route from Being. This apophatic evasiveness of *khora* has been noted by Jacques Derrida, who writes: "It does not have the characteristics of an existent, by which we mean an existent that could be receivable in the *ontologic*, that is, those of an intelligible or sensible existent. There is *khôra*, but the *khôra* does not exist."[5]

Strangely however, *khora* does not only drive apophatic quiverings on the edge of the ontological; this strange figure from a Platonic past also appears at crucial moments of repetition and creativity in the writings of Deleuze and Whitehead. In a way reminiscent of the "bastard reasoning" of *khora* in the *Timaeus*,[6] Deleuze once confessed his way of staying within philosophy as a queer venture of begetting philosophy with monstrous bastards:

> I suppose the main way I coped with it at the time was to see the history of philosophy as a sort of buggery or (it comes to the same thing) immaculate conception. I saw myself as taking an author from behind and giving him a child that would be his own offspring, yet monstrous. It was really important for it to be his own child, because the author had to actually say all that I had him saying. But the child was bound to be monstrous too, because it resulted from all sorts of shifting, slipping, dislocations and hidden emissions that I really enjoyed.[7]

John Rajchman contends that bastard logic as found in the Platonic *khora* is suitable to explain the Deleuzian project of the overturning of Platonism.[8] If *khora* presents us with a potential for Faberian de-ontologization, might that queer "shifting, slipping, dislocations and hidden emissions," that Deleuzian repetition/folding, have something in common with *khora*'s "bastard reckoning?" Deleuze reads Plato against Plato, pointing to tumultuous passages in Plato's writing for overturning Platonism. He looks back to the *Timaeus* and points out how Plato's thought constantly destabilizes its own transcendence, how the yearning for the transcendent One is always punctuated by embodiment:

> The poisoned gift of Platonism is to have introduced transcendence into philosophy, to have given philosophy a plausible philosophical meaning (the triumph of the judgment of God). This enterprise runs against the numerous paradoxes and aporias, which concern precisely, the status of the doxa (*Theatetus*), the nature of friendship and love (*Symposium*) and the irreducibility of an immanence of the earth (*Timaeus*).[9]

The *khora* is not explicitly mentioned in this reference to earthly immanence, but it is obviously the troubling element in *Timaeus* to which Deleuze refers. Deleuze writes: "There are not two 'paths' as Parmenides' poem suggests, but a single 'voice' of Being, which includes all its modes, including the most diverse, the most varied, the most differenciated."[10] Platonism established the distinction between order and chaos, clear thought and contradiction. The Platonic chaos is an undifferentiated abyss, a lack of order a nonbeing. If Plato presents chaos as an undifferentiated abyss, a lack of order, a nonbeing,[11] Deleuze's project is focused on reaching a place where the Platonic Ideas and the simulacra can no longer be separated, where the pure can no longer be set aside from the impure, an affirmation of a rhythmic chaos. In difference to the Platonic depth, the Deleuzian groundlessness is an porous abyss, full of surfaces and differences. "It is as the ground rose to the surface, without ceasing to be ground."[12] If Plato constitutes chaos and nonbeing in sharp contrast to Being, nonbeing in Deleuzian thought is a method of questioning, a "(non)-being or, better still, ?-being."[13] Grounding and ungrounding, or even grounding and grinding are not opposites in Deleuzian thought, but two aspects of the same reality, deconstructive and reconstructive forces. Deleuze has also described this (non)being as a fold, a concept to be revisited in his book on Leibniz and Whitehead, *The Fold*:

> It is as if there was an opening, a gap an ontological "fold" which relates being and the question to one another. In this relation, being is difference

itself. Being is also non-being, but non-being is not the being of the negative, rather it is the being of the problematic, the being of problem and question.[14]

According to Deleuze, the single voice of Being is constantly created and increased, in the same sense as Whitehead's creativity is the open condition of all evolution. In *The Fold*, Deleuze writes of Whitehead: "Even God desists from being a Being who compares worlds and chooses the richest compossible. He becomes Process, a process that at once affirms incompossibilities and passes through them."[15] Whitehead's definition of creativity as the principle of novelty, "the many become one and are increased by one,"[16] could thus as well have come from Deleuze's pen. He wants to visualize difference without having to sacrifice oneness, and oneness without sacrificing novelty.

"How can the Many become the One?" Deleuze asks, and searches for an answer by putting Whitehead and Plato in a dialogue. If the Platonic *khora* has signaled the negative way in the history of philosophy, Deleuze also claims *khora* for univocity and difference. One of many images Plato used for the *khora* is the sieve that sifts all things, "like grain that is sifted by winnowing sieves or other such implements. They are carried off and settled down, the dense and the heavy ones in one direction, and the rare and light ones to another place."[17] Deleuze answers his own question of the oneness of the many: "A great screen has to be placed in between them. Like a formless elastic membrane, an electromagnetic field, or the receptacle of the *Timaeus*, the screen makes something issue from chaos, and *even if this something differs only slightly*."[18]

For Deleuze, the key to the complex question of the One and the Many lies in Gottfried Wilhelm Leibniz's monad—with some important help from Whitehead. Leibniz imagined a whole world inside a monad, consisting of possible events and things, which fitted the world ("compossibles"). Outside the monad, in other monads were "incompossibles," which would make the world and its laws contradictory. According to Leibniz, the compossibles of our world were chosen by God, and as such, this world is the best of all possible worlds. If the walls between the monads would be broken down and the compossibles mixed with the incompossibles, we would experience chaos instead of the divine harmony.[19] Deleuze argues that Leibniz was able to develop the concept of the monad further than the Neoplatonists who invented it, by means of a mathematical discovery. Instead of the neoplatonic monad as "a unity that envelops a multiplicity developing the One in the manner of 'series',"[20] Leibniz introduces the infinite series into his system (*infini* in French meaning both infinite and unfinished). The world, according to Deleuze, is comprised only of individual experiences, which all express the world in their own singular way. Deleuze turns his attention to the structure of the monad, which is for him designed like a Baroque house. In contrast to the neoplatonic pattern, which would allow for endless floors of emanation, the Baroque monad has only two floors. The upper floor is closed and private without windows, but the lower floor is public and the senses are its open windows. Deleuze cannot accept Leibniz's assumption of the divine harmony. To be able to take the monad out of the Baroque house, Deleuze makes use of Whitehead's "prehension,"[21] and erases the walls that distinguish between compossibles and incompossibles.[22]

Whitehead described God as being dipolar, i.e., having a primordial and a consequent nature; "an infinite ground for all mentality."[23] The primordial nature is an infinite positive feeling, the "free, complete, primordial, eternal, actually deficient and unconscious," while the consequent nature of God is realized within physical experience, in bodies, in a world: "determined, incomplete, 'consequent,' 'everlasting,' fully actual and conscious."[24] For Whitehead, God, by this constant actualization in the world, is "the goad towards novelty,"[25] symbolizing freedom and unity, the many and the one in contrast and unity with the world. At the very end of *Process and Reality*'s cosmological speculations, Whitehead makes a theological move. He likens his God to the platonic Eros of the Universe, who has an appetite for harmony, truth, and beauty and works towards these goals by persuasion rather than coercion. Whitehead depicts a God who is present in everything and keeps a memory of every event, omnipresent in exactly the same way every prehension is interrelationally everywhere. "In a certain sense, everything is everywhere at all times."[26] God for him suffers with everyone and everything and is continually luring the creation towards greater harmony; "the suffering God as the great companion—the fellow-sufferer who understands."[27]

In *Adventures of Ideas*, in sharp contrast to *Process and Reality*'s suffering-companion-God, Whitehead speaks about God as the lure or Eros of the Universe that has fully emerged into the process of universal creativity. I argue that the Whiteheadian God Deleuze describes in *The Fold*, is more in line with *Adventures of Ideas* than *Process and Reality*. If Whitehead has already placed a *khoric* sieve between the Many and the One in *Adventures of Ideas*, this move is reiterated in Deleuze's *The Fold*. Thus, the Deleuzian-Whiteheadian appropriation of the Platonic Receptacle may prove to be an important factor for a possible de-ontologization.

Deleuze's use of Whitehead is eclectic, focusing on God as process, the sieve (or the receptacle) and the divine appetite. The receptacle becomes a screen for Deleuze, where Nature's patterns and repetitions are actualized and realized in bodies, in a life, a world, a thousand plateaus of the lines of flight. If, for Deleuze, Plato's *khora* serves as a symbol of earth and immanence, as a sieve filtering the many and the One, the *khora*/receptacle becomes a recurring theme in Whitehead's cosmological scheme in *Adventures of Ideas*. In a strikingly similar move to Deleuze's khoric immanence, Whitehead's *khora* safeguards unity, necessity, and immanence of the whole system and creates a solution to the isolation of the Leibnizian monads. Whitehead writes:

> The Receptacle, as discussed in the *Timaeus*, is the way in which Plato conceived the many actualities of the physical world as components in each other's natures. It is the doctrine of the immanence of Law, derived from the mutual immanence of actualities. It is Plato's doctrine of the medium of intercommunication.
>
> Thus finally we can understand that the Receptacle, according to Plato, the Void, according to Lucretius, and God, according to Leibniz, play the same part in cosmological theory.[28]

Whitehead presents the Receptacle as "the general interconnectedness of things, which transforms the manifoldness of the many into the unity of the one."[29] Thus, for Whitehead, the Adventure and the Receptacle complement each other for a unity of all entities, the latter is devoid of forms, the former is full of it. The receptacle safeguards immanence, the adventure (or the movement towards harmony, truth, beauty and peace) is the principle of transcendence.

Even the modest, omnipresent, emphatic God, who lures the creation towards harmony in *Process and Reality*, would bear too much transcendence and human projection to look authentic in a Deleuzian system. But, as already stated, the Companion God is not the only way in which Whitehead expresses divine reality in his texts. The Adventure/Receptacle seems to present us with a different model. In crafting the concept of the Adventure, Whitehead makes the traditional, Platonic move of granting truth, goodness, and beauty a prioritized ontological status where tragedy is viewed as a form of beauty. Whitehead's optimism is vastly different from Deleuze's Spinozist proclivities that would make truth, goodness, and beauty relevant to the one experiencing these traits (ontological parallelism).[30]

Moving back to Faber's threefold operation of de-ontologization, as "aesthetic reality," "expressive in/difference" and "escatological adventure," transforming ontology to aesthetics helps Faber to safeguard the alterity of God.[31] The in/difference of God is Faber's formulation of the way in which Whitehead integrates God and creativity in *Adventures of Ideas:* "The Adventure of the Universe starts with the dream and reaps tragic beauty. This is the secret of the union of Zest with Peace:—That the suffering attains its end in a Harmony of Harmonies . . . In this way the World receives its persuasion toward such perfections as are possible for its diverse, individual occasions."[32] In/difference for Faber denotes both something in-difference and beyond difference.[33] Faber's eschatological reality of God is influenced by Whitehead's "Adventure."[34] Faber writes: "Whitehead writes: 'God is "in coming" but never "coming to be"; God subsists as "unification," but never as unity; God insists neither as "being" nor as "becoming," but ever as what I shall call eschatological ad-vent.'"[35] With regards to the threefold operation, I worry that a Godhead who comes out of the future has already closed the future. But I can partake fully in Faber's advent, if its eschatology holds fast to its own apophatic promises, of keeping the future and all its texts open, creating new escape routes from the frozen forms of ontology.

The stratification of ontology is for Deleuze and Guattari conducted by a three-headed menace: "the organism, significance, and subjectification."[36] This menace is the "judgment of God," of an analogical theology that hides its God where it cannot be affected and judges, conducts, chooses, and organizes the world from a safe, untouchable place. To escape the judgment of this systematic God, one needs to be on a constant flight, in constant movement, developing special techniques of mimicking the strata. "You have to keep enough of the organism for it to reform each dawn; and you have to keep small supplies of significance and subjectification, if only to turn them against their own systems when the circumstances demand it."[37] Deleuze and Guattari describe signification and subjectification as the domains of semiotics and psychoanalysis. Deleuze and Guattari reject the "oedipalization" of the major schools of psychoanalysis, because in their view psychoanalysis tends to reduce the world to a metaphysical drama of "daddy-mommy-me," which occasionally takes the guise of a domesticated *khora*. Deleuze and Guattari show reservations for the way in which Julia Kristeva[38] uses the Platonic *khora* in her semiotics.

> Should we say that there are signs on all the strata, under the pretext that every stratum includes territorialities and movements of deterritorialization

and reterritorialization? This kind of expansive method is very dangerous, because it lays the ground-work for or reinforces the imperialism of language, if only by relying on its function as universal translator or interpreter. It is obvious that there is no system of signs common to all strata, not even in the form of a semiotic "chora" theoretically prior to symbolization.[39]

I have elsewhere argued that Kristeva's embodied and rhythmic *khora* has important insights to give to discourses on the edge of the postmodern abyss of being, and would therefore not be as quick to sweep her off the de-ontological table as Deleuze and Guattari.[40] However, given that *khora* serves both as the substratum of Western cosmologies and its ambiguous, apophatic disturber, who receives all but takes no form of its own, how can one save *khora* from *khora*, or de-ontologize the *khoric* God from the onto-God of universal language? If there are apophatic traits at the heart of Deleuze's project of overturning ontology, that discourse slides from *khora* into the strangest places. In a section on semiotics in *A Thousand Plateaus*, Deleuze and Guattari have smuggled in a strange discourse of God, which may be helpful for teasing out some qualities of the Whiteheadian/Deleuzian *khora*. "God is a Lobster," Deleuze and Guattari say, "or a double pincer, a double bind."[41]

What could be so divine about lobsters? John Protevi explains the articulations of the Deleuze-Guattari's Lobster-God as stratification and de-stratification, where the Lobster-God both builds new spaces and tears them down, so that new dimensions may be added. He stresses the immanence of the Lobster-God; it is a living being in the sea of many in the sea, one of the processes of nature.

> The Lobster as organism is doubly articulated, the result of the process of stratification symbolized by the Lobster-God. But the abstract machine of nature is not just stratification producing organisms, but also destratification producing the plane of consistency. So the Lobster-God is neither transcendent, nor is he all of nature, but only one aspect of nature as abstract machine of stratification *and* destratification. *The partiality of the Lobster-God*.[42]

This Lobster that is neither this nor that, not transcendent nor wholly of nature seems to drill apophatically into Protevi's language of stratification and destratification. Protevi, however does not inquire into why the image of a lobster was chosen—why not a bat, worm, an eagle, or a tick? Why lobster and what has the lobster in common with Plato's Receptacle or *khora*, which we have just offered as a paradigm for de-ontologization?

For me, the lobster is a profound image of divine reality. The lobster is a creature on the edge of the abyss, where the shore ends and the depth begins. The water permeates the lobster thoroughly through its shell. The lobster sheds its shell many times over its lifespan and therefore can never be tagged or organized. Its giant pincers catch and crush a lot of food. They also can be easily trapped in fishermen's nets. The lobsters therefore can be seen as catchers and crushers, who also can be easily caught in a theological system. Deleuze and Guattari describe later in *A Thousand Plateaus* a certain periodical lobster migration north of the Yucatan peninsula, a travel that cannot be associated with egg-laying but is somehow related to the cosmic forces.[43] The lobster, in its relationship to the cosmic, continually runs away from its own transcendence, creates a line of flight. It is a creature of the sea, not the sea-maker, an "accident" in Whitehead's sense. If the Deleuzian God would consent to Whitehead's "great companion the fellow sufferer who understands"[44] it has to be in the way Isabelle Stengers explains Whitehead's God's companionship.

> When Whitehead writes that God is the great companion, the fellow sufferer who understands, it seems to me important to take "understanding" as devoid of any paternalistic connotation. God does not understand in the sense of understanding why the actual entity missed the best its initial aim proposed, and excusing it because of love; It understands in unison of becoming.[45]

The Lobster-God does not create *ex nihilo*, rather it makes strata out of old strata, shapes new lines of flight, by folding and unfolding, as the Platonic sieve that winnows a Joycean "chaosmos" from chaos, the screen makes something issue from chaos, *even if this something differs only slightly*.[46] This chaosmos no longer consists of the unified, divinely ordered cosmos in contrast to an engulfing, mythic chaos of Western cosmologies, but rather of many patterns and orders that rise out of the abyss of creativity, a plurality of cosmoses and chaoses. Catherine Keller points to the significance of the Deleuzian chaosmos for feminist theology:

> The distinction of chaosmos from chaos, like that of connection from fusion, guards against the dedifferentiation or dissolution. It seeks to protect the difference of the other from self as well as of self from loss in the other. But if such protection is sought through the erection of a boundary against all chaos, a symbolic apparatus of domination will be required to maintain it. And that domination will produce its feminine Other as complement and threat.[47]

May we read the Lobster as a symbol of creative chaosmos? Of that which winnows and receives as *khora*, shelled, but never tagged with double pincers? And which yet slides out of the ontological robes that the Platonic *khora* has been clothed in, some of which are sexist? Recalling Deleuze's queer confession of philosophical-homosexual coupling, of monstrous conceptions, of "all sorts of shifting, slipping, dislocations and hidden emissions that I really enjoyed,"[48] what might the lobster/*khora* de-ontologize? For Marcella Althaus-Reid, the Lobster-God bears the mark of a radical queering of theology, which destabilizes the sexual codes of society. Such stripping of language calls for radical *kenosis* of theological language, and no longer resembles its own sexual productions or representations.[49]

> God is an articulation between the interstices of this double process of unity and dispersion. Deleuze and Guattari call this articulation the Lobster God. But the Lobster God is not the whole of it . . . So "God is not everything" means that God needs to be thought of as in transit, or in a process of extreme heterosexual kenosis or disembowelling simply by acknowledging that God is only a part in the articulation of desire and sexuality. God is not an ultimate or a total source. God the Lobster shows us a path of God (the Trinity) as an articulation of a limited exercise of kenosis.[50]

Advocating Althaus-Reid partial sensitivities, I propose to call this approach to de-ontologization, this movement of creation, the lobster, the grinding/grounding work of stratification and destratification, "the ground behind every other ground," "the (non)being as an ontological fold," the screen that makes something issue from chaos even ever so slightly, by the name of *khora*, following Deleuze's gentle hint in *The Fold* and evoking the immanence of the earth.

CHAPTER 11

Uninteresting Truth? Tedium and Event in Postmodernity

Catherine Keller

Truthiness Triumphant

On the first airing of his fake news show, *The Colbert Report*, comedian Stephen Colbert offered the now-classic alternative to old-fashioned, factual truth-claims: the word "truthiness." Truthiness, declared Colbert, wearing his satiric persona as television commentator, is a kind of unquestionable truth of the heart. The left doesn't get it; they are "all fact, no heart." "Face it, folks," he announced, "we are a divided nation. Not between Democrats and Republicans . . . no, we are divided between those who think with their head, and those who *know* with their *heart*." Of an infamously under-qualified nominee for United States Supreme Court, he said, for instance: "If you 'think' about Harriet Miers, of course her nomination's absurd. But the president didn't say he 'thought' about his selection. He said this: 'I know her heart.' . . . And what about Iraq? If you 'think' about it, maybe there are a few missing pieces to the rationale for war. But doesn't taking Saddam out 'feel' like the right thing?"[1]

If the punch lines have mercifully lost some of their punch, post-Bush, their philosophical pertinence persists. Whiteheadians will recognize that the trope of truthiness answers to the diagnosis that introduces *Process and Reality*: that of the "life tedium" produced by the "differences of tempo between the mere emotions and the conceptual experiences."[2] The political abyss between the heart and the head—if we adopt Colbert's caricature of the red and the blue—may be said to exemplify that "tedium" at the national scale. As the unquestionable certainties of the right wrapped themselves in the mantle of the Christian nation, the left was left behind. The situation suddenly shifted dramatically, due to a presidential candidate who did not rely upon the secular left's predilection for wonkish facticity, but who sought to heal both the style and the content of the red/blue split. The success of that endeavor—key to the kind of mobilizations needed to deal, for instance, with the *facts* of climate change—will depend in part upon whether progressive thought can coordinate those differences of tempo. Colbert's clue remains timely: If for us "truth" is nothing *more* than facts, we will not be able to overcome the less-than-factual truthiness. For of course the epistemological status of a fact is rightly shaky in a relativistic universe. If truth is reducible to fact, it is no wonder that a certain postmodern relativism lurks beneath the surface of every progressive passion. We suffer our own heart/head tedium, which conservatives perceive rather accurately. In order now to progress beyond a heady (!) electoral triumph to a sustainably shared future, we may wish to heal—and to *hearten*—our own discourse of truth.

In the context of this volume, for which the "postmodern" (despite or because of its vagueness) contributes the medium of the sharable, I presume that the very concept of truth has turned tedious on us. The inflated certainties of modernity, themselves mimicking the theological absolutes they meant to supercede, continue quite unceremoniously to collapse. Truth, indeed, has seemed not only elusive but uninteresting—or rather, merely *interested*. So the tedium of truth "feels," to thinking people, like a boredom tinged with cynicism. The tedium has intensified over a century of the death of God among the head-people. Arguably, the entrenchment of cultural secularism helped to provoke (in the United States, at least) the organized reactions among the heart-folk. Nietzsche recognized with celebration and foreboding that God's death expresses a rigorous truthfulness directed against delusion. He also knew that it pulls Truth itself with it, in God's wake. Poststructuralism can be said to theorize that wake. If continental thought, in the Nietzschean heritage, comprises the cutting edge of philosophical postmodernism, Whiteheadians, less cutting and edgy, claim the deeper postmodernism. Refusing to dissociate from either truth or God, the process postmodernism might count Nietzsche as an uncle rather than a progenitor.[3]

Whitehead finds, in religion, "an ultimate craving to infuse into the insistent particularity of emotion that non-temporal generality which primarily belongs to conceptual thought alone." In other words, he has diagnosed the tedium as the breakdown of that "supreme fusion."[4] And so, process thought comes by its theology honorably. In this exercise, I do not propose to analyze the political media of truth-production. But, if the satire of truthiness reminds us of the concrete stakes of theory, it may also help to prevent paternalistic (not to say tedious) abstraction in the methodological comparison of poststructuralism and process thought. What Deleuze might call their "convergent divergence" seems to me only to increase in intensity as its implications and applications unfold. This divergence cannot even be caricatured as that of head-versus-heart truths, even if process thought *thinks* more about feeling and the problem of the binary. Nor is the divergence political, per se. French postmodernism, by whatever name, has been preoccupied with ethico-political questions of justice.[5] Process theology comprises a theological counter-imperialism prolific in texts and diverse in strategies.[6]

I am wondering, however, what a possible poststructuralist evolution of process thought signals for our capacity to make truth-claims: whether they are factual, political, cosmological or, yes, theological. How can it not inhibit our capacity to make *hearty* claims, to lay claims upon ourselves and upon others, that commit us to high fidelity in language and a coordination of tempo in life?

We have been accustomed, within the process paradigm, to a modest and fluid form of the theory of truth as correspondence.[7] The defense of correspondence as such is not part of Whitehead's argument or priority. On the contrary, his oft-cited claim—that "it is more important that a proposition be interesting than that it be true"—undoes the flat realism associated with most correspondence theories of truth.[8] Yet Whitehead nonetheless considers every proposition (whether or not it gets interesting) either true or false. It refers to a world beyond the language of the claim. And this referentialism swells in *Adventures of Ideas* into the definition of Truth as the conformity of Appearance to Reality.[9] Whiteheadians today tend to minimize these capitalized Ideas. It is eighty years later, and we have read Foucault. We attend to the delusions and the legitimations of Power producing Truth. How shall we speak truth to power when truth is already power?

Truthiness today, with its folksy Christian feelings lubricating the power drive of an empire, seems unlikely to be answered simply by unmasking its falsehoods. Yet for both poststructuralists and process thinkers, the capacity for *truthfulness*, which is to say *honesty* in the address of our shared world, would seem to be at stake. "Those who, like us, confess the humility of our condition should not be left to shiver through the night of truth all alone."[10] Thus John D. Caputo, as he supplements Foucault's "truth of truth." Yet poststructuralism renders us habitually self-conscious when we wish to speak of the reality of that world, and the truth or untruth of claims about it. Judith Butler, reading the later Foucault, who disavowed any "self-satisfied form of constructivism," thus encapsulates the dilemma: "Insofar as we do tell the truth, we conform to a criterion of truth, and we accept that criterion as binding upon us."[11] I'm going to suggest—in conversation necessarily with a variety of poststructuralisms that will allow me to address a cultural mood rather than an author's idiosyncrasy—that while this bind may worsen the tedium, it also can fuel Whitehead's salubrious critique of abstractions.

Conformation and Deconstruction

The incompatibility between process thought and poststructuralism belongs to that wider antagonism that can be framed in terms of realism and anti-realism. Epistemologically, it could be caricatured as a war between the troops of Truth and the guerilllas of anti-Truth. These crass binaries do highlight real difference. Whitehead occasionally makes himself an easy target of anti-realism: "Apart from blunt truth, our lives sink decadently amid the perfume of hints and suggestions. The blunt truth that we require is the conformal correspondence of clear and distinct Appearance to Reality."[12] This is a clear and distinct reassertion of a theory of truth as correspondence. So we might ask (blasphemously) whether his true/false propositionalism actually contributes to the tedium. He sounds, here, almost as if he is defending Truth against that relativism, the heir of which is deconstruction.

Derrida early defined deconstruction as "the de-sedimentation . . . of all the significations that have their source in . . . the logos. Particularly the signification of truth. All the metaphysical determinations of truth."[13] Down another branch, Deleuze and Guattari insist that "philosophy does not consist in knowing and is not inspired by truth."[14] While in the same book they signal a surprising solidarity with Whitehead, they remain firmly aligned with a third branch (pardon my arborealism), that of Foucault. The latter announces that "truth is a thing of this world: it is produced only by virtue of multiple forms of constraint. And it induces regular effects of power. Each society has its regime of truth."[15] The political meaning of "constraint" may shed troubling light on Whitehead's notion of "conformation." Whitehead could seem to be exemplifying, not deconstructing, a regime of truth; he would seem to advance a notion of truth as the agreement between a proposition and its referent, based on a realism that seems epistemologically conservative today.

We Whiteheadians, however, hear irony rather than pomp in his capitalized Truth and Beauty, Appearance and Reality; what he calls the "truth-relation" lies "below the stale presuppositions of verbal thought."[16] After all, he already has dissolved the substantial subjects and objects between which the standard correspondence of truth could take place at all, offering instead a polyrhythmic feedback loop of complex interrelations between the proposition and its logical subject. His truth, with its process of *con*-formation, is precisely not a conformity of verbal statements to objects in reality, let alone an otherworldly donation. It is a subtle medium for the mutual participation of the becoming subject and select prehended objects of its emergence.[17] The knowing is at base a feeling, wherein may lie the truth that truthiness apes and manipulates.

"A propositional feeling is a lure to creative emergence in the . . . future."[18] As such a lure, the truth-relation cannot support claims of certainty. It does not refer to an already settled world. Whitehead's truth concept does, however, entail a certain fidelity to the given, a conservation that will appear conservative when progressive thought has lost its moorings in the actual world. But that actuality in Whitehead is always as such emergent: only as past, rather than as actual, is it given. When the given reality has been transmuted into a propositional feeling, in which the possible truth of that proposition gets interesting—it has undergone the complex mediations that require the constant critique of abstractions.[19]

Philosophy as "critic of abstractions" entails "an analysis of their origination" according to which "spoken language is merely a series of squeaks."[20] Such critique of the "fallacy of misplaced concreteness," of abstractions confused with actualities, of the delusions of speech as a mirror of origin, approaches as a procedure the radicality and purpose of deconstruction. Both process and deconstruction perform a de-sedimentation that undermines the privilege of the spoken *logos*.

So Whitehead's insistence that "it is more important that a proposition be interesting than that it be true" may, after all, resemble the general poststructuralist boredom with "truth." It is the judgment of true versus false that Whitehead finds in itself uninteresting—except when conjoined to a lure, an Eros, when summoning up "new resources of feeling," indeed ultimately of Beauty. Mere truth versus falsehood is. for him, no more inspiring to philosophy than it is for Deleuze and Guattari. It remains incapable of the deconstruction of its own political and metaphysical determinations. He does not thereby put truth under erasure. But neither does a serious poststructuralist.

Foucault, for example, does not (contrary to rumor) merely debunk truth as power. In fact, he protests—against a tedium he himself has intensified?—that he is "no theoretician of power. The question of power in itself doesn't interest me."[21] On the contrary, he insists: "My problem never ceased to be always the truth, speaking truth, *wahr-sagen*—that is, the speaking of truth—and the relationship [*le rapport*] between speaking truth and the forms of reflexivity, the reflexivity of self on self."[22] Butler, reading him closely while resisting any truth-language of her own, notes humorously: "When he claims that he has always had at the forefront of his mind the problem of truth-telling itself, he may or may not be telling the truth."[23] For truth-telling remains a problem, a problem set by the terms of any regime in which truth can be told. But he does strain mightily, within the terms of his own problematic, to prevent the paralyzing effect of his own concept of truth-regimes. Thus, he concludes that the "essential political problem for the intellectual [is] that of ascertaining the possibility of constituting a new politics of truth."[24] Foucault here was transposing Nietzsche into the context of the twentieth-century European science and state.

When we transpose Whitehead into the same context, we might think that he, too, was reading Nietzsche. Just after the diagnosis of the tedium and the importance of philosophy as the bridge between science and religion, crucial to healing the supreme fusion, Whitehead asserts that, in the "demand for intellectual justification of brute experience," European science is only a "variant form of religious interest. Any survey of the scientific devotion to 'truth,' as an ideal, will confirm this statement."[25] Similarly, Nietzsche argued that "it is still a metaphysical faith upon which our faith in science rests—that even we knowers of today, we godless anti-metaphysicians, still take our fire, too, from the flame lit by the . . . Christian faith which was also Plato's faith, that God is truth, that truth is divine."[26] He does not worship at the altar of that flame but he hardly calls us ("we" godless anti-metaphysicians, we deconstructors *avant la lettre*) to extinguish the fire. On the contrary, the will not to deceive, not to deceive even myself, which he calls "this unconditional will to truth," drives his thinking.[27]

Whitehead's parallel relocation of science to the history of Christianity smacks of Nietzschean irony. But, at the same time, it recapitulates his stated faith: "To know that in being ourselves we are more than ourselves."[28] That "more" opens the self into its boundless world, never captured in language, never absent from language. In the excess of a multi-tempoed universe, that irreducible, never quite nameable "more"—of our self and every other—claims of us a cosmopolitan politics in the fullest sense, in precisely the sense of the Whiteheadian/Deleuzian philosopher of science Isabelle Stengers's neologism, or verbal rhizome, *cosmopolitique*.[29] But in terms of the present problematic is it not a work of truth, or of truthfulness, that opens any given self into its fullness—its "more"?

In methodologically divergent, but not necessarily antagonistic ways, religion and science may both be said to dis/close that opening into the more. According to Whitehead both infuse "conceptual generality" into "the insistent particularity" of experience—either of the emotion of the experiencing subject or of the "detailed facts" of the "objects" of experience. Whitehead effects a constructive criticism, a deconstruction *avant la lettre* rather than a destruction of Christian theology vis-à-vis the science it provoked. He does not mean to expunge truth of its divine traces. To the contrary, already in the opening of *Process and Reality*, truth shows its theological colors. "The truth itself is nothing else than how the composite natures of the organic actualities of the world obtain adequate representation in the divine nature. Such representations compose the 'consequent nature' of God, which evolves in its relationship to the evolving world."[30]

Analogously, Whitehead translates power into "the principle that the reasons for things are always to be found in the composite nature of definite actual entities—in the nature of God for reasons of the highest absoluteness, and in the nature of definite temporal actual entities for reasons which refer to a particular environment."[31] In other words, God, power, and truth are de-sedimented and reconstructed in the same motion of thought, the very motion by which a relationalism of composite events takes the place of the changelessly unifying simples.

The deity thus proposed breaks up from within any theology—let alone ontotheology—of a changeless, apathetic *logos*. For God as "the fellow-sufferer who understands" emerges as a paraphrase for the infinite sensitivity, indeed vulnerability, unfolded in the theology of that composite, consequent nature.[32] Such a theology does perform propositions, if not creedal ones. More precisely than any secularism ever can, its theological propositions may be helping, here and there, to untie the "'tied' imagination"[33] of the propositions of an omnipotent providence and supernatural reward that pump the born-again heart of U.S. truthiness.

If Whitehead uses the name of God as a name for the widest space and perspective of that more, he does so in resistance to the entire tradition of a static self-identical omnipotence. The space of that more, when it registers as the place of composition in and so of God, might be read of the surface of the Johannine locution "in spirit and in truth." To speak or to act "in truth" is not to possess a truth, but to participate knowingly in that excess—in a fullness that exceeds the sum of its own finitudes. The "death of God" no more captures its infinite complication than does any proposition about God.

Truth-Event

Still, this sort of theological truth-work might seem to suck process thought far away from the poststructuralist tradition. But this would only be true if, first, Nietzsche were not from the start recognizing the insoluble dilemma of the fiery truth drive that shatters the idol of God and yet burns with a divine fire; and, second, if the poststructuralist tradition were not outgrowing its own dead God and its near proscription of truth-talk.

This latter hope I find embodied in John D. Caputo's recent work *The Weakness of God: A Theology of the Event*.

This text, the event of a Derridean *philosopher* turning constructively to theology, performs one long deconstruction of the omnipotence of God, riffing on the creation from chaos from one testament, while leaning on Paul's "strength made perfect in weakness" from the other. As to the truth regimes of divine power, he writes: "How in God's name are we going to settle these wars over the name of God? That belligerence, that mundane militancy, arises from reducing an event to a name, from trapping the truth of the event inside a name, which is what happens in a strong theology."[34] Process theologians, no doubt, will persist in our arguments for an alternative strength, a different concept of power—a relational peacemaking potency—rather than acquiesce in the weakness of which the process God always already has been accused.[35] Nonetheless the Caputan weakness does not resemble certain troubling theologies of the cross, which, to the horror of feminist theologians, ipso facto idealize suffering. It does not inflate a salutary divine vulnerability into salvation by sadomasochism. It is attempting to claim a truth—or, as Caputo prefers, to be claimed by a truth—embodied in resistance to the truth regimes of Power. It is of course thinking through Foucault, not Whitehead. Yet perhaps because of its passion for theological questions, it would not stop, for instance, where Foucault does: "The subject is capable of truth, such as it is, but the truth is not capable of saving the subject."[36] Nor would it stop with Butler's Foucauldian affirmation that such irony "does not preclude the possibility that some change may happen along the way."[37] It does not stabilize the real possibilities of change into a metaphysics of presence, however—as Whiteheadian eternal objects might tempt us to do. It lets them emerge at the edge of the impossible. There, the "event harbored in the name of God" becomes—possible.[38] The truth of that event may not save us—but neither can it rule out the event designated by the symbols of salvation.

The Weakness of God is, as it turns out, one of the rare poststructuralist texts to make overtures both to Whitehead and his theological heirs. Caputo's sense of "event" would bear serious comparison to Whitehead's "actual occasion," especially in that earlier, less atomist version that Deleuze, in a chapter entitled "The Event," proposes for his own neo-Leibnizian philosophical chaosmos.[39] Caputo's theology of the event converges upon the Deleuzian event, the very meeting point with Whitehead in *The Fold*. Yet his terms are drawn largely from Derrida, with overtones of Paul—the power made perfect in weakness. Nietzsche, Kierkegaard, and Levinas form the chorus. Precisely because the "causal efficacy" to which his own project conforms caries the poststructuralist tradition in undiluted form, its porosity toward process theology is all the more promising. Porosity here signals its possible shift from the aporia of mere disjunction, from the merely impossible, to a possible rapprochement.

In terms of the possibility of a deconstructive theology, Caputo has long challenged "a/theologian" Mark C. Taylor's definition of deconstruction as the hermeneutics of the death of God.[40] For Caputo, a radical hermeneutics passes through the death of God by way of a certain Levinasian '*adieu a Dieu*': "to stay in tune with the event that happens in the name of God," writes Caputo, "we may need to suspend that very name. For it is only by loving and welcoming the stranger, by responding *in the name of* the God who loves the stranger, that God can be God. I pray God to rid me of God." He thus cites a great moment in Christian apophasis. But he doesn't stay there: "The name of God," writes Caputo, "must be translated into an event, and the event must be translated into a deed. This is a translation into justice that precedes truth, or a translation into truth in the Augustinian sense of *facere veritatem*, 'in spirit and in truth.'"[41]

Whether that justice, strictly speaking, precedes truth or rather actualizes it, the space of the event, like that of the *more*, hosts the Johannine theologoumenon. In the face of the truthiness of postmodern politics, such uninhibited truth-talk is good news: If deconstruction is not gospel, the gospel's deconstructive edge may be translating its way toward an effectual theopolitics.

Caputo's buoyant style, charged with a playful rhetoric at once passionate and confessional, may contribute as much to a non-tedious truthfulness as does his argument: "I have been haunted and unhinged by the love of an event that is harbored by this name, by desiring and being desired by this event, hoping and praying to be visited by the truth of this event."[42] Such a confession, postmodern in its Augustinianism to be sure, unsatisfying to any nostalgia for a God once made fully present, may offer a discursive balm for the postmodern tedium. "I am shaken by the uncontainability of the event that the name of God contains, by the trauma of the truth promised under the name of God."[43] This ethico-mystical poststructuralism—a deconstruction with heart—performs its own version of the "supreme fusion." It thereby circumvents, sans metaphysics, the nihilism to which its own tradition is tempted. Or perhaps more precisely, it *deepens* the nihilism, until the *nihil* opens into the deep, the *tehom* of its own "more."[44] With its apophatic theology of divine vulnerability, this poststructuralism opens itself to its own downright kataphatic affinities with process theology. In this, Caputo's work surfaces, I suspect, a repressed depth of poststructuralism itself. For in the naming of that "more" with names resistant to both the positivist claims of heady atheism and a heart-felt religion, a fresh event and process of truth may be in the works.

Truthworks

This exercise means only to outline new relations forming within a truth-process, a doing *of* truth that is a word *in* process. Such truth-work is characterized by attention to the limits of its own language. Those limits harbor the oceanic "more." They cannot contain or exclude its depth—for that *tehom* appears on the very face of our relations to each other. It surfaces in our politics. The truth-process takes place where the particular conveys its intensity to a conceptual generality, in Whitehead's sense— and thus exposes itself to limitation and correction by that excess of its own relevance. That relevance is relève, lifted into attention, felt by much more than a mind. We feel our propositions are truthful to the extent they dis/close the fullness itself: as articulated in the subject's interdependence with its others, its neighbors, strangers, enemies, its world. That fullness need not be infinitized theologically in order to find formulations that support a process theological version of the truth-process. For instance, Butler's developing relationalism of mutual recognition—read from Hegel and Foucault—opens into this interdependence that resists every closure. "I cannot muster the 'we,'" she writes, "except by finding the way in which I am tied to 'you,' by trying to translate but finding that my own language must break up and yield if I am to know you."[45] Such truth-work requires both epistemic humility and connectional courage—from *coeur*, heart. Its epistemology would attend less to *how* we know what we know and more to how we *do not know* what we know; and how we know that we do not know: *de docta ignorantia*. The apophatic depth surges, uninvited, into the most secular of poststructuralist politics: for "we must recognize that ethics requires us to risk ourselves precisely at moments of unknowingness, when what forms us diverges from what lies before us."[46] For the truth-relation always precedes and exceeds any correspondence of my knowing and your being, of proposition and reality. It does not, however, exclude correspondence but precisely requires it, as an event of knowing, of fluent, passing co-responsiveness between your words and my reality—as between correspondents who are already different by the time their letters arrive, only to change each other further.

Nor does that truth-work preclude such conformation as we cherish under the banner of "facts." Indeed, factual truth, Arendt warned all too astutely, is always an early victim of totalitarianism.[47] Truthiness is a folksy face of totalizing power. In the face of the current conformity of the U.S. media to corporate and political propaganda—fortuitously mocked at the comic edges of the media themselves—we are surely challenged to outgrow any callow relativism. We need trusty propositions, faithfully narrating what has been in order to keep open the democratic space in which the shared future is negotiated.

In that space we do not forfeit, but rather enlarge, a fidelity to the real, to the given, that allows truth to be tested. The freedom of the future, with its becoming-truths, is only proposed for a world that includes, in the jargon, the proposition's logical subjects of physical feeling.[48] The trustworthiness of truth takes place, if it does, when a present event makes of itself a space of relation that we might as well call an inter-becoming. In its always frail and finite opening into the boundless—always intimate, always cosmopolitical—the unknowable future emerges from the felt past.

A conformation of appearance to reality is the least interesting baseline of trusty propositions. Truth gets interesting only as the multiple media of appearance propose, to reality, some barely possible future.

Might we transcribe the language of "true proposition" to that of a trusty proposal? A proposal lures. It makes erotic proposals. Every truth-claim proposes a possible future, even if it is just to commend a proposition as worthy of credence. Lure and trust, Eros and agape, work synergistically in the event of the truth-process. Be it the uninteresting probability of the sun setting tonight or of the interesting improbability of the messianic age—the truth-relation, in Whitehead's language, is a "pledge for the future."[49] This language of commitment comes far closer than that of true versus false propositions to the biblical vocabulary of truth, *emet v'emunah* (faithful and trustworthy); as truth in English shares the root of troth, trust. We used to "pledge our troth." Truth then is not certainty or conformity but the pledge of trustworthiness within the field of the relation; the more interesting is the truth at hand, the more it opens into the unknowable future, and the more its trustworthiness must prove itself, come true, make free, take place in that opening. It is not conformity but con-formation, the forming-together of the future by its universe of participants. If our hearts are in it, if we pledge our truth, our troth, for that future, we do so within the space of the more. *Coram deo*.

As Caputo puts it, sounding almost Whiteheadian, "the truth of the event harbored by the name of God triggers the potencies that stir in things, releasing their pent-up charges of divinity."[50] If a true proposition is not after all merely the opposite of false, but is always "more"—the "more" is surely harbored by the specific eco-social, and always political, context in which the terms of either/or facts are negotiated—along with "the Truth of supreme Beauty."[51] The regimes of truthiness will not be answered by more strident critique or more absolute counter-Truth, but they might get offset, if not displaced, by the coordinated tempos of a truth-work that is by definition a work-in-process; truth in process and in relation, that is, in *intéresse*, the inter-being that is as such inter-becoming.

Process thought will energize more possible trustworthiness and more cosmopolitics within the flux than does poststructuralism. Poststructuralism will continue to unhinge and undo us with more difference, indeed more messianic impossibility, within the event. To open process thought to a more "interesting" notion of truth than even Whitehead's, a notion after all more Whiteheadian, will at least permit more vital cultural collaborations in theory. But it might also put in practice more coalitional cures for that tedium. Of course the explication of the terms of such coalitions will undo prior rhythms of discourse. As Butler says of the ethics of our interdependence: "Our willingness to become undone in relation to others constitutes our chance of becoming human."[52] And our chance of becoming human may hinge now on our willingness to become undone in relation to all the other species.

In the face of the terrifying odds against this all-too-interesting truth-work, we inter-becoming creatures are invited to pledge our troth.

To get our hearts and heads together, in truth, for the sake of that "more" that we so becomingly, and never quite, are.

NOTES

INTRODUCTION: NEGOTIATING BECOMING
Roland Faber

1. See WP, p. 85.
2. More hidden for Whitehead, but see J. Thomas Howe, *Faithful to the Earth: Nietzsche and Whitehead on God and the Meaning of Human Life* (Lanham, U.K.: Rowman & Littlefield, 2003).
3. Friedrich Nietzsche, *On the Genealogy of Morals* (New York: Vintage, 1969), p. 45.
4. I borrow this term from the Japanese philosopher Tanabe Hajime, *Philosophy as Metanoetics* (Berkeley: University of California Press, 1986).
5. PR, p. 23.
6. Ibid., p. 7.
7. Ibid., p. 24.
8. AI, p. 237.
9. NP, p. 47.
10. WP, p. 21.
11. Ibid., p. 59.
12. Ibid., p. 158.
13. GT, p. 43.
14. Ibid.
15. Ibid., p. 33.
16. See BC, p. 287.
17. PR, p. xi.
18. See David Ray Griffin, *Whitehead's Radically Different Postmodern Philosophy: An Argument for Its Contemporary Relevance* (Albany: State University of New York Press, 2007).
19. See Ken Wilber, *Integral Spirituality: A Startling New Role for Religion in the Modern and Postmodern World* (Boston: Shambala, 2006).
20. See G. Lucas, *Hegel and Whitehead: Contemporary Perspectives on Systematic Philosophy* (Albany: State University of New York Press, 1986).
21. See Steven Best and Douglas Kellner, *Postmodern Theory: Critical Interrogation* (New York: Guilford Press, 1991).

22. See George Lucas, *The Rehabilitation of Whitehead: An Analytic and Historical Assessment of Process Philosophy*, (Albany: State University of New York Press, 1989).

23. PR, p. 7.

24. See David Ray Griffin et al, *Founders of Constructive Postmodern Philosophy: Peirce, James, Bergson, Whitehead, and Hartshorne*, (Albany: State University of New York Press, 1993).

25. See Catherine Keller and Anne Daniell, eds., *Process and Difference: Between Cosmological and Poststructuralist Postmodernism* (Albany: State University of New York Press, 2002).

26. It is interesting that not only Deleuze did not believe in the death of philosophy—in remaining a post-structuralist thinker—and even being interested in systematic thought and metaphysics (see N, p. 136), but that this seems to be an expression of broader movement, as can be seen in the later works of J. Baudrillard, M. Serres or B. Latour.

27. See J. Williams, *The Transversal Thought of Gilles Deleuze: Encounters and Influences* (Manchester: Clinamen Press, 2005).

28. DR, pp. 284–285.

29. Ibid., p. 284.

30. Ibid., p. 285.

31. See Roland Faber, "Whitehead at Infinite Speed: Deconstructing System as Event," in *Schleiermacher and Whitehead: Open Systems in Dialogue*, ed. C. Helmer, M. Suchocki, and J. Quiring (Berlin: de Gruyter 2004), pp. 39–72.

32. See TF, pp. 76–82.

33. See CV.

34. DR, p. 285.

35. IM, p. 25.

36. PR, p. 113.

37. See CN, pp. 165–172.

38. See CN, pp. 79–81.

39. See TF, p. 134.

40. See LS, p. 111.

41. TF, p. 79.

42. CV. See LS, pp. 4–11.

43. See TF, pp. 59–75.

44. See AI, p. 263.

45. See LS, p. 174.

46. TF, p. 81.

47. Ibid., p. 134.

48. Ibid., p. 79.

49. GT, p. 14.
50. See GT, p. 12.
51. GT, pp. 14–15.
52. See GA, ch. 1.
53. CN, p. 13.
54. Ibid., p. 17.
55. Ibid., p. 16.
56. SMW, p. 51.
57. PR, p. 26.
58. S, p. 26.
59. See PR, pp. 83–129.
60. S, p. 27.
61. See GA, pp. 30–40.
62. See GT, p. 15.
63. PR, p. 89.
64. See GT, p. 69. In an interesting sense, we could say that Whitehead's cosmological analysis relates to Butler's, culturally critical critique like mathematics to physics: His "deconstructive" power seems to be based in a more universal (generally relational) analysis (that he terms "metaphysics") that, if we find the right point of experimental and experiential application, begin to speak and offer new resources—although as long as this is not seen, it cannot be used. This is precisely what Whitehead was demanding of this "metaphysics"—that it be able to be applied and modified by its application in experiences and experiments (see PR, pp. 3–5).
65. GT, p. 23.
66. While Deleuze goes even further in this shift to "spatial" expressions of the event, Butler always seems to include the diachronic perspective of performance as important to her deconstruction of substantial identity. Whitehead, on the other hand, is classically perceived to have given the temporal expression of performance higher significance (epochal theory of time). Yet, Deleuze has a complex theory of time. See LS, pp. 276–279, which Whitehead counters with his spatial expressions of events (coordinate analysis of events).
67. Ibid., 37.
68. Ibid., 39.
69. See DR, pp. 66–69.
70. See AI, p. 168.
71. GT, p. 41.
72. DR, p. 125.
73. GT, p. 41.
74. PR, p. 109.

75. PR, p. 220.
76. GT, p. 41.
77. GT, pp. 43–44.
78. GT, p. 44.
79. See BC, p. 282.
80. See Annika Thiem, *Unbecoming Subjects: Judith Butler, Moral Philosophy, and Critical Responsibility* (New York: Fordham University Press, 2008), 78–9.
81. GT, p. 173.
82. GT, p. 175.
83. GT, p. 177.
84. GT, p. 179 (italics added).
85. For the importance of the two World Wars as actor in the downfall of humanism, see Stephanie Moses, "From Rosenzweig to Levinas: Philosophy of War," in *Political Theologies: Public Religions in a Post-Secular World*, ed. Hent de Vries and Lawrence E. Sullivan (New York: Fordham University Press, 2006), 231.
86. DR, p. 128.
87. What has stunned many commentators in Whitehead is the fact that in analyzing human experience, in the end what has disappeared is the specific human existence, human subjectivity, and the extraordinary place it is given in the world (of experiences, of things, of Being). But this is a misperception of Whitehead's interest. When he analyses "experience," he never engages "introspection" by privileging human experience. On the contrary, he wanted to deconstruct this human privilege in experience—as can be seen in his notion of "prehension" that takes the conscious (human) aspect of "apprehension" away (see SMW, p. 69) and his widely misunderstood "emotional language" when he talks about a cosmology of experience, feeling, intensities, and so on (see AI, p. 186).
88. See G. Gutting, *French Philosophy in the Twentieth Century* (Cambridge: Cambridge University Press, 2001), pp. 234–257.
89. See M. Foucault, *The Order of Things* (New York: Vintage, 1973), p. 385: "Rather than the death of God—or, rather, in the wake of that death and in profound correlation with it—what Nietzsche's thought heralds is the end of his murderer."
90. See J. Heartfield, *The "Death of the Subject" Explained* (Sheffield: Hallam University Press, 2002).
91. See M. Foucault, *Discipline and Punish: The Birth of the Prison* (New York: Vintage, 1995); *Madness and Civilization: A History of Insanity in the Age of Reason* (New York: Vintage, 1988).
92. See Jean-François Lyotard, *The Postmodern Condition: A Report on Knowledge* (Manchester, U.K.: Manchester University Press, 1989), p. xxiv.

93. Louis Althusser, *The Future Lasts a Long Time* (London: Vintage, 1994), p. 218.

94. See Jean Baudrillard, *The Illusion of the End* (Stanford, Calif.: Stanford University Press, 1994).

95. See J. Derrida, *A Derrida Reader: Between the Blinds* (Hemel Hempstead: Harvester, 1991) p. 65.

96. S. Žižek, ed., *Mapping Ideology* (London: Verso, 1994).

97. See J. Derrida, *Of Spirit: Heidegger and the Question* (Chicago: Chicago University Press, 1991), p. 40. While Heidegger in his letter recognized "humanism" to presuppose the old metaphysics he wanted to convert in his fundamental ontology, Derrida draws the even more radical conclusion that its substantialism/subjectivism leads to human catastrophe.

98. While this is more obvious for Butler and Deleuze, being based in the post-structuralist movement, which was growing out of a historical antithesis to phenomenology and its privileging not only of human experience but of "experience" as such—understood as introspection—thereby deconstructing it as formed by pre-individual structures, Whitehead's non-privileging still seems to be based on "experience." Moreover, we could understand *Process and Reality* as an analysis of experience because, "apart from the experiences of subjects there is nothing, nothing, nothing, bare nothingness" (PR, p. 167), but he was never interested in "introspection" because the "requisite evidence cannot be gained by mere acts of direct introspection conducted at one epoch by a few clear-sighted individuals" (AI, p. 164). His interest in the most general *structures* of experience (see PR, pp. 3–4) puts him—especially in the way he understand them as subject-forming—in the structuralist context, and in not believing that *the* structure can ever be found because "we cannot produce that final adjustment of well-defined generalities which constitute a complete metaphysics" (AI, p. 145), he might be named a forbearer of "post-structuralism." His rigorous opposition to the "dogmatic fallacy" of metaphysics and his complicated interest in "truth and interest" makes him naturally a near-ancestor of Deleuze.

99. GT, p. 33.

100. See GT, p. 3.

101. PLP, p. 2.

102. GT, p. 40.

103. GT, p. xxv.

104. PLP, p. 3.

105. PLP, p. 10.

106. See BC, p. 285.

107. See BTM, pp. 187–222. See also Slavoj S. Žižek, "The Matrix: Or, The Two Sides of Perversion," in *The Matrix and Philosophy: Welcome to the Desert of the Real*, William Irwin (Chicago: Open Court, 2003), pp. 240–266.

108. See AO, p. 10.
109. AO, p. 8.
110. AO, p. 13.
111. See AI, pp. 201–205.
112. See PR, pp. 34–35.
113. See S, pp. 66–75.
114. PR, p. 88.
115. S, p. 79.
116. S, p. 88.
117. S, p. 66.
118. S, p. 76.
119. S. Žižek, *The Sublime Object of Ideology* (London: Verso, 1989), p. 73.
120. See GT, p. 43.
121. See A. Badiou, *Infinite Thought: Truth and the Return to Philosophy* (New York: Continuum, 2003), pp. 3–4.
122. This is a long standing criticism of Whitehead—from the perspective of a "modern" philosophy, phenomenology, existentialism, or Neothomism—which all the more strengthens the thesis of an intimate relation of Whitehead's impulse to think with that of post-structuralist flavor.
123. TF, p. 81.
124. TP, p. 238.
125. Ibid.
126. TP, p. 232.
127. PR, p. 22.
128. TP, p. 238.
129. PR, p. 21.
130. TP, p. 238.
131. See PR, p. 7.
132. See DR, p. 36.
133. TF, p. 13.
134. TF, p. 137.
135. See TF, p. 20.
136. See LS, p. 144.
137. N, p. 158.
138. See TP, pp. 3–25.
139. See TF, pp. 4–5.
140. See TF, p. 135.
141. See WP, pp. 15–34.
142. See TF, p. 16.
143. See TF, p. 79.
144. The misunderstanding of A. Sokol and J. Bricmont, *Intellectual Impostures* (London: Profile Books, 1998) and the whole discussion on the "science

wars" in accusing, e.g., Deleuze of scientific imposture (misuse of scientific concepts) relies on the *presupposition* of Sokol's view of scientific *independence*, which is exactly a *substantiating isolation* presupposing and executing the substantial subject (of the scientist) as being in control of the reality investigated and not being a part of it. The fluent conceptualization in Deleuze, however, is not to dissolve science—far from that! (see WP, pp. 1–12)—but to perform a non-substantive philosophical discourse, which is always the *event* of conceptualization.

145. TP, p. 249.
146. See TP, pp. 474–500.
147. See TP, pp. 232–309.
148. See DR, pp. 35–42.
149. See M. Foucault, "A Preface to Transgression," in *Essential Works of Michel Foucault, 1954–1984, vol. 2: Aesthetics, Method, and Epistemology* (New York: The New Press, 1997–99), pp. 69–87.
150. CV.
151. PR, p. 20.
152. 1PR, p. 19.
153. See TF, pp. 76–82.
154. PR, p. 18.
155. This seems to be more obvious for Deleuze than for Whitehead, for whom there is a God and a teleological element (the initial aim from God). But in Whitehead both elements do not amount to any eschatological closure or ontologically unilateral transcendence. The universe is more open than one might expect; certainly more open than any cyclical universe of the Absolute (as in Hegel).
156. See J. Bradley "Transcendentalism and Speculative Realism in Whitehead," *Process Studies* 23, no. 3 (1994): pp. 155–191.
157. PR, p. 104.
158. PR, p. 105.
159. Ibid.
160. In this sense, the cosmological approach is also a radical consequence of the grand in/humanism 1. Against the privileging of *consciousness* as the primordial source for meaning—as in Descartes' (*ego cogito*), Kant's (transcendental subject) and Sartre's (being-for-itself)—it is not reconstructed in its unconscious structures. Moreover, against the privileging of the psychological approach to humanism, consciousness is deconstructed in a *social* context, that is, that it privileges the Western social construct of a psyche over against the "savage" mind—as Claude Lévi-Strauss, *The Savage Mind* (Chicago University of Chicago Press, 1966), pp. 247–248, has demonstrated against Sartre. Even further, with Bruno Latour, *Politics of Nature: How to Bring the*

Sciences into Democracy (Cambridge, Mass.: Harvard University Press, p. 204), the privileging of *human* societies over nature is deconstructed in favor of a community of becoming-social. This is where Whitehead's concept of society radically goes beyond the binominals of society/nature, value/fact, culture/technology, body/soul, psyche/society, humans/non-humans into a "democracy of fellow creatures" (PR, p. 50)—with their own regional differences beyond any privilege (see PR, pp. 83–129).

161. See TP, p. 24.
162. See TP, pp. 228–231.
163. See AI, pp. 69–87.
164. GT, p. 179.
165. BTM, p. 188.
166. See BTM, p. 277n2.
167. See BTM, p. 41.
168. See GT, p. 106.
169. PLP, p. 5.
170. See PLP, pp. 2–3.
171. BTM, p. 204.
172. BTM, p. 188.
173. See Slavoj Žižek, *For They Know Not What They Do* (London: Verso, 1991), p. 112.
174. BTM, p. 190.
175. GT, p. 6.
176. See BTM, p. 195.
177. BTM, pp. 206–207.
178. BTM, p. 196.
179. See BTM, pp. 206–207.
180. BTM, p. 198.
181. Ibid.
182. See L. Irigaray, *Speculum of the Other Woman* (Ithaca, N.Y.: Cornell University Press, 1985), pp. 168–179.
183. BTM, p. 37.
184. See BTM, p. 41.
185. See BTM, p. 40.
186. BTM, p. 43.
187. See BTM, p. 41.
188. See BTM, p. 39.
189. GT, p. 102.
190. See Julia Kristeva, *Revolution in Poetic Language* (New York: Columbia University Press, 1984).
191. GT, p. 102.

192. See GT, pp. 101–118. See also Julia Kristeva, *Desire in Language: A Semiotic Approach to Literature and Art* (New York: Columbia University Press, 1980).
193. See GT, p. 105.
194. See BTM, pp. 41–42.
195. GT, p. 115.
196. GT, p. 104.
197. GT, pp. 104–105.
198. See BTM, p. 195.
199. BTM, p. 195.
200. BTM, p. 207.
201. As Butler notes, Rosi Braidotti has made the case that Butler lives off a "theology of lack" instead of a plenitude of affections. However, Butler's defense is interesting because she relates this "positivity" of affections to Braidotti's "materialist" interpretation of Deleuze, and her inclination to follow Hegel's "negativity" instead as an indication that she might be a "bad materialist." See UG, pp. 195–198. In fact, the Spinozism of all of them—Braidotti, Butler, and Deleuze—doesn't strike me as materialist at all. The impression might be connected to the fact that Deleuze rejects psychoanalysis, while Butler includes the psychic in the social construction as irreducible to it (against Foucault but with Lacan), as does Braidotti, as Butler assumes with Braidotti's reading of Irigaray. For Deleuze, however, it is about the "Idea" of multiplicity as one of affirmation instead of a negative dialectic (see DR, pp. 26–27).
202. LS, p. 172.
203. In Rosi Braidotti's interpretation, her "materialist" (Spinozist) reading of the terms "affectivity, intensity and speed" are affirmative while "psychoanalysis expresses a very negative set of forces: it is the morality of the confession, the priestly or 'pastoral' guidance so dear to Foucault, but distasteful to Deleuze's post-humanist secular mind-set"; Rosi Braidotti, *Metamorphosis: Towards a Materialist Theory of Becoming* (Cambridge: Polity, 2002), p. 98.
204. See LS, pp. 172–173. See also M. Hardt, *Gilles Deleuze: An Apprenticeship in Philosophy* (Minneapolis: University of Minnesota Press, 1995). pp. 1–25.
205. DR, p. 57.
206. See WP, pp. 35–60.
207. LS, p. 175.
208. See WP, pp. 156–157.
209. See LS, p. 279.
210. LS, p. 129.

211. TP, pp. 150–151.
212. See AO, pp. 8–13.
213. See LS, p. 172.
214. LS, p. 173.
215. LS, p. 172.
216. LS, p. 279.
217. TP, pp. 153–154.
218. TP, p. 155
219. TP, pp. 156–157.
220. TP, p. 150.
221. GT, p. 110.
222. In this sense, for Kristeva, the exclusion (suppression) of the semiotic is a necessity that creates language and human culture; it is, as in Žižek, the "Real" as the excluded "obscene underside" of all discursivity that can be broken down only by violating the incest taboo (see GT, p. 110). See also Slavoj Žižek, *Welcome to the Desert of the Real: Five Essays on September 11 and Related Dates* (London: Verso, 2002).
223. GT, p. 105.
224. See J. Derrida, "Geschlecht. Sexual Difference, Ontological Difference," in *Research in Phenomenology* 13 (1983): p. 72.
225. Elizabeth Grosz, *Space, Time, and Perversion: Essays on the Politics of Bodies* (New York: Routledge, 1995), p. 78.
226. See AO, p. 8.
227. See TP, p. 150.
228. AI, p. 134.
229. PR, p. 23.
230. See PR, p. 23.
231. See PR, p. 95.
232. See AI, p. 113.
233. See PR, pp. 20–21.
234. LS, p. 176.
235. PR, p. 95.
236. See PR, p. 72.
237. See PR, p. 4.
238. PR, p. 110.
239. PR, p. 98.
240. See BTM, p. 188.
241. PR, pp. 205–206.
242. PR, p. 110.
243. Ibid.
244. PR 20–1.

245. PR, pp. 106–107.

246. PR, p. 224. In opposition to Kristeva, Whitehead does not exclude the multiplicity of libidinal desires in order to create societies, but understands them as necessary elements of a complexity that allows for human subjectivity and human societies to occur—but for the price of an always-lingering chaos of destruction.

247. PR, p. 314.

248. PR, p. 107.

249. Ibid.

250. See PR, p. 41.

251. See AI, p. 259.

252. See AI, p. 256.

253. It is here that Butler's "non-materialism" of the psyche is connected to Whitehead's proposition that "Consciousness is the feeling of negation" (PR, p. 162) and that "negative judgment is the peak of mentality" (PR, p. 5). In fact, negativity, as in Hegel, is not a matter of materialism as in Braidotti, but of intensity. In this connection, Butler is correct to assume that Braidotti does not get rid of negativity, that is, as in Whitehead, of "suffering as suffering, but that, methodologically, she would seek to identify these sites of fracture and mobility as conditions for new possibility" (UG, p. 195).

254. See PR, p. 26.

255. See GA, ch. 2.

256. See AI, p. 198.

257. AI, p. 259.

258. Here, Whitehead's concept of "contrast" does not reduce oppositions under a unification, a One, a reduction of multiplicity to identity, but, as in Deleuze, leads to a new "distribution of intensities," which are what Deleuze calls the "nomadic distribution" (LS, p. 102) that only happens if difference is not seen already as difference of identities or with identity as ideal—both based on a process of "auto-unification" or "self-creativity."

259. See AI, p. 276.

260. PR, p. 103.

261. PR, p. 72.

262. PR, p. 105.

263. See AI, p. 295.

264. See PR, p. 103.

265. PR, p. 163.

266. See PR, p. 279.

267. PR, p. 23.

268. See PR, p. 26.

269. See AI, p. 261.

270. GT, p. 117.

271. Keller and Daniell, ed., *Process and Difference*, p. 16.

272. Deleuze's quasi-causality (see LS, p. 176) of the pre-symbolic realm of intensities is not so much causal efficacy as a surface effect of causality, much like the form of Whitehead's *final* causality. "The 'lure for feeling' is the final cause guiding the concrescence of feelings" (PR, p. 185). Yet for both it is the effect that generates it own causes.

273. Many commentators describe Whitehead's discovery, which he also calls "prehension," his single most important philosophical contribution. See E. Kraus, *The Metaphysics of Experience: A Companion to Whitehead's* Process and Reality (New York: Fordham University Press, 1998).

274. PR, p. 81.
275. S, p. 58.
276. See S, pp. 13–16.
277. See S, p. 56.
278. See S, p. 23.

279. See, S, p. 21. Here, Whitehead's *mixture* as complexity is related to Deleuze's process of folding (explication/implication). See Latour, p. 191: "We shall always go from the mixed to the still more mixed, from the complicated to the still more complicated, from the explicit to the implicit." Although Deleuze differentiates between evolution and becoming (see TP, p. 238), the assemblage of folds/vibrations, as explained in his 1987 lecture on Whitehead, implicates a symbiosis that would amount to the emergence of "presentational immediacy" in Whitehead.

280. S, p. 35.
281. See AI, pp. 184–186.
282. PR, p. 46.
283. S, p. 44. For Butler's "fate of law," see CC, p. 215.
284. See S, p. 66.
285. S, p. 43.

286. PR, p. 50. In this definitely non-Lacanian approach, Whitehead and Deleuze rather strongly resonate with Jean-Francois Lyotard, *Discourse, figure* (Paris: Klincksieck, 1971). His understanding of a pre-Oedipal realm of desires is, in a sense, an interesting parallel idea: It is not produced by the Oedipal Symbolic, and it opens a possibility to think through and beyond the psychological impact of more radical, political implications.

287. GT, p. 112.
288. See S, p. 18.
289. S, p. 7.
290. S, p. 56.
291. S, pp. 30–31.

292. S, p. 10.

293. In this sense, the Symbolic is a *relation* of a pre-Symbolic difference that becomes *in* symbolic relation signifier and signified, but is, per se, neither (neither meaning nor sign; see S, p. 10). This would open interesting new questions on *what constitutes a sign*—in relation to Ferdinand de Saussure, Lacan, and Roland Barthes. In any case, the pre-symbolic aspects are not realms without "interpretation"—there is no such thing as facts without interpretation (see PR, pp. 14–15)—but somehow constituted by their difference as *potentiality* of semiotic relations (see S, p. 6). In fact, for Whitehead, they are never existing in themselves and are always already *in symbolic transfer*, i.e., in semiotic interference so that we could even say that they are "products" of the semiotic activity in the sense that the symbolism is a mode of self-production, which is the becoming of events (see S, pp. 8–10). Whitehead's odd formulation of the "infallibility" (S, p. 6) of the pre-Symbolic aspects of "direct recognition" is not to install a pre-symbolic truth, but to say that that the problem of truth only arises with the symbolic transfer (see S, pp. 6–7; pp. 19–21).

294. S, p. 7.

295. S, p. 63.

296. See LS, pp. 278–279. This accusation haunts Whitehead's reception since the beginning, not bound to, but especially akin to, all non-Idealistic philosophies, post-Hegelian or otherwise. It is always the stumbling bock of any appropriation of Whitehead in any contemporary philosophical discourse.

297. See F. Nietzsche, *The Gay Science* (London: Vintage, 1974), §§ 108, 125, 343.

298. WP, p. 43. See also M. Bryden, ed., *Deleuze and Religion* (London: Routledge, 2001).

299. See PL, pp. 101–127, and also her newer work on Walter Benjamin, CC, p. 201–219.

300. BC, p. 278.

301. AI, p. 121.

302. See RM, p. 66.

303. RM, p. 68.

304. See RM, pp. 74–75.

305. RM, p. 76.

306. RM, p. 37.

307. See SMW, pp. 178–179. The history of "process theology" is in itself a pluralist multiplicity of approaches, based mostly on Whitehead's explorations, especially in *Religion in the Making* and *Process and Reality*, and should not be conflated with a (fortunate or unfortunate) spiritualization of Whitehead's philosophy. It has developed in remarkably different directions in

exploring the "function" of the Divine in the Chaosmos *through* Whitehead's cosmology. See Roland Faber, *God as Poet of the World: Exploring Process Theologies* (New York: Fordham University Press, 2008). Variable also in its motives and interests, the variety ranges from a "philosophical theology"—J. Cobb, *A Christian Natural Theology: Based on the Thought of Alfred North Whitehead* (Louisville: Westminster John Knox Press, 2007)—to a Christian theology—see M. Suchocki, *God—Christ—Church: A Practical Guide to Process Theology* (New York: Crossroad, 1995); from a Buddhist philosophy—Steven Odin, *Process Metaphysics and Hua-Yen Buddhism: A Critical Study of Cumulative Penetration vs. Interpenetration* (Albany: State University of New York Press, 1988)—to a pluralist philosophy of religion—David Ray Griffin, ed., *Deep Religious Pluralism* (Louisville, Ky.: WJK, 2005); and even, in taking up post-structuralist augmentations, to a veritable post-structuralist account of a theology of becoming—Catherine Keller, *Face of the Deep: A Theology of Becoming* (New York: Routledge, 3003).

308. TP, p. 150.

309. See LS, p. 172. The Whiteheadian "initial aim" from God to issue any process of concrescence has a resemblance to this Leibnizian pre-established organization, but, in fact, should not be confused with it because it is not about order but intensity (see PR, p. 244).

310. AO, p. 13.

311. LS, p. 172.

312. See TF, p. 73.

313. LS, p. 176.

314. LS, p. 172.

315. See LS, pp. 278–279.

316. TF, p. 81.

317. GT, p. 38.

318. See AI, p. 168.

319. AI, p. 169.

320. See CC, pp. 210–11.

321. Ibid., p. 215.

322. PR, p. 7. Non-temporality or "eternity" is not a problem here because it is precisely a mark of the *Aeonic* tome of the Event in Deleuze, which is also "an incorporeal, unlimited, and empty form of time" and "eternal" in the sense of the "eternal return" (LS, p. 62).

323. PR, p. 31.

324. Ibid., p. 32.

325. Ibid., p. 84.

326. PR, p. 45. In more technical terms: While it may be doubted that Whitehead understood God's "primordial nature" (realm of the potential) as

an effect of the world, he held the "consequent nature" (realm of actualities) to be such an effect (see PR, p. 32), in the context of the *superjectivity*—God being the primordial accident of creativity—we may question whether or not all these aspects of God rest on creativity and are its "effect," in the same sense in which Deleuze knows of the realm of the effects as quasi-causes of the process (see LS, pp. 169–170).

327. LS, p. 107. This prefigures Butler's criticism of the Law and Nietzsche's view that it is nothing but the exclusion of becoming for Being.

328. See LS, p. 279.

329. See PR, p. 88.

330. LS, p. 172.

331. PR, p. 47.

332. AI, p. 296.

333. Ibid., p. 295.

334. PR, p. 348. Whitehead's God does not reflect Butler's power beyond the Law as the redeemer of guilt that is still an effect of that Law; see CC, pp. 214–5.

335. See PR, pp. 346–347.

336. AI, p. 106.

337. AI, p. 286.

338. PR, p. 350. How this *limit* relates to Lacan's and Žižek's "Real" still is an open question. While all understand it as limit, Whitehead's limit (of the BwO) is *not* the excluded but indicates *non-exclusion*. *As* non-excluded, it is in itself the *impossible* event. From a Whiteheadian perspective, however, it would be interesting to ask the question whether the limit, which, in a sense, is an "exclusion" as no event can realize it—except the limit itself, the impossible event—is God. God, then, remains the only event that has no "Real" as limit and therefore is the internal reversion of "the Real." In this sense, God is not "the Real" and not part of it; God is not the projection of the unspeakably excluded, but the limit of the attainment of the unspeakable as pure intensity—which, of course, is "excluded" in any event.

339. See LS, p. 172. See Jeff Bell, *Philosophy at the Edges of Chaos: Gilles Deleuze and the Philosophy of Difference* (Toronto: University of Toronto Press, 2006), pp. 190–192.

340. See AI, pp. 133–134. Whitehead's naming of God as the "principle of limitation" (see SMW, p. 178) is *not* a proof to the contrary because it does not function to install order but intensity; besides, it functions as the principle of *irrationality* in which it is itself the *limit* of any rational order: not in negation, but in *affirmation* of the event!

341. PR, p. 67.

342. See AI, p. 113.

343. PR, pp. 342–343.

344. God as *limit* of the BwO is an *infinitely attaining* body, never reaching fulfillment of a full BwO or a "presented" B *with* O.

345. PR, p. 111.

346. PR, p. 105.

347. Ibid.

348. RM, p. 160.

349. AI, p. 236.

350. TP, p. 154.

351. MG, p. 106.

352. IM, p. 26.

353. PR, p. 7.

354. Ibid.

355. PR, p. 244. See also Masao Abe, "Mahayana Buddhism and Whitehead," in Abe, *Zen and Western Thought* (Honolulu, 1985), pp. 152–170.

356. IM, p. 25.

357. See PR, p. 30.

358. IM, p. 27.

359. Ibid., p. 31.

360. See PR, p. 345.

361. IM, p. 26.

362. See PR, pp. 349–351.

363. Imm., p. 90.

364. Ibid.

365. See PR, p. 345.

366. Imm., p. 80.

367. Ibid., p. 82.

368. See R. Faber, "'The Infinite Movement of Evanescence'—The Pythagorean Puzzle in Plato, Deleuze, and Whitehead," *American Journal of Theology and Philosophy* 21 (2000): pp. 171–199 and R. Faber, "De-Ontologizing God: Levinas, Deleuze, and Whitehead," in C. Keller and A. Daniell, eds., *Process and Difference: Between Cosmological and Poststructuralist Postmodernism* (Albany: State University of New York Press, 2002), pp. 209–234.

1. WHITEHEAD, POST-STRUCTURALISM, AND REALISM
Keith Robinson

1. Much of this "early" reaction to Derrida seems based on an at times willful misreading of his work, readings that Derrida always vigorously disputed. For a striking example of the latter, see Derrida's *Limited Inc.* (Chicago: Northwestern University Press, 1988).

2. Giorgio Agamben uses the "immanence-transcendence" distinction to characterize different tendencies in continental thought in *Potentialities:*

Collected Essays in Philosophy (Stanford, Calif: Stanford University Press, 1999). In his "Deleuze and Derrida, Immanence and Transcendence: Two Directions in Recent French Thought" in *Between Deleuze and Derrida*, ed Paul Patton, John Protevi (New York: Continuum, 2003), pp. 46–66, Dan Smith has explored the immanence-transcendence distinction in relation to Deleuze and Derrida and points out, rightly I think, that the "choice" between transcendence and immanence should ultimately be evaluated in the ethical/political domain.

3. While completing final revision of this paper, I came across Lee Braver's interesting book *A Thing of This World* (Chicago: Northwestern University Press, 2007). Braver reads continental philosophy since Kant through the lens of anti-realism and uses this lens as a rapprochement for the division between continental and analytic. Although this is an interesting and worthwhile project, my own use of the realism–anti-realism distinction would suggest the need for a parallel project in relation to "continental realism."

4. PR, pp. xii–xiii.

5. Simon Critchley and Dominique Janicaud would dispute this reading of Heidegger. Heidegger does of course say here that the task is now to "cease all overcoming." See S. Critchley, "The Overcoming of Overcoming: On Dominique Janicaud," *Continental Philosophy Review* 36 (December 2003).

6. DR, pp. 64–66.

7. DR, p. 222.

8. Putnam's sense of internalism is an anti-realism since it is opposed to what he calls "externalism," which is the "God's eye view" external to correspondence. Internalism for Putnam is an account of objects in the world that can only make sense from within a description. Here I contrast Deleuze's own critique of "external" difference with his preference for internal difference. See H. Putnam, *Reason, Truth and History* (New York: Cambridge University Press, 1981), especially ch. 3, pp 49–74.

9. DR, p. 208.

10. PR, pp. 7, 10–11.

11. PR, p. 11 (italics added).

12. D, p. 139.

13. PR, p. 11.

14. See my Introduction to *Deleuze, Whitehead and Bergson: Rhizomatic Connections*, ed. Keith Robinson (New York: Palgrave Macmillan, 2008).

15. PR, p. 166.

16. PR, p. 167.

17. PR, p. 156.

18. SMW, p. 58.

19. PNK, pp. 8–9.

20. PR, p. 78.

21. In his *Intensive Science and Virtual Philosophy* (London: Continuum, 2002), Manuel DeLanda argues for Deleuze as a "realist" but not in the sense I argue for here. DeLanda's realism is more of a traditional "metaphysical realism" in that he argues that for Deleuze the world exists independently of the mind. This isn't particularly helpful in Deleuze's case since DeLanda doesn't articulate his positions in accordance with these standard rubrics and therefore tends to ignore Deleuze's "transcendentalism" and the sense in which Deleuze's "constructivism" is not making claims about the existence of certain kinds of material entities but giving a speculative account of the *conditions* of the world.

22. I am influenced here by James Bradley's "Transcendentalism and Speculative Realism," *Process Studies* 23 (Fall 1994).

23. PR, p. 113.

24. PR, p. 72.

25. Elsewhere I have given a more detailed account of Whitehead's analysis of temporalization in terms of the creative processes of "concrescence" and "transition" that parallels in some respects Deleuze's accounts of actualization. See my "The New Whitehead? An Ontology of the 'Virtual' in Whitehead's Metaphysics," *Symposium* 10, no. 1 (Spring 2006).

26. PR, p. 72.

2. NOMAD THOUGHT: DELEUZE, WHITEHEAD, AND THE ADVENTURE OF THINKING
Jeff Bell

1. DR, p. 293.
2. Ibid., p. 147.
3. NT, p. 142.
4. DR, pp. 284–285.
5. AI, p. 279.
6. Ibid., p. 276.
7. Ibid., p. 278.
8. n numerous places Nietzsche expresses his exasperation with the decadence of culture in which he was writing. Heidegger, in *Being and Time*, writes of the dominance of the "they," or how we, among other things, "read see, and judge about literature and art as they see and judge . . ." *Being and Time*, trans. John Macquarrie and Edward Robinson (New York: Harper & Row, 1962), p. 164. The title of Spengler's influential book, *The Decline of the West* (New York: Vintage Press, 2006), speaks for itself, as does Allan Bloom's more recent work, *The Closing of the American Mind* (New York: Simon and Schuster, 1998).

9. EP, p. 172.
10. P, p. 232 (translation mine).
11. TP, p. 8.
12. Rhizome and multiplicity are used interchangeably by Deleuze and Guattari. See, for instance, TP, p. 9: "The point is that a rhizome or multiplicity never allows itself..."
13. TP, p. 21.
14. PR, p. 406.
15. M, pp. 285–286.
16. GT, p. 9.
17. Ibid., p. 21.
18. Ibid., p. 19–20.
19. Ibid., p. 181.
20. Ibid., p. 185.
21. Ibid.
22. Ibid., p 188.
23. See my book *Deleuze's Hume: Culture, Criticism, and the Scottish Enlightenment* (Edinburgh: Edinburgh University Press, forthcoming), where this problem is explored in detail.
24. LS, p. 151.
25. David Sudnow, *Ways of the Hand* (Cambridge, Mass.: Harvard University Press, 1978), p. 15.
26. Ibid., p. 25.
27. Double articulation is yet another key concept in Deleuze's work. For more, see TP, pp. 40–41, as well as Deleuze and Guattari's discussion of sedimentary rocks in the "On the Geology of Morals" chapter.
28. TP, p. 40.
29. PR, p. 256.
30. Ibid.
31. LS, p. 116.
32. AI, p. 259.
33. Ibid., p. 211.
34. Ibid., p. 207.
35. Ibid., p. 258.
36. Ibid., p. 204.
37. PR, p. 131.
38. Friedrich Nietzsche, *Human All Too Human*, trans. Marion Faber (Lincoln: University of Nebraska Press, 1984), p. 283.
39. PR, p. 408.
40. Ibid.
41. LS, p. 102.

42. GA, p. 8.
43. Ibid., p. 17.
44. Ibid., p. 135.
45. Ibid., p. 43.
46. Ibid., p. 42.
47. M, p. 287.
48. AI, p. 93.
49. See Nietzsche, *Thus Spoke Zarathustra*, in *The Portable Nietzsche*, ed. and trans. Walter Kaufmann (New York: Penguin Books, 1954), p. 164: "Far from the market place and from fame happens all that is great: far from the market place and from fame the inventors of new values have always dwelt."
50. NT, p. 148.

3. TRANSCENDENTAL EMPIRICISM IN DELEUZE AND WHITEHEAD
Steven Shaviro

This chapter originally appeared as part of Chapter 2 of my book *Without Criteria: Kant, Whitehead, Deleuze, and Aesthetics* © MIT 2009, published by The MIT Press.

1. DR, pp. 284–285.
2. For Whitehead's list of categories, see PR, pp. 20–28.
3. PR, p. 18.
4. DR, pp. 284–285.
5. PR, p. 20.
6. Ibid., p. 151.
7. As Keith Robinson forcefully puts it:

> the key context for understanding ... Whitehead is to refuse to read Whitehead as simply a pre-Kantian metaphysical realist. ... Rather, Whitehead's pre-Kantianism plays much the same role in his thought as it does in Deleuze: a way of approaching and confronting the aporias of Kantianism as preparation for the laying out of an essentially post-Kantian philosophy of creativity and becoming. Whitehead is a deeply post-Kantian philosopher in much the same way that Deleuze is post-Kantian. (Keith Robinson, "The New Whitehead? An Ontology of the 'Virtual' in Whitehead's Metaphysics," *Symposium* 10, no. 1 [Spring 2006]: p. 72)

8. DR, pp. 168–170.
9. NP, pp. 51–52.
10. LS, p. 102.
11. NP, p. 89.
12. DR, p. 211.
13. Ibid., pp. 211–212.
14. Ibid., p. 212.

15. Ibid., p. 211.
16. Ibid., p. 208.
17. Gilbert Simondon, *L'individuation à la lumière des notions de forme et d'information* (Grenoble: Million, 2005).
18. Manuel DeLanda, *Intensive Science and Virtual Philosophy* (New York: Continuum, 2002).
19. LS, p. 4.
20. "The subjectivist principle is, that the datum in the act of experience can be adequately analysed purely in terms of universals. . . . The sensationalist principle is, that the primary activity in the act of experience is the bare subjective entertainment of the datum, devoid of any subjective form of reception. This is the doctrine of mere sensation" (PR, p. 157).
21. TP, p. 12.
22. DR, p. 143.
23. LS, p. 6.
24. Ibid., p. 7.
25. Ibid., p. 6.
26. Ibid., p. 33.
27. Ibid., p. 164.
28. Ibid., p. 95.
29. Ibid., p. 7.
30. Ibid., p. 165.
31. Ibid., p. 170.
32. Robinson, "The New Whitehead?" p. 72.
33. PR, p. 22.
34. Ibid., p. 29.
35. Ibid., p. 191.
36. Ibid., p. 23.
37. Ibid., pp. 48, 158.
38. Ibid., p. 186.
39. Ibid., p. 44.
40. Ibid., pp. 52, 149.
41. Ibid., p. 40.
42. Ibid., pp. 148–149.
43. Ibid., p. 44.
44. Ibid., p. 291. It is important to recall here that, for Whitehead, all entities feel and have feelings, and not just sentient ones.
45. Ibid., p. 114.
46. Ibid., p. 22.
47. Ibid., p. 29.
48. Ibid., p. 44.

49. Ibid., p. 23.

50. Ibid., p. 188.

51. The actual and the potential thus reciprocally determine one another in Whitehead, much as the actual and the virtual are reciprocally determining in Deleuze. James Williams rigorously examines "the concept of reciprocal determination" in both thinkers. See *The Transversal Thought of Gilles Deleuze: Encounters and Influences* (Manchester: Clinamen Press, 2005), pp. 77–100.

52. PR, p. 239.

53. Ibid., p. 239.

54. Ibid., p. 41.

55. Ibid., pp. 41–42. Strictly speaking, Whitehead uses the term "negative prehension" to designate both the exclusion of an actual entity and the exclusion of an eternal object. But although a negative prehension of an actual entity "may eliminate its distinctive importance," nevertheless "in some way, by some trace of causal feeling, the remote actual entity is [still] prehended positively. In the case of an eternal object, there is no such necessity" (p. 239; see also p. 219: "All the actual entities are positively prehended, but only a selection of the eternal objects"). Actual entities, you might say, can only be excluded via something like (psychoanalytic) repression, while eternal objects can actually be dismissed, without residue, when subject to a negative prehension. This follows from the very nature of eternal objects: that, although they are real, they are not "facts," and they have no causal efficacy.

56. PR, pp. 42–43.

57. Ibid., p. 29.

58. Ibid., p. 239.

59. Ibid., pp. 43–44.

60. Ibid., p. 239.

61. DR, p. 168.

62. PR, p. 169.

63. Ibid., p. 137.

64. LS, p. 164.

65. Immanuel Kant, *Critique of Pure Reason*, trans. Werner Pluhar (Indianapolis, Ind.: Hackett, 1996), p. 8.

66. Ibid., p. 735.

67. I have already mentioned Deleuze's rejection of questions of legitimation, his desire "to have done with the judgment of God." But Deleuze's immanent and constructivist mode of thought also, in its own way, involves a kind of critical self-reflexivity, and thereby poses the transcendental question of the *limit*: "You never reach the Body without Organs, you can't reach it, you are forever attaining it, it is a limit" (TP, p. 150). An experimental, constructivist practice seeks to affirm itself to the full extent of what it can do

(a concept that Deleuze develops in his discussions of Spinoza's *conatus*, and Nietzsche's doctrine of active forces). But this means precisely pushing a force, or a practice, to its limits, and confronting the Body without Organs as ultimate limit. This is where we face the question of blockages and flows, "emptied bodies" and "full ones," accomplishments and further problematizations.

Whitehead, for his part, is always circumspect in his critiques. When he discusses other philosophical systems, he always recognizes their validity within limits, but criticizes the attempt to push beyond these limits:

> The chief error in philosophy is overstatement. The aim at generalization is sound, but the estimate of success is exaggerated. There are two main forms of such overstatement. One form is what I have termed elsewhere the "fallacy of misplaced concreteness." . . . The other form of overstatement consists in a false estimate of logical procedure in respect to certainty, and in respect to premises. (PR, pp. 7–8)

In many ways, this is very close to Kant's project of rejecting the dogmatic excesses of rationalism, but without adopting, in their place, a generalized (and eventually self-discrediting) skepticism. The difference, of course, is one of affect or temperament: Whitehead's genial and relaxed mode of critique is far removed from Kant's high seriousness and severity.

68. Immanuel Kant, *Perpetual Peace and Other Essays*, trans. Ted Humphrey (Indianapolis, Ind.: Hackett, 1983), p. 41.

69. Michel Foucault, *Ethics: Subjectivity and Truth*, ed. Paul Rabinow, trans. Robert Hurley, et al (New York: The New Press, 1997), p. 319.

70. Foucault, *Ethics*, p. 309.

71. Foucault, *Ethics*, p. 319.

72. WP, p. 75.

73. MT, p. 174.

4. CAN WE BE WOLVES? INTERSECTIONS BETWEEN DELEUZE'S DIFFERENCE AND REPETITION AND BUTLER'S PERFORMATIVITY
Andrea M. Stephenson

1. N, p. 6.
2. UG, p. 233.
3. GT, p. 184.
4. n this volume, the reader will find chapters that discuss Whitehead, Butler, and Deleuze, some that address Whitehead and Deleuze, and still others that explore Whitehead and Butler. The one relationship that is missing is the one between Butler and Deleuze, which is what this chapter will address. The reader will find that many of the Whiteheadian ideas from the

other chapters share an affinity with the concepts in this chapter, and I encourage the reader to exercise her creativity in making those connections.

5. Rosi Braidotti defends a type of Deleuzian materialistic theory of sexual difference in *Metamorphosis: Towards a Materialist Theory of Becoming* (Cambridge: Polity, 2002). Butler, who takes issue with the lack of the negative in Deleuze, comments: "I am not a very good materialist" (UG, 198). Catherine Keller notes, "I am not sure Deleuze is either" (e-mail message to the author, April 2009).

6. GA, p. 37.

7. TP, p. 30.

8. Roland Faber (comment to author in editing notes for "Can We Be Wolves," March 2009).

9. DR, p. 5 (italics added). Transgression here refers to the transgression of boundaries and norms and includes transgression of norms set by society, transgression of the ideals of family and friends, transgression of the boundaries of the self, and so forth. The notion of subversion in Butler is used similarly, as will be seen later in the chapter.

10. DR, p. 24.

11. DR, p. 76.

12. DR, p. 21.

13. GT, p. 178 (italics added).

14. GT, p. 185.

15. TP, p. 28.

16. Ibid.

17. The title of this section, "The Wolf Is the Pack," is from TP, p. 31.

18. See GT.

19. WS, p. 4.

20. WS, p. 30.

21. WS, p. 31.

22. WS, p. 58.

23. WS, p. 67.

24. GA, p. 8.

25. TP, p. 29

26. GA, p. 8.

27. TP, p. 29.

28. TP, p. 35.

29. DR, p. 191.

30. TP, p. 29.

31. GT, p. 42.

32. WS, p. 69.

33. GA, p. 132.

34. TP, p. 37.
35. DR, p. 257.
36. The title of this section, "The Wolf-Man Keeps Howling," is from TP, p. 38.
37. WS, p. 51.
38. UG, p. 198.
39. GA, p. 34.
40. GA, p. 101.
41. TP, p. 29.
42. Though this love is certainly not the type of power-seeking, possession-desiring love that is critiqued by Butler in her work on gender and identity, it is, nevertheless, also not a sterile, ethereal love, but a real material love. A love that acknowledges the very intimate way in which we are implicated not only in each other's physical lives but in our very experience of who we are.
43. TP, p. 35.

5. BUTLER AND WHITEHEAD ON THE (SOCIAL) BODY
Michael Halewood

1. M. Fraser, "What is the matter of feminist criticism?" in *Economy and Society* 31, no. 4 (November 2002): p. 610.
2. According to Whitehead, the bifurcation of nature is that mode of thought, characteristic of modernity, that conceives reality as split into two realms. One realm is the underlying causal realm that is out-there in nature and makes up real reality. The other realm is that of the perceptions and experiences of such a realm by [human] subjects. Between the two realms lies a practical and conceptual gulf—see CN, pp. 26–48.
3. K. Barad, "Getting Real: Technoscientific Practices and the Materialization of Reality," *differences: A Journal of Feminist Cultural Studies* 10, no. 2, 1998: pp. 87–128; M. Fraser, "What is the Matter of Feminist Criticism?" *Economy and Society* 31, no. 4, (November 2002): pp. 606–625; V. Kirby, *Telling Flesh. The Substance of the Corporeal*, (London: Routledge, 1997); V. Kirby, "Human Nature" *Australian Feminist Studies* 14, no. 29, 1999: pp. 19–29; S. Sandford. "Contingent Ontologies. Sex, Gender and 'Woman' in Simone de Beauvoir and Judith Butler" in *Radical Philosophy* (September/October 1999): pp. 18–29.
4. BTM, p. 4.
5. Ibid., p. 9.
6. Ibid., p. 245.
7. Ibid., p. 10.
8. Ibid., p. 244.

9. UG, p. 48.
10. See UG, pp, 43–48.
11. UG, p. 53.
12. PL, p. 33.
13. Kirby, *Telling Flesh*, p. 2.
14. Kirby, *Telling Flesh*, p. 5.
15. UG, p. 44.
16. P. Cheah, "Mattering" in *Diacritics* 26, no. 1 (1996): p. 108.
17. Ibid., p. 113.
18. Ibid., p. 114.
19. Ibid., pp. 116–117.
20. Ibid., p. 119.
21. Ibid., p. 121.
22. Fraser, "What is the matter," p. 613.
23. E. A. Wilson, "Introduction: Somatic Compliance—Feminism Biology and Science," *Australian Feminist Studies* 14, no. 29 (1999): p. 16.
24. PL, p. 43.
25. UG, p. 195.
26. Ibid., p. 198.
27. Ibid., p. 52.
28. PL, p. 20.
29. Ibid., p. 26.
30. UG, p. 185.
31. Ibid., p. 180.
32. Ibid., p. 202.
33. See MT, p. 211 and PR, pp. 246–247.
34. PR. p. xi.
35. CN, p. 53.
36. SMW, p. 99.
37. MT, p. 157.
38. Ibid.
39. MT, p. 167.
40. See PR, p. 184.
41. Ibid., p. 62 (italics added).
42. PR, p. 108.
43. Michael Halewood, "On Whitehead and Deleuze—The Process of Materiality," in *Configurations* (Baltimore, Md.: Johns Hopkins, 2007).
44. PR, p. 240.
45. Ibid., p. 160.
46. Ibid., p. 151.
47. Ibid., p. 203.

48. PL, p. 27.
49. Ibid., p. 45.
50. D. Debaise, *Un empirisme spéculative. Lecture de Procès et réalité de Whitehead* (Vrin: Paris. 2006), pp. 133ff.
51. PR, p. 34.
52. Debaise, pp. 135–136.
53. While Whitehead's thoughts on "life" shall not be dealt with in detail here, it is important to state that "there is no absolute gap between 'living' and 'non-living' societies" (PR, p. 102).
54. PR, p. 99.
55. Ibid., p. 119.
56. Ibid., pp. 178–79
57. AI, p. 189.
58. BTM, p. 108.
59. UG, p. 197.
60. PL, p. 28.

6. CONFLICT
Isabella Palin

1. I have in mind Whitehead's conception of the function of propositions as developed by Isabelle Stengers when she writes of their "problematic" character: how they serve to render the givens of a problem indeterminate as regards the role they will be brought to play in a possible solution. See Isabelle Stengers, *Penser avec Whitehead* (Paris: Editions du Seuil, 2002), pp. 27–29.
2. GA, pp. 100–101.
3. See Butler's examples in PL, pp. 12–15.
4. Hannah Arendt, *On Violence* (New York: Harcourt, Brace & World, 1970), pp. 35–40.
5. Ibid., pp. 40–41 (italics added).
6. Ibid., p. 56.
7. GA, p. 100.
8. UG, pp. 105–106.
9. GA, pp. 22–26.
10. Ibid., p. 22.
11. "[A] masculine gender is formed from the refusal to grieve the masculine as a possibility of love; a feminine gender is formed (taken on, or assumed) through the incorporative fantasy by which the feminine is excluded as a possible object of love, an exclusion never grieved, but 'preserved' through the heightening of feminine identification itself." (BTM, p. 235. Quoted in Elena Loizidou, *Judith Butler: Ethics, Law, Politics* [New York: Routledge-Cavendish, 2007], p. 37)

12. GA, p. 23.
13. Ibid., p. 25.
14. PL, p. 15.
15. Ibid., p. 34.
16. At times, Butler concludes her arguments with calls of this type. See, for instance, PL, p. 127.
17. GA, pp. 85–87. See also pp. 10–12.
18. Ibid., pp. 130–132.
19. PL pp. 10–11.
20. NP, p. 62n2; also p. 3. Compare with p. 212: "There is no creation in the proper sense of the word except insofar as we, far from separating life from what it can do, use the excess in order to invent new forms of life." (All translations from French my own.)
21. See NP, pp. 90–94, where Deleuze describes how the creation of new values is very different from any fight for the attribution of established values, or from warring, rivalry, and also the judgment of comparison. See also p. 97, on giving value and meaning.
22. NP, p. 118.
23. See Stengers, *Penser avec Whitehead*, pp. 26–27, and D, pp. 7–9.
24. AI, p. 170.
25. MT, pp. 50–52.
26. NP, pp. 3–6.
27. FR, pp. 8, 18–20. Compare with p. 33.
28. Arendt, *On Violence*, pp. 79–81; PL, p. 11.
29. AI, p. 66.
30. See WS, pp. 20–27, and Butler, "Competing Universalities," in *Contingency, Hegemony, Universality: Contemporary Dialogues on the Left*, ed. Judith Butler, Ernesto Laclau, and Slavoj Žižek (New York: Verso, 2000), pp. 166–168, 177. See also Arendt, *On Violence*, p. 52: "Power springs up whenever people get together and act in concert, but it derives its legitimacy from the initial getting together, rather than from any action that may then follow. . . . Violence can be justifiable, but it never will be legitimate."
31. AI, p. 54 (italics added).
32. Ibid., p. 66.
33. "Merely Cultural," quoted in Loizidou, *Judith Butler*, p. 130. See also "Competing Universalities," pp. 166–168, on how translation is not the same as arguing an identitarian position.
34. PL, p. xiv.
35. Ibid., p. 151.
36. See The Initiative and Referendum Institute, http://www.iandrinstitute.org/ (US) and http://www.iri-europe.org/ (Europe); and the

Belgian organization Democratie.Nu, http://www.democratie.nu/links/ onderzoek/ (links to research on direct democracy) and http://democratie.nu/ algemeen/intro/referendum.html ("Three Steps and Seven Modalities" suggesting requirements for the practical implementation of direct democracy to ensure it fulfils its aims, for those of you who read Dutch).

37. Arendt, *On Violence*, p. 41

38. See James Surowiecki, *The Wisdom of Crowds: Why the Many Are Smarter Than the Few and How Collective Wisdom Shapes Business, Economics, Societies and Nations* (New York: Random House, 2004).

39. See NP, p. 93, where Deleuze describes the distinction between the will to power (creative of values) and *wanting* power (a fight for the attribution of established, represented values).

40. UG, p. 226.

41. Arendt, *On Violence*, p. 41.

42. Arendt, *On Violence*, p. 52.

7. BECOMING THROUGH MULTIPLICITY: STAYING IN THE MIDDLE OF WHITEHEAD'S AND DELEUZE-GUATTARI'S PHILOSOPHIES OF LIFE
Luke B. Higgins

1. Catherine Keller, *The Face of the Deep: A Theology of Becoming* (New York and London: Routledge, 2003), and *Apocalypse Now and Then: A Feminist Guide to the End of the World* (Boston: Beacon Press, 1996).

2. Roland Faber, "In the Wake of False Unifications: Whitehead's Creative Resistance against Imperialist Theologies" (Claremont, Calif.: Claremont School of Theology, Lecture, March 2005).

3. My discussion of Deleuze-Guattari in this chapter will focus primarily on their work *A Thousand Plateaus*.

4. PR.

5. The concept of survey at infinite speed is developed most explicitly in their work *What Is Philosophy?*

6. For Whitehead, there is no definitive separation between these two: "The body, however, is only a peculiarly intimate bit of the world" (PR, p. 81). Deleuze-Guattari's philosophy similarly sees the body as existing on a larger continuum populated throughout by nonhuman entities. This close association between body and ecosystem in both thinkers' work makes a significant contribution to ecological philosophy—a point I will take up later in this chapter.

7. TP, p. 8.

8. Ibid., p. 81.

9. Ibid., pp. 8–9.

10. Ibid., p. 245.

11. Ibid., p. 22.

12. Philosopher of science Isabelle Stengers emphasizes this "societal" level of Whitehead's analysis in her quite Deleuzian reading of Whitehead. See Isabelle Stengers, *Penser avec Whitehead: Une libre et sauvage création de concepts* (Paris: Seuil, 2002).

13. PR, p. 283.

14. See endnote 5.

15. PR, p. 102.

16. Ibid., p. 107.

17. Ibid., p. 103

18. Ibid., pp. 101–103.

19. Ibid., p. 102.

20. Ibid., p. 105.

21. Ibid., p. 105.

22. Deleuze-Guattari's mostly pejorative use of the term "organism"— referring to those transcendent organizational structures that restrictively impose themselves on the flows of the Body without Organs—stands in marked contrast to Whitehead's positive, constructive use of this same term to describe the relational and ecological aspects of his philosophy (a "philosophy of organism"). As will become clearer below, I suggest that near-opposite meanings are invoked by these two uses of the term.

23. TP, p. 150.

24. Ibid., p. 161.

25. PR, pp. 107–108.

26. TP, p. 158.

27. Ibid., p. 160.

28. Ibid., p. 161.

29. This commitment is inspired in part by the political ideas around ecology set forth by Bruno Latour in his *Politics of Nature: How to Bring the Sciences into Democracy*, trans. Catherine Porter (Cambridge, Mass.: Harvard University Press, 2004).

30. TP, p. 161.

31. Meister Eckhart, "Sermon 5b" in *Meister Eckhart: The Essential Sermons, Commentaries, Treatises, and Defense*, trans. Edmond Colledge and Bernard McGinn (New York: Paulist Press, 1981), p. 184.

8. SURRATIONALITY AND CHAOSMOS: FOR A MORE DELEUZIAN WHITEHEAD (WITH A BUTLERIAN INTERVENTION)
Roland Faber

1. Jacques Derrida, "Différance," in *Margins of Philosophy*, tr. Alan Bass (Chicago: University of Chicago Press, 1982), p. 10.

Notes to pages 157–60   245

2. See Luce Irigaray, *The Sex Which Is Not One* (Ithaca, N.Y.: Cornell University Press, 1985).

3. See GT, pp. 11–33.

4. See Keller, *Face of the Deep: A Theology of Becoming* (London: Routledge, 2003), pp. 3–40.

5. "The world is no accomplice of our cognition. There is no pre-discursive provision that makes the world lean toward us" (Michel Foucault, "The Order of Discourse"—my own translation).

6. TP, p. 24.

7. See PR, p. 22.

8. TP, p. 84.

9. PR, p. 103.

10. See PR, p. 105.

11. TP, p. 25.

12. TF, p. 81.

13. PR, p. 21.

14. TF, p. 81.

15. PR, p. 350.

16. AI, p. 134.

17. WP, p. 35.

18. TF, p. 81.

19. GT, p. 69.

20. Ibid., p. 14.

21. Ibid., p. 33.

22. See Constantine V. Boundas, "Deleuze–Bergson: An Ontology of the Virtual," in *Deleuze: A Critical Reader*, ed. Paul Patton (Oxford: Blackwell, 1996), pp. 81–106.

23. See C1, p. 10.

24. WP, p. 35.

25. TP, p. 12.

26. PR, p. 209.

27. See Alain Badiou, *Deleuze: The Clamor of Being* (Minneapolis: University of Minnesota Press, 1997), pp. 9–30; see also David Griffin, et al, *Founders of Constructive Postmodern Philosophy: Peirce, James, Bergson, Whitehead, and Hartshorne* (Albany: State University of New York Press, 1993).

28. PR, p. xii.

29. AI, p. 223.

30. TF, p. 81.

31. See PR, p. 209.

32. PR, p. 230 (second italics added).

33. See PR, p. 48.

34. See Ivor Leclerc, "Whitehead and the Dichotomy of Rationalism and Empiricism," in *Whiteheads Metaphysik der Kreativität: Internationales Whitehead-Symposium Bad Homburg 1983*, ed. Friedrich Rapp and Reiner Wiehl (Freiburg: Karl Alber, 1986), pp. 13–32.

35. Lyman T. Lundeen, *Risk and Rhetoric in Religion: Whitehead's Theory of Language and the Discourse of Faith* (Philadelphia: Fortress, 1972), p. 93.

36. PR, pp. 20–27.
37. Ibid., p. 8.
38. Ibid., p. 20.
39. See PR, p. 4.
40. PR, p. 46.
41. DR, p. 57.
42. SMW, p. 178.
43. PR, p. 90.
44. AI, p. 52.
45. Friedrich Nietzsche, *On the Genealogy of Morals* (New York: Vintage, 1969), p. 45.
46. PR, p. 23.
47. See PR, p. 4
48. See PR, p. 3.
49. See PR, p. 48; see also Roland Faber, "'O Bitches of Impossibility!'—Programmatic Dysfunction in the Chaosmos of Deleuze and Whitehead," in *Deleuze, Whitehead, and Bergson: Rhizomatic Connections*, ed. Keith Robinson (New York: Palgrave MacMillan, 2009), pp. 200–219.

50. See Michel Weber, *Whitehead's Pancreativism: The Basics* (Frankfurt: Ontos, 2006), pp. 65–182.

51. See MT, p. 174.
52. Ibid.
53. PR, p. 42.
54. SMW, p. 192.
55. AI, p. 257.
56. Ibid., p. 296.
57. TF, p. 82.
58. See John Marks, *Gilles Deleuze: Vitalism and Multiplicity* (London: Pluto Press, 1998), pp. 78–90.

59. WP, p. 42.
60. AI, p. 134.
61. Ibid., p. 295.
62. Here is a common tradition, in which Whitehead and Deleuze converse with Derrida; see Jacques Derrida, "Chora," in *Choral Works: A Collaboration between Peter Eisenman and Jacques Derrida*, ed. Jeffrey Kipnis (New York, 1993).

63. See Roland Faber, "Bodies of the Void: Polyphilia and Theoplicity," in *Apophatic Bodies: Negative Theology, Incarnation, and Relationality*, ed. Chris Boesel and Catherine Keller (New York: Fordham University Press, 2010), pp. 200–223.

64. AI, p. 144.

65. See Dorothea Olkowski, *Gilles Deleuze and the Ruin of Representation* (Berkeley: University of California Press, 1998), pp. 47–54.

66. See DI, pp. 9–14.

67. See PR, p. 43.

68. See, e.g., the "hard core common sense" doctrines in David Griffin, *Reenchantment without Supernaturalism: A Process Philosophy of Religion* (Ithaca, N.Y.: Cornell University Press, 2001), pp. 5–7.

69. See Roland Faber, "Wahrheit und Maschine: Wider das transsilvanische Argument von der Gewalt im Erkenntnisdiskurs," *Labyrinth* 3 (2001) at http://labyrinth.iaf.ac.at/2001/Faber.html.

70. Robert Nozick, *Philosophical Explanations*. 15th ed. (Cambridge, Mass.: Harvard University Press, 2003), p. 4.

71. AI, p. 52.

72. Ibid., p. 25.

73. CI, p. 10.

74. See Charles Hartshorne, *The Divine Relativity: A Social Conception of God* (New Haven, Conn.: Yale University Press, 1948), p. 88.

75. See PR, p. 4.

76. See Stascha Rohmer, *Whiteheads Synthese von Kreativität und Rationalität: Reflexionen und Transformationen in Alfred North Whiteheads Philosophie der Natur*, Alber Thesen, vol. 13 (Freiburg: Alber, 2000), pp. 122–149.

77. WP, p. 41.

78. See PR, p. 24.

79. See PR, p. 95; see Genesis 1:2.

80. See AI, p. 211.

81. AI, pp. 295–296.

82. AI, p. 177; see also Roland Faber, "Whitehead at Infinite Speed: Deconstructing System as Event," in *Schleiermacher and Whitehead: Open Systems in Dialogue*, ed. Christine Helmer, Marjorie Suchocki, and John Quiring (Berlin: de Gruyter, 2004), pp. 39–72.

83. Faber, "Whitehead at Infinite Speed," pp. 71–2. "Irrational" forces utilize structures for their interests; surrational critique, therefore, restores the importance of "structures" against this biased irrationalism.

84. See RM, p. 67.

85. AI, p. 150.

86. See AI, p. 246.

87. See N 167–182. See also Ian Buchanan and Claire Colebrook, ed., *Deleuze and Feminist Theory* (Edinburgh University Press, 2000), and Sheila Davaney, ed., *Feminism and Process Thought* (New York: Edwin Mellen Press, 1981).

88. See CT, pp. 177–9.

89. See GT, p. 38.

90. See BTM, pp. 121–142. For a good overview of this process of subjectification, see Annika Thiem, *Unbecoming Subjects: Judith Butler, Moral Philosophy, and Critical Responsibility* (New York: Fordham University Press, 2008), pp. 21–50.

91. See BTM, pp. 187–222. This holds true also for her later investigation of censorship as the condition of the constitution of subjects of language; see ES, p. 140.

92. GA, pp. 22–26.

93. It is difficult to follow a thinker in her structural repetitions when this thinker is still in development. With Butler, I sense an increasing sensitivity for, and approximation with, Whitehead in these matters. Social construction is the basis for Whitehead's understanding of novelty, not its enemy. Butler's newer approach seems to indicate the same kind of move: that the opaqueness of the subject that does not allow one to give an account of oneself without becoming fictitious, is, at the same time, in this function the well for performativity as novelty. Here, the *khoric* space that she has struggled with in relation to Kristeva and Irigaray reappears in Butler.

94. See Tamsin Lorraine, *Irigaray & Deleuze: Experiments in Visceral Philosophy* (Ithaca, N.Y.: Cornell University Press, 1999), pp. 142–164.

95. See NP, pp. 162–164.

96. DR, p. 40.

97. Ibid., p. 41.

98. Ibid., p. 67.

99. See Michael Hardt, *Gilles Deleuze: An Apprenticeship in Philosophy* (Minneapolis: University of Minnesota Press, 1995).

100. This shift appears in the early GT, ch. 1, as well as in the current GA, ch. 1—that is, it seems to be a constant in her work.

101. See DI, p. 124.

102. GA, p. 16.

103. Ibid., p. 37.

104. That performativity as the interplay of necessity and novelty is not a "game" but has its tragic implications of fate is demonstrated by Butler's reference to the case of David Reimer and other cases of gender-performativity; see UG, and Judith Butler, "Doing Justice to Someone: Sex Reassignment and Allegories of Transsexuality," *GLQ: A Journal of Lesbian and Gay Studies* 7, no. 4 (2001): pp. 621–36.

105. PR, p. 4.
106. GA, p. 78.
107. PR, p. 5.
108. AI, p. 106.
109. Ibid., p. 42.
110. See PR, p. 95.
111. PR, p. 42.
112. Ibid., p. 43
113. SMW, p. 178.
114. Ibid.
115. DR, p. 42.
116. DR, p. 42; see also Roland Faber, "'The Infinite Movement of Evanescence'—The Pythagorean Puzzle in Plato, Deleuze, and Whitehead," *American Journal of Theology and Philosophy* 21 (2000): pp. 171–199.
117. DR, p. XXI.
118. SMW, pp. 10–11.
119. For a most interesting introduction of the problem of liberation and the relation of freedom to destiny, see Jean Baudrillard, *Impossible Exchange* (London: Verso, 2001), pp. 51–89.
120. See Roland Faber, "Whitehead at Infinite Speed," pp. 39–72.
121. See BTM, pp. 27–56.
122. UG, p. 198.
123. UG, p. 195.
124. See PR, p. 110; N, p. 149.
125. See G. Kline, "Begriff und Konkreszenz: über einige Gemeinsamkeiten in den Ontologien Hegels und Whiteheads," in *Whitehead und der Deutsche Idealismus*, ed. George Lucas and Antoon Braeckman (Bern: Peter Lang, 1990), pp. 145–161; see also C. Macherey, "Who's Afraid of Hegelian Wolfs?" in *Deleuze: A Critical Reader*, ed. Paul Patton (Oxford: Blackwell, 1996), pp. 114–138.
126. See WP, pp. 45–49; This goes beyond and, at the same time, is nothing but the criticism, as it is normally stated, that dialectic is not radical enough because it remains within the concept of the Same. The Same, however, is the transcendence per resemblance; see Hardt, *Gilles Deleuze*, p. 8.
127. See DI, pp. 117–127.
128. Especially in the form of "negative prehensions" of exclusion of actualities and eternal object to become an affirmed part of a new actuality. Nevertheless, both reinstate affirmation as a basic move: first, by understanding "positive prehension" as a basic move of repetition in the occasion, the repetition of the subjective form; and second, by leaving direct or indirect traces of the "cut away" actualities and eternal objects—the former always leaving

traces of their exclusion; the latter always leaving a whole in the systematic vibration of eternal objects in their "relational essence."

129. "Le premier stade c'était le "many," des vibrations n'importe comment, des vibrations aléatoires. Pour ceux qui connaissent Bergson, peut-être que vous vous rappelez la splendide fin de Matière et Mémoire, le fond de la matière est vibration et vibration de vibrations" (CV).

130. C1, p. 10.
131. PR, p. 4.
132. Ibid., p. 79.
133. Ibid., p. 163.
134. Ibid., p. 22.
135. Ibid., p. 167.
136. For the discussion on Whitehead and Hegel, see George Lucas, *Hegel and Whitehead: Contemporary Perspectives on Systematic Philosophy* (Albany: State University of New York Press, 1986).
137. PR, p. 25; see also Roland Faber, "Trinity, Analogy and Coherence," in *Trinity in Process: A Relational Theology of God*, ed. Joseph Bracken and Marjorie Suchocki (New York: Continuum, 1997), pp. 147–171.
138. PR, p. 22.
139. Ibid., p. 279.
140. Ibid., p. 147.
141. FR, p. 4.
142. PR, p. 105.
143. Ibid., p. 104.
144. Ibid., p. 103.
145. Ibid., p. 72.
146. Ibid., p. 105.
147. See GA, ch.1.
148. GT, p. 96.
149. WP, p. 21.
150. See GT, p. 6–7.
151. See Ibid., p. 46.
152. PR, p. 36.
153. On "mutual immanence" in Whitehead, see Roland Faber, *Prozeßtheologie: Zu ihrer Würdigung und kritischen Erneuerung* (Mainz: Grünewald, 2000), pp. 264–294.
154. PR, p. 7.
155. See Julia Kristeva, *Revolution in Poetic Language* (New York: Columbia University Press, 1984), pp. 25–31.
156. GT, p. 104.
157. Ibid., p. 116.

158. Ibid., p. 115.

159. Ibid., pp. 38–39, 46, 48–49, 94–95.

160. For the term "heterogeneous" in relation to Whitehead, see Gregory Vlastos, "Organic Categories in Hegel and Whitehead," in *Alfred North Whitehead. Essays in His Philosophy*, ed. George Kline (Englewood Cliffs, N.J.: Prentice-Hall, 1963), p. 159.

161. For the application to the important "reciprocal determination" of the Virtual and the Actual in Deleuze and Value and Actuality in Whitehead, see Roland Faber, "De-Ontologizing God: Levinas, Deleuze, and Whitehead," in *Process and Difference: Between Cosmological and Poststructuralist Postmodernism*, ed. Catherine Keller and Anne Daniell (Albany: State University of New York Press, 2002), pp. 209–234, and James Williams, *The Transversal Thought of Gilles Deleuze: Encounters and Influences* (Manchester: Clinamen Press, 2005), pp. 77–100.

162. GA, pp. 26–30.

163. Ibid., ch. 3. It is interesting that Butler's later approach to the inescapable "lateness" of the subject that cannot become self-transparent without becoming abstract or fictitious not only mirrors Derrida's critique of (a metaphysics of) "Presence," but also Whitehead's differentiation into two modes of perception, of which "presentational immediacy" not only is always "too late" but abstract and fictitious in its self-construction. See S, passim.

164. LS, p. 116.

165. SMW, pp. 10–11.

166. See IM, pp. 25–32.

167. PR, p. 244.

168. Ibid.

169. PR, p. 67.

170. See Roland Faber, *God as Poet of the World: Exploring Process Theologies* (New York: Fordham University Press, 2008), pp. 132–140.

171. SMW, p. 178.

172. Tim Clark, "A Whiteheadian Chaosmos? Process Philosophy from a Deleuzian Perspective," in *Process and Difference*, ed. Keller and Daniell, p. 202.

173. TP, p. 20; see also "Bitches," in *Process and Difference*, ed. Keller and Daniell, p. 123.

174. See DR, p. 40.

175. See WP, p. 42.

176. See SMW, p. 107.

177. See AI, p. 150; Faber, *God as Poet*, pp. 141–144.

178. See RM, pp. 89–90.

179. See AI, p. 134.

180. See PR, p. 21.
181. Ibid.
182. See PR, p. 46.
183. See SMW, p. 179.
184. See PR, p. 348.
185. This is nicely demonstrated by Steven Shaviro; see "Deleuze's Encounter with Whitehead" (www.shaviro.com/Othertexts/DeleuzeWhitehead.pdf).
186. AI, p. 113.
187. See RM, p. 62.
188. LS, p. 102.
189. AI, p. 168. Against the proposed resemblance of God with the Self-I, see Jeff Bell, *Philosophy at the Edges of Chaos: Gilles Deleuze and the Philosophy of Difference* (Toronto: University of Toronto Press, 2006), p. 190.
190. PR, p. 346.
191. See PR, p. 349; see also Elizabeth Kraus, *The Metaphysics of Experience: A Companion to Whitehead's* Process and Reality (New York: Fordham University Press, 1998), pp. 168–184.
192. See PR, p. 225.
193. See PR, p. 105. If there is any consciousness in God, as there is in Whitehead's understanding of the mutual immanence of God's natures, it is not an individual Self-Consciousness, but rather the most objective mode of non-individualistic and pre-personal (or even hyper-personal) intensity/creativity, only comparable to Deleuze's "pure (non-subjective) consciousness" of his late text "Immanence—A Life"; see IM, pp. 29–30. As in Whitehead, it is a perfect statement of what in Whitehead includes the virtuality of the eternal objects in God's primordial nature and the actualizations in God's consequent nature.
194. See Roland Faber, "The Infinite Movement of Evanescence," pp. 188–191. Especially in his two articles from 1941, "Immortality" and "Mathematics and the Good," Whitehead not only shows the most radical reconstructions of all of his ultimates in terms of one another, but almost a dissolution.
195. WP, p. 43; this has to be said against simplifications. See Keith Pearson, "Pure Reverse: Deleuze, Philosophy, and Immanence," in *Deleuze and Religion*, ed. Mary Bryden (London: Routledge, 2001), pp. 141–155.
196. SMW, p. 18.
197. WP, p. 42.
198. LS, p. 95.
199. LS, p. 56.
200. AI, p. 295.

201. PR, p. 105.
202. LS, p. 95.
203. LS, p. 102.
204. AI, p. 134.
205. See AI, pp. 295–296.
206. See Christoph Kann, *Fußnoten zu Platon: Philosophiegeschichte bei A. N. Whitehead*. Paradeigmata, vol. 23 (Hamburg: Meiner, 2001), p. 210.
207. AI, p. 133.
208. See IM, pp. 29–30.
209. See Imm., pp. 90; see also Faber, "De-Ontologizing," pp. 219–220, and Faber, "Bodies of the Void." In *Apophatic Bodies*, ed. Boesel and Keller, pp. 217–223.
210. Although Deleuze's account would also have to be understood as creation, and not as mere organization; see Hardt, *Gilles Deleuze*, p. 18.
211. See LS, p. 116.
212. In Faber, "Evanescence," and "De-Ontologizing," I have opted to understand this Divine principle as *in/difference* (neither being able to be conceptualized *as* difference, nor *in* difference, nor *beyond* difference (for that matter), but beyond the *duality* of the ontological difference and the *duality* of the "magic formula," indicating *in/different insistence on difference*.
213. PR, p. 35; see also Keith Robinson, "The New Whitehead? An Ontology of the Virtual in Whitehead's Metaphysics," *Symposium* 10, no. 1 (2006): pp. 69–80.
214. WP, p. 60.
215. AI, p. 169.

9. DIVINE POSSIBILITIES: BECOMING AN ORDER WITHOUT LAW
Alan R. Van Wyk

1. A recent collection of articles appearing under the heading of Political Theology—*Political Theologies: Public Religions in a Post-Secular World*, ed. Hent de Vries and Lawrence Sullivan (New York: Fordham University Press, 2006)—for example, contains thirty-four entries, almost exclusively from philosophers and political theorists.
2. Judith Butler, "Precarious Life" in PL, pp. 128–151; CC, pp. 201–219.
3. Isabelle Stengers, *Penser avec Whitehead; Une libre et sauvage création de concepts* (Paris: Éditions du Seuil, 2002), p. 13.
4. PR, p. 207; SMW, p. 173.
5. PR, p. 105.
6. In BTM, an already religiously inflected rendering of assumption becomes the key critical concept through which Butler is able to both counter any supposed misreading of her earlier work and advance performativity

beyond a mere performance. Assumption comes to designate the functional logic by which the law creates sexed subjects through "citational practices instituted within a juridical domain—a domain of constitutive restraints. The embodying of sex would be a kind of 'citing' of the law, but neither the sex nor the law can be said to preexist their various embodying and citings." BTM, especially ch. 3: "Phantasmic Identification and the Assumption of Sex."

7. PL, xiii.
8. PL, p. 135.
9. PL, p. 135.
10. PL, p. 137.
11. CC, p. 205.
12. CC, p. 212.
13. CC, p. 204.
14. CC, p. 209.
15. There has always been, within Butler's work, a critique of the theological. As Adam Kotsko has recently shown, this has not been directly against theology itself, but rather against the "avowedly secular thinkers who take up positions that seem to Butler to function theologically" (Adam Kotsko, "The Failed Divine Performative: Reading Judith Butler's Critique of Theology with Anselm's *On the Fall of the Devil*." *Journal of Religion* 88, no. 2 (April 2008): p. 210). Within this critique, the theological designates for Butler, in part, a conceptualization of power modeled on sovereign divine power. With this, the theological designates the fixing of the relation between temporality and causation, whereby power itself operates with a linear temporality matched by a single causation, both grounded in and through a prior subject that is subsequently bound to its own lawful or unlawful acting. The theological becomes a way of designating the religious binding of subjects in and to the law of their own subjugation. A binding that itself is occluded and disappears in its very operation.
16. PL, p. 138.
17. CC, p. 214.
18. CC, p. 217.
19. CC, p. 216.
20. CC, pp. 216–217.
21. CC, p. 219.
22. 22. For a further exploration of Butler's continued conversation with Giorgio Agamben concerning sacred life, see Elena Loizidou, *Judith Butler: Ethics, Law, Politics* (New York: Routledge, 2007), especially "Double Law."
23. 23. PL, p. 135.

24. CC, p. 210.
25. CC, p. 219.
26. See Lewis S. Ford, *Transforming Process Theism*, SUNY Series in Philosophy, foreword by Robert Cumming Neville (Albany: State University of New York Press, 2000), especially Part 1.
27. Ford, *Transforming Process Theism*, p. 44.
28. PR, p. 207. In *Science and the Modern World*, this proposal is made with reference to Aristotle, whose "consideration of this metaphysical question [of God] was entirely dispassionate; and he was the last European metaphysician of first-rate importance for whom this claim can be made. After Aristotle, ethical and religious interests began to influence metaphysical conclusions" (SMW, p. 173).
29. PR, p. 343.
30. PR, p. 342.
31. PR, p. 88.
32. PR, p. 7.
33. PR, p. 88.
34. PR, p. 105.
35. PR, p. 83.
36. See Judith A. Jones, *Intensity: An Essay in Whiteheadian Ontology* (Nashville, Tenn.: Vanderbilt University Press, 1998).
37. PR, p. 65.
38. SMW, p. 174; PR, p. 244.
39. PR, p. 31.
40. PR, p. 40.
41. Steven Shaviro, *Without Criteria: Kant, Whitehead, Deleuze, and Aesthetics* (Cambridge, Mass: The MIT Press, forthcoming). See especially "God, or the body without organs."
42. PR, p. 40.
43. SMW, p. 178.
44. CC, pp. 201–202.
45. PR, p. 244.
46. PR, p. 43.
47. CC, p. 208.
48. PR, p. 43.
49. PR, p. 244.
50. PR, p. 83.
51. PR, p. 43.
52. PR, p. 88.
53. PR, p. 343.

54. PR, p. 225.

55. In this sense, Catherine Keller's *Face of the Deep: A Theology of Becoming* (New York: Routledge, 2003) is the prolegomena for any possible secular political theology.

56. PR, p. 21.

57. PR, p. 84.

58. For Whitehead, "order" in its primary designation refers to that which is ordered for an individual actual occasion. All social order is, for Whitehead, derivative from this primary meaning of order (PR, p. 89).

59. In its metaphysical sense, a society is, for Whitehead, "a nexus of actual entities which are 'ordered' among themselves" (PR, p. 89). This ordering is a shared ordering, being based not on an imposition of order, but rather on an eliciting of an complex of eternal objects which is the societies defining characteristic (PR, p. 92).

60. PR, p. 108.

61. PR, p. 105.

62. AC. See especially "Promiscuous Obedience."

63. CC, p. 218.

64. CC, p. 219.

65. As Butler parenthetically notes, "(The messiah is that which will never appear in time.)" CC, p. 218.

66. PR, p. 214.

67. PR, p. 104.

68. PR, p. 105.

69. AI.

10. "GOD IS A LOBSTER": WHITEHEAD'S RECEPTACLE MEETS THE DELEUZIAN SIEVE
Sigridur Gudmarsdottir

1. Roland Faber, "De-Ontologizing God: Levinas, Deleuze, and Whitehead," in *Process and Difference: Between Cosmological and Poststructuralist Postmodernisms*, ed. Catherine Keller and Anne Daniell (Albany: State University of New York Press, 2002), p. 210.

2. The terms univocal and equivocal come from Aristotelian philosophy; see Aristotle, *Categories* I.1a. Also see section 2 of Aristotle, *Categories* I. on *univocity of being (via univoca)*. *Equivocity of being (via negativa)* means that there is radical difference between Being and beings—human words and knowledge are not capable of revealing Being. *Eminence of being (via eminentiae)* stresses that words can denote Being, but in a sublime way.

3. Possible affinities between Deleuze's univocal ontology and mystical, neoplatonic thought has been argued by both philosopher Alain Badiou and

theologian Oliver Davies. Badiou claims that Deleuze's enterprise of multiplicity and becomings is bound to collapse because of his yearning for the One, which for Badiou is nothing else than a Platonism with a face-lift. Badiou defines Deleuze's philosophy as "classical," "systematic," "ascetical," and "organized through a metaphysics of the One" in spite of its post-structural, anti-Platonic appearance. Badiou accuses Deleuze of smuggling transcendence into a discourse on immanence. For Badiou, any grounding is a return to foundationalism, to Plato, or rather to Plotinus, to the One. In spite of an often appreciative and nuanced relation to Deleuze, Badiou states his own manifesto in contrast to Deleuze: "The One is not, there are only actual multiplicities, and the ground is void." Alain Badiou, *Deleuze: The Clamor of Being*, trans. Louise Burchill (Minneapolis: University of Minnesota Press, 1999), p. 53. If Badiou worries about a transcendent bastard in the lair of immanence, Oliver Davies worries about a potential Deleuzian collapse into immanence. Davies notes the similarities between Deleuze's philosophy of difference, the Plotinian One, and Meister Eckhart's *unum indistinctum*. He argues that Deleuze's project of overturning Platonic representationalism has rendered difference transcendental by removing it from the scope of representation. For Davies, Deleuze's persistent hope is in the possibility of thinking difference, which brings him close to theological, apophatic discourse. If the diverse intuitions of Badiou and Davies are to be trusted, Deleuze's thought seems to offer a discourse that resides on the edge of the philosophical and the theological and expresses, in Davies words, "a certain familiar tension, which—despite the absence of any rhetoric of grace or participation seems ... to be natively and ecstatically theological." Oliver Davies, "Thinking Difference: A Comparative Study of Gilles, Deleuze, Plotinus and Meister Eckhart," in *Deleuze and Religion*, ed. Mary Bryden (London/New York: Routledge, 2001), pp. 82, 85.

4. "Timaeus" 50b-c. Plato, *Complete Works*, ed. John Cooper and D. S. Hutchinson, trans. Donald Zeyl (Indianapolis, Ind.: Hackett Publishing Company, 1997), p. 1253.

5. Jacques Derrida, *On the Name*, ed. Thomas Dutoit, trans. David Wood and John P. Leavey (Stanford, Calif.: Stanford University Press, 1995), p. 97.

6. Plato, *Timaeus* 49a.

7. N, p. 6.

8. John Rajchman, *The Deleuze Connections* (Cambridge, Mass.: The MIT Press, 2000), p. 61.

9. E, p. 137.

10. DR, p. 36.

11. DR, p. 274. See also LS, pp. 106–107, 139–140.

12. DR, p. 28. The word *fond* and the cognate *fondement* that Deleuze uses in *Logic of Sense* and *Difference and Repetition* can have many meanings in

French. Louise Burchill, translator of Badiou, distinguishes well between the two terms; however, Badiou refuses this Deleuzian distinction between *fond* and *fondement*. "*Fond:*" "a nonmediated formless 'bottom'—that is if it is a 'ground' in the sense of an underlying reality or basis of 'what is,' is one that lies behind every other 'ground' capable of explaining a sufficient reason for the 'world' as it appears, and that for this reason may be said to be differentiated from *le sans-fond* or 'the groundless' less in terms of its 'nature' than by the relations that it enters into or that are established between its components." "*Fondement:*" "the 'foundation' or 'ground' that precisely results from the 'operation of logos, or of sufficient reason' and serves as the underpinning for the forms of representation." Louise Burchill, "Translators Preface: Portraiture in Philosophy, or Shifting Perspectives," in *Deleuze: The Clamor of Being*, Alain Badiou (Minneapolis: University of Minnesota Press, 1999), p. xviii. The translator of *Difference and Repetition*, Paul Patton, calls both *fond* and *fondement* "ground." Catherine Keller has proposed to call representational thought "founding" and "foundation," but the "nonmediated formless 'bottom'"—to borrow Burchill's phrase—"grounding" and "ground"; cf. Catherine Keller, "Introduction," in *Process and Difference*, ed. Keller and Daniell, pp. 12–13. According to Burchill, French philosophical dictionaries classify *fond* more as an aesthetic word, i.e., "background," while *fondement* is applied both as Keller's "ground" and "foundation." While Keller's distinction between the two concepts is helpful, the complicated history of the word "ground" probably always will render the term ambiguous, and therefore also apophatically attractive.

13. DR, p. 64. Patrick Hayden offers helpful remarks on Deleuzian (non)being:

> Deleuzian (non)being is at the heart of being in the form of the problematic structure of objects, the nexus of problem and question. (Non)being is the difference internal to things, the positivity of what not yet has been created . . . the necessary problematizing element of being that is expressed in questioning rather than negation. (Patrick Hayden, *Multiplicity and Becoming* [New York: Peter Lang, 1998], p. 17)

14. DR, p. 67.
15. TF, p. 81.
16. PR, p. 21.
17. "Timaeus" 52e. Plato, *Complete Works*, p. 1255.
18. TF, p. 76.
19. TF, p. 63. On the divine harmony, see the last five articles in Leibniz's *Monadology*.
20. Ibid., p. 23.

21. Whitehead uses the term prehension to denote "an apprehension which may or may not be cognitive" (SMW, p. 69), and refers to an apprehension of nature: "Nature is that which we observe in perception through the senses. In this sense perception we are aware of something which is not thought and which is self contained for thought" (CN, p. 3).

22. The basic structure of the Whiteheadian system is the actual occasion, which prehends or relates to other actual occasions. The "congruence" or "nexus" of actual occasions or "actual entities" is called an event. "I shall use the term 'event' in the more general sense of a nexus of actual occasions, interrelated in some determinate fashion in one extensive quantum. An actual occasion is the limiting type of an event with only one member" (PR, p. 73).

23. Ibid., p. 348.

24. Ibid., p. 345.

25. Ibid., p. 88.

26. SMW, p. 91.

27. PR, p. 351.

28. AI, p. 172. See also "Plato's doctrine of the real Receptacle [*hypodoche* and *khora*] and Epicurus's doctrine of the real Void [*to kenon*], differ in some details. But both doctrines are emphatic assertions of a real communication between ultimate realities" (AI, pp. 171).

29. AI, p. 192.

30. "This is why Spinoza stands fundamentally apart from all the theses of his time, according to which Evil is nothing, and the Good causes one to be and to act. The Good, like Evil, is meaningless. They are beings of reason or imagination that depend entirely on social signs, on the repressive system of rewards and punishments" (SP, p. 73).

31. "If aesthetic reality is thought without God, then the moment of alterity disappears. If aesthetic reality is thought, however without the immanence of creativity, then it loses its character of novelty" (Faber, "De-Ontologizing," p. 231).

32. AI, p. 381.

33. "The paradox of Alterity and self-creative Immanence can only be resolved within . . . the ultimate intersection of both Worlds *beyond* their difference" (Faber, "De-Ontologizing," p. 221).

34. "The Adventure of the Universe starts with the dream and reaps tragic beauty. This is the secret of the union of Zest with Peace:—That the suffering attains its end in a Harmony of Harmonies. . . . In this way the World receives its persuasion toward such perfections as are possible for its diverse, individual occasions" AI, p. 381.

35. Faber, "De-Ontologizing," p. 222.

36. TP, p. 159. See also Ian Buchanan, *Deleuzism: A Metacommentary* (Durham, N.C.: Duke University Press, 2000), pp. 122–127 for a good explanation of stratification.

37. TP, p. 160.

38. Kristeva speaks about two registers in language, the semiotic and symbolic, where the semiotic is also called the name of the Platonic Receptacle. Kristeva speaks about *khora* as abjected and repressed in language because it bears memories of the maternal. Kristeva's work is based on Lacanian individuation in language, while Deleuze is critical of the psychoanalytical framework.

39. TP, p. 65.

40. Chapter 2 in Sigridur Gudmarsdottir, "Abyss of God: Flesh, Love and Language in Paul Tillich" (Ph.D. diss., Drew University, 2007).

41. TP, p. 40.

42. John Protevi, "The Organism as the Judgment of God. Aristotle, Kant and Deleuze on Nature (That is, on Biology, Theology and Politics)," in *Deleuze and Religion*, ed. Mary Bryden (London: Routledge, 2001), p. 39.

43. TP, p. 549.

44. PR, p. 351.

45. Isabelle Stengers, "Beyond Conversation: The Risk of Peace," in *Process and Difference*, ed. Keller and Daniell, p. 240.

46. TF, p. 76.

47. Keller, *Face of the Deep*, p. 87.

48. N, p. 61.

49. Marcella Althaus-Reid, *The Queer God* (London: Routledge, 2003), p. 65.

50. Ibid., p. 68.

11. UNINTERESTING TRUTH? TEDIUM AND EVENT IN POSTMODERNITY
Catherine Keller

1. Excerpts from the October 17, 2005 episode of *The Colbert Report*, Stephen Colbert; see Wikipedia entry at http://en.wikipedia.org/wiki/Truthiness. Like Jon Stewart, Colbert lampoons the sort of patriotic Fox News programs that currently dominate the U.S. media.

2. PR, p. 16.

3. For an exploration of process postmodernism, see *Process and Difference: Between Cosmological and Poststructuralist Postmodernisms*, ed. Catherine Keller and Anne Daniell (Albany: State University of New York Press, 2002).

4. PR, p. 16.

5. Foucault's entire oeuvre is an exposition of the interface of power, knowledge, and social institutions. The writings of Deleuze and Guattari are

immersed in their critique of despotic regimes, as in the two volumes of *Capitalism and Schizophrenia*. So also Jacques Derrida, *Specters of Marx*, on the "undeconstructible of justice": "What remains irreducible to any deconstruction, what remains as undeconstructible as the possibility itself of deconstruction is, perhaps, a certain experience of the emancipatory promise." Derrida, *Specters of Marx: The State of the Debt, the Work of Mourning, and the New International*, trans. Peggy Kamuf (London: Routledge, 1994), 59.

6. See for example, John B. Cobb, Jr. and David Ray Griffin, *Process Theology: An Introductory Exposition* (Louisville, Ky.: Westminster John Knox Press, 1976); Catherine Keller, *God and Power: Counter-Apocalyptic Journeys* (Minneapolis, Minn.: Fortress Press, 2005); Jay McDaniel and Donna Bowman, ed. *Handbook of Process Theology* (St. Louis, Mo.: Chalice Press, 2006); Roland Faber, *God as Poet of the World: Exploring Process Theologies* (Louisville, Ky.: Westminster John Knox Press, 2008).

7. David Ray Griffin, *Whitehead's Radically Different Postmodern Philosophy: An Argument for its Contemporary Relevance* (Albany: State University of New York Press, 2007), ch. 5, especially p. 90.

8. PR, p. 259.

9. AI, esp. ch. XVI.

10. At the theological edge of deconstruction, Caputo demonstrates how the problem of truth will not be solved by an epistemological definition of truth, by what Foucault called "the truth of truth." John D. Caputo, *More Radical Hermeneutics: On Not Knowing Who We Are* (Bloomington: Indiana University Press, 2000), pp. 17ff.

11. GA, p. 121.

12. AI, p. 250.

13. Jacques Derrida, *Of Grammatology*, trans. Gayatri Chakravorty Spivak (Baltimore, Md.: Johns Hopkins University Press, 1976), p. 10.

14. WP, pp. 7 & 82.

15. Michel Foucault, *Power/Knowledge: Selected Interviews and Other Writings 1972–1977*, ed. Colin Gordon (New York: Pantheon, 1980), 131.

16. AI, p. 267.

17. Ibid., p. 242.

18. PR, p. 263.

19. "It follows that in the pursuit of truth even physical feelings must be criticized, since their evidence is not final apart from an analysis of their origination. This conclusion merely confirms what is a commonplace in all scientific investigation, that we can never start from dogmatic certainty" (PR, p. 264).

20. Ibid.

21. Michel Foucault, "How Much Does It Cost for Reason to Tell the Truth?" in *Foucault Live*, ed. Sylvie Lotringer, trans. John Johnston (New York: Semiotext(e), 1989), p. 254.

22. Foucault as cited in Butler, with her translational annotations, GA, p. 121.

23. GA, p. 122.

24. Foucault, *Power/Knowledge*, p. 131.

25. PR, p. 16.

26. Nietzsche's interrogation doesn't stop there: "But what if this were to become more and more difficult to believe, if nothing more were to turn out to be divine except error, blindness, the lie—if God himself were to turn out to be our longest lie?" Friedrich Nietzsche, *The Gay Science*, ed. Bernard Williams, trans. Josefine Nauckhoff (Cambridge: Cambridge University Press, 2001), Section 344, bk. 5, p. 201, his emphasis.

27. Nietzsche, *The Gay Science*, Section 344. Of course, in another context one might ask whether, in order to escape the vicious circle of truth, the truth of the God whom he unmasks as the ultimate lie, he spins into the Dionysian cruelty Irigaray so cannily unmasks in her guise as *Marine Lover of Friedrich Nietzsche*.

28. SMW, p. 18.

29. Isabelle Stengers, *Cosmopolitique* (Paris: La Découverte, 2003).

30. PR, pp. 12–13.

31. Ibid., p. 19.

32. Ibid., p. 351.

33. Ibid., p. 263.

34. John D. Caputo, *The Weakness of God: A Theology of the Event* (Bloomington: Indiana University Press, 2006), p. 296.

35. See, classically, the process theological critique of omnipotence in David Ray Griffin, *God, Power and Evil: A Process Theodicy* (Louisville, Ky.: Westminster John Knox Press, 2004).

36. Cited and translated in GA, p. 130.

37. Ibid.

38. Caputo, *Weakness*, p. 285.

39. TF. For discussion of the relation of Deleuze and Whitehead, see the essays by Keller and Faber in *Process and Difference*, ed. Keller and Daniell.

40. As he has done carefully before, as in *The Prayers and Tears of Jacques Derrida: Religion without Religion* (Bloomington: Indiana University Press, 1997), p. 14.

41. Caputo, *Weakness*, pp. 271–272, his emphasis. Pushing Eckhart's prayer, "So therefore let us pray to God that we may be free of 'God.'" Meister Eckhart, "Sermon 52: Beati pauperes spiritu, quoniam ipsorum est

regnum caelorum (Mt. 5:3)," in *Meister Eckhart: The Essential Sermons, Commentaries, Treatises, and Defense*, trans. and with introduction by Edmund Colledge and Bernard McGinn (Mahwah, N.J.: Paulist Press, 1981), 200.

42. Caputo, *Weakness*, p. 284.
43. Ibid., p. 285.
44. Caputo, *Weakness*, p. 284.
45. PL, p. 49. On "relationality," p. 23.
46. GA, p. 136.
47. Hannah Arendt, "Truth and Politics," in *The Portable Hannah Arendt*, ed. Peter Baehr (London: Penguin, 2000), pp. 545–575. She was thinking not just about the first half of the twentieth century but about the gathering power of capital.
48. "In the integrated objective datum the physical feeling provides its determinate set of actual entities, indicated by their felt physical relationships to the subject of feeling. These actual entities are the logical subjects of the proposition" (PR, p. 257). "The logical subjects, are nevertheless, in fact actual entities which are definite in their realized mutual relatedness. Thus the proposition is in fact true, or false. But its own truth, or its own falsity, is no business of a proposition" (Ibid., p. 258).
49. AI, p. 251.
50. Caputo, *Weakness*, p. 285.
51. AI, p. 267.
52. GA, p. 36.

BIBLIOGRAPHY

Abe, Masao. *Zen and Western Thought*. Honolulu: University of Hawaii Press, 1985.
Agamben, Giorgio. *Potentialities: Collected Essays in Philosophy*. Stanford, Calif.: Stanford University Press, 1999.
Allison, David B., ed. *New Nietzsche*. Cambridge, Mass.: The MIT Press, 1977.
Althaus-Reid, Marcella. *The Queer God*. London: Routledge, 2003.
Althusser, Louis. *The Future Lasts a Long Time*. London: Vintage, 1994.
Arendt, Hannah. *On Violence*. New York: Harcourt, Brace & World, 1970.
———. "Truth and Politics." In *The Portable Hannah Arendt*, edited by Peter Baehr, 545–575. London: Penguin, 2000.
Aristotle. *Categories*.
Armour, Ellen, and Susan St. Ville, eds. *Bodily Citations: Religion and Judith Butler*. New York: Columbia University Press, 2006.
Badiou, Alain. *Deleuze: The Clamor of Being*. Minneapolis: University of Minnesota Press, 1997.
———. *Infinite Thought: Truth and the Return to Philosophy*. New York: Continuum, 2003.
Barad, K. "Getting Real: Technoscientific Practices and the Materialization of Reality." *differences: A Journal of Feminist Cultural Studies* 10, no. 2 (1998): 87–128.
Baudrillard, Jean. *Impossible Exchange*. London: Verso, 2001.
Bell, Jeff. *Deleuze's Hume: Culture, Criticism, and the Scottish Enlightenment*. Edinburgh: Edinburgh University Press, forthcoming.
———. *Philosophy at the Edges of Chaos: Gilles Deleuze and the Philosophy of Difference*. Toronto: University of Toronto Press, 2006.
Best, Steven, and Douglas Kellner. *Postmodern Theory: Critical Interrogation*. New York: Guilford Press, 1991.
Bloom, Allan. *The Closing of the American Mind*. New York: Simon and Schuster, 1998.
Boesel, Chris, and Catherine Keller. *Apophatic Bodies: Negative Theology, Incarnation, and Relationality*. New York: Fordham University Press, 2010.

Bradley, J. "Transcendentalism and Speculative Realism in Whitehead." *Process Studies* 23, no. 3 (1994): 155–191.
Braidotti, Rosi. *Metamorphosis: Towards a Materialist Theory of Becoming.* Cambridge: Polity, 2002.
Braver, Lee. *A Thing of This World.* Chicago: Northwestern University Press, 2007.
Bryden, Mary, ed. *Deleuze and Religion.* London: Routledge, 2001.
Buchanan, Ian. *Deleuzism: A Metacommentary.* Durham, N.C.: Duke University Press, 2000.
Buchanan, Ian, and Claire Colebrook, eds. *Deleuze and Feminist Theory.* Edinburgh: Edinburgh University Press, 2000.
Butler, Judith. *Antigone's Claim: Kinship between Life and Death.* New York: Columbia University Press, 2000.
———. *Bodies That Matter: On The Discursive Limits of "Sex."* New York: Routledge, 1993.
———. "Critique, Coercion, and Sacred Life in Benjamin's 'Critique of Violence.'" In *Political Theologies: Public Religions in a Post-Secular World*, edited by Hent de Vries and Lawrence E. Sullivan, 201–19. New York: Fordham University Press, 2006.
———. "Doing Justice to Someone: Sex Reassignment and Allegories of Transsexuality." *GLQ: A Journal of Lesbian and Gay Studies* 7/4 (2001): 621–36.
———. *Excitable Speech: A Politics of the Performative.* New York: Routledge, 1997.
———. *Gender Trouble: Feminism and the Subversion of Identity.* New York: Routledge, 1999.
———. *Giving an Account of Oneself.* New York: Fordham University Press, 2005.
———. *Precarious Life: The Power of Mourning and Violence.* New York: Verso, 2006.
———. *The Psychic Life of Power.* Stanford, Calif.: Stanford University Press, 1997.
———. *Undoing Gender.* New York: Routledge, 2004.
Butler, Judith, Ernesto Laclau, and Slavoj Žižek, eds. *Contingency, Hegemony, Universality: Contemporary Dialogues on the Left.* New York: Verso, 2000.
Butler, Judith, and Gayatri Chakravorty Spivak. *Who Sings the Nation State: Language, Politics, Belonging.* New York: Seagull, 2007.
Caputo, John D. *More Radical Hermeneutics: On Not Knowing Who We Are.* Bloomington: Indiana University Press, 2000.
———. *The Prayers and Tears of Jacques Derrida: Religion without Religion.* Bloomington: Indiana University Press, 1997.

———. *The Weakness of God: A Theology of the Event*. Bloomington: Indiana University Press, 2006.
Cheah, P. "Mattering." *Diacritics* 26, no. 1 (1996): 108–139.
Cobb, John B., Jr., *A Christian Natural Theology: Based on the Thought of Alfred North Whitehead*. Philadelphia: Westminster Press 1974.
Cobb, John B., Jr. and David Ray Griffin. *Process Theology: An Introductory Exposition*. Louisville, Ky.: Westminster John Knox Press, 1976.
Colbert, Steven. *The Colbert Report*, October 17, 2005.
Crary, Jonathan, and Sanford Kwinter, eds. *Incorporations*. New York: Zone Books, 1992.
Critchley, Simon. "The Overcoming of Overcoming: On Dominique Janicaud." *Continental Philosophy Review* 36 (December 2003).
Davaney, Sheila, ed. *Feminism and Process Thought*. New York: Edwin Mellen Press, 1981.
de Vries, Hent, and Lawrence E. Sullivan, eds., *Political Theologies: Public Religions in a Post-Secular World*. New York: Fordham University Press, 2006.
Debaise, D. *Un empirisme spéculative. Lecture de Procès et réalité de Whitehead*. Paris: Vrin, 2006.
DeLanda, Manuel. *Intensive Science and Virtual Philosophy*. London: Continuum, 2002.
Deleuze, Gilles. *Cinema 1: Movement-Image*. Minneapolis: University of Minnesota Press, 1986.
———. *Desert Islands and Other Texts 1953–1974*. Paris: Semiotext(e), 2004.
———. *Difference and Repetition*. New York: Routledge, 1994.
———. *Essays: Critical and Clinical*. Minneapolis: University of Minnesota Press, 1997.
———. *Expressionism in Philosophy: Spinoza*. New York: Zone Books, 1990.
———. *The Fold: Leibniz and the Baroque*. Minneapolis: University of Minnesota Press, 1992.
———. *Logic of Sense*. New York: Columbia University Press, 1990.
———. *Negotiations, 1972–1990*. New York: Columbia University Press, 1990.
———. *Nietzsche and Philosophy*. New York: Columbia University Press, 1983.
———. *Pourparles, 1972–1990*. Paris: Les Editions de Minuit, 1990.
———. *Pure Immanence: Essays on A Life*. New York: Zone Books, 2005.
———. *Spinoza, A Practical Philosophy*. San Francisco: City Lights Books, 1988.
Deleuze, Gilles, and Felix Guattari. *Anti-Oedipus: Capitalism and Schizophrenia*. Minneapolis: University of Minnesota Press, 1983.
———. *Kafka: Pour une littérature mineure*. Paris: Les Editions de Minuit, 1975.
———. *A Thousand Plateaus*. Minneapolis: University of Minnesota Press, 1987.

———. *What is Philosophy?* New York: Columbia University Press, 1994.
Deleuze, Gilles, and C. Parnet. *Dialogues*. London: Athlone, 1987.
Derrida, Jacques. *A Derrida Reader: Between the Blinds*. Hemel Hempstead: Harvester, 1991.
———. "Geschlecht. Sexual Difference, Ontological Difference." *Research in Phenomenology* 13 (1983): p. 72.
———. *Limited Inc*. Chicago: Northwestern University, 1988.
———. *Margins of Philosophy*. Translated by Alan Bass. Chicago: University of Chicago Press, 1982.
———. *Of Grammatology*. Translated by Gayatri Chakravorty Spivak. Baltimore, Md.: Johns Hopkins University Press, 1976.
———. *Of Spirit: Heidegger and the Question*. Chicago: University of Chicago Press, 1991.
———. *On the Name*. Edited by Thomas Dutoit, translated by David Wood and John P. Leavey. Stanford, Calif.: Stanford University Press, 1995.
———. *Specters of Marx: The State of the Debt, the Work of Mourning, and the New International*. Translated by Peggy Kamuf. London: Routledge, 1994.
Eckhart, Meister. *Meister Eckhart: The Essential Sermons, Commentaries, Treatises, and Defense*. Translated by Edmond Colledge and Bernard McGinn. New York: Paulist Press, 1981.
Faber, Roland. "Bodies of the Void: Polyphilia and Theoplicity." *Apophatic Bodies: Negative Theology, Incarnation, and Relationality*, ed. Chris Boesel and Catherine Keller. (New York: Fordham University Press, 2010): 200–223.
———. "De-Ontologizing God: Levinas, Deleuze, and Whitehead." *Process and Difference: Between Cosmological and Poststructuralist Postmodernism*, ed. C. Keller and A. Daniell. (Albany: State University of New York Press, 2002): 209–234.
———. *God as Poet of the World: Exploring Process Theologies*. Louisville, Ky.: Westminster John Knox Press, 2008.
———. "In the Wake of False Unifications: Whitehead's Creative Resistance against Imperialist Theologies." Claremont, CA: Claremont School of Theology Lecture, March 2005.
———. "'The Infinite Movement of Evanescence'—The Pythagorean Puzzle in Plato, Deleuze, and Whitehead." *American Journal of Theology and Philosophy* 21 (2000): 171–199.
———. "'O Bitches of Impossibility!'—Programmatic Dysfunction in the Chaosmos of Deleuze and Whitehead." In *Deleuze, Whitehead, and Bergson: Rhizomatic Connections*, edited by Keith Robinson, 200–219. (New York: Palgrave MacMillan, 2009).
———. *Prozeßtheologie: Zu ihrer Würdigung und kritischen Erneuerung*. Mainz: Grünewald, 2000.

———. "Trinity, Analogy and Coherence." In *Trinity in Process: A Relational Theology of God*, edited by Joseph Bracken and Marjorie Suchocki, 147–171. New York: Continuum, 1997.

———. "Wahrheit und Maschine: Wider das transsilvanische Argument von der Gewalt im Erkenntnisdiskurs." *Labyrinth*. Vol. 3 (2001).

———. "Whitehead at Infinite Speed: Deconstructing System as Event." *Schleiermacher and Whitehead: Open Systems in Dialogue*. ed. C. Helmer, M. Suchocki, and J. Quiring. (Berlin: de Gruyter 2004): 39–72.

Ford, Lewis. *Transforming Process Theism*. New York: State University of New York Press, 2000.

Foucault, Michel. *Discipline and Punish: The Birth of the Prison*. New York: Vintage, 1995.

———. *Essential Works of Michel Foucault, 1954–1984, Vol. 2: Aesthetics, Method, and Epistemology*. New York: The New Press, 1997–99.

———. *Ethics, Subjectivity and Truth*. Ed. Paul Rabinow, Vol. 1, *Essential Works of Foucault*. Translated by Robert Hurley et al. New York: The New Press, 1997.

———. "How Much Does It Cost for Reason to Tell the Truth?" In *Foucault Live*, edited by Sylvie Lotringer, translated by John Honston, 233–56. New York: Semiotext[e], 1989.

———. *Madness and Civilization: A History of Insanity in the Age of Reason*. Vintage, 1988.

———. *The Order of Things*. New York: Vintage, 1973.

———. *Power/Knowledge: Selected Interviews and Other Writings 1972–1977*. Edited by Colin Gordon. New York: Pantheon, 1980.

Fraser, M. "What is the matter of feminist criticism?" *Economy and Society* 31, no. 4 (November 2002): 606–625.

Griffin, David Ray. *Deep Religious Pluralism*. Louisville, Ky.: WJK, 2005.

———. *Founders of Constructive Postmodern Philosophy: Peirce, James, Bergson, Whitehead, and Hartshorne*. Albany: State University of New York Press, 1993.

———. *God, Power and Evil: A Process Theodicy*. Louisville, Ky.: Westminster John Knox Press, 2004.

———. *Reenchantment without Supernaturalism: A Process Philosophy of Religion*. Ithaca: Cornell University Press, 2001.

———. *Whitehead's Radically Different Postmodern Philosophy: An Argument for Its Contemporary Relevance*. Albany: State University of New York Press, 2007.

Grosz, Elizabeth. *Space, Time, and Perversion: Essays on the Politics of Bodies*. New York: Routledge, 1995.

———. *Volatile Bodies. Toward a Corporeal Feminism*. Bloomington: Indiana University Press, 1994.

Gudmarsdottir, Sigridur. "Abyss of God: Flesh, Love and Language in Paul Tillich." Ph.D. diss. Madison, N.J.: Drew University, 2007.
Gutting, Gary. *French Philosophy in the Twentieth Century*. Cambridge: Cambridge University Press, 2001.
Hajime, *Philosophy as Metanoetics*. Berkeley: University of California Press, 1986.
Halewood, M. "On Whitehead and Deleuze—The Process of Materiality." *Configurations* 13 (2007): 55–74.
Hardt, Michael. *Gilles Deleuze: An Apprenticeship in Philosophy*. Minneapolis: University of Minnesota Press, 1995.
Hartshorne, Charles. *The Divine Relativity: A Social Conception of God*. New Haven: Yale University Press, 1948.
Hayden, Patrick. *Multiplicity and Becoming*. New York: Peter Lang, 1998.
Heartfield, James. *The "Death of the Subject" Explained*. Sheffield, U.K.: Hallam University Press, 2002.
Heidegger, Martin. *Being and Time*. Translated by John Macquarrie and Edward Robinson. New York: Harper & Row, 1962.
Helmer, Christine, Marjorie Suchocki, and John Quiring, eds. *Schleiermacher and Whitehead: Open Systems in Dialogue*. Berlin: de Gruyter 2004.
Howe, Thomas J. *Faithful to the Earth: Nietzsche and Whitehead on God and the Meaning of Human Life*. Lanham: Rowman & Littlefield, 2003.
Irigaray, Luce. *Speculum of the Other Woman*. Ithaca, N.Y.: Cornell University Press, 1985.
———. *This Sex Which Is Not One*. Ithaca, N.Y.: Cornell University Press, 1985.
Irwin, William, ed. *The Matrix and Philosophy: Welcome to the Desert of the Real*. Chicago: Open Court, 2003.
Jones, Judith. *Intensity: An Essay in Whiteheadian Ontology*. Nashville, Tenn.: Vanderbilt University Press, 1998.
Kann, Charles. *Fußnoten zu Platon: Philosophiegeschichte bei A. N. Whitehead*. Paradeigmata, vol. 23. Hamburg: Meiner, 2001.
Kant, Immanuel. *Critique of Pure Reason*. Translated by Werner Pluhar. Indianapolis, Ind.: Hackett, 1996.
———. *Perpetual Peace and Other Essays*. Translated by Ted Humphrey. Indianapolis, Ind.: Hackett, 1983.
Keller, Catherine. *Face of the Deep: A Theology of Becoming*. New York: Routledge, 2003.
———. *God and Power: Counter-Apocalyptic Journeys*. Minneapolis, Minn.: Fortress Press, 2005.
Keller, Catherine, and Anne Daniell, eds. *Process and Difference: Between Cosmological and Poststructuralist Postmodernism*. Albany: State University of New York Press, 2002.

Kerin, J. "The Matter at Hand: Butler, Ontology and the Natural Sciences" *Australian Feminist Studies* 14, no. 29 (1999): 91–104.

Kipnis, Jeffrey, ed. *Choral Works: A Collaboration Between Peter Eisenman and Jacques Derrida.* New York: Monacelli Press, 1993.

Kirby, V. "Human Nature." *Australian Feminist Studies* 14, no. 29 (1999): 19–29.

———. *Telling Flesh: The Substance of the Corporeal.* London, Routledge: 1997.

Kline, George, ed. *Alfred North Whitehead. Essays in His Philosophy.* Engelwood Cliffs, N.J.: Prentice-Hall, 1963.

Kotsko, Adam. "The Failed Divine Performative: Reading Judith Butler's Critique of Theology with Anselm's *On the Fall of the Devil.*" *Journal of Religion* 88, no. 2 (April 2008): 209–225.

Kraus, Elizabeth. *The Metaphysics of Experience: A Companion to Whitehead's Process and Reality.* New York: Fordham University Press, 1998.

Kristeva, Julia. *Desire in Language: A Semiotic Approach to Literature and Art.* New York: Columbia University Press, 1980.

———. *Revolution in Poetic Language.* New York: Columbia University Press, 1984.

Latour, Bruno. *Politics of Nature: How to Bring the Sciences into Democracy.* Cambridge, Mass.: Harvard University Press, 2004.

Levi-Strauss, Claude. *The Savage Mind.* Chicago: Chicago University Press, 1966.

Loizidou, Elena. *Judith Butler: Ethics, Law, Politics.* New York: Routledge-Cavendish, 2007.

Lorraine, Tamsin. *Irigaray & Deleuze: Experiments in Visceral Philosophy.* Ithaca, N.Y.: Cornell University Press, 1999.

Lucas, George. *Hegel and Whitehead: Contemporary Perspectives on Systematic Philosophy.* Albany: State University of New York Press; 1986.

———. *The Rehabilitation of Whitehead: An Analytic and Historical Assessment of Process Philosophy.* Albany: State University of New York Press, 1989.

Lucas, George, and Antoon Braeckman, eds. *Whitehead und der Deutsche Idealismus.* Bern: Peter Lang, 1990.

Lundeen, Lyman. *Risk and Rhetoric in Religion: Whitehead's Theory of Language and the Discourse of Faith.* Philadelphia: Fortress, 1972.

Lyotard, Jean-Francois. *Discourse, figure.* Paris: Klincksieck, 1971.

———. *The Postmodern Condition: A Report on Knowledge.* Manchester, U.K.: Manchester University Press, 1989.

McDaniel, Jay, and Donna Bowman, eds. *Handbook of Process Theology.* St. Louis, Mo.: Chalice Press, 2006.

Marks, John. *Gilles Deleuze: Vitalism and Multiplicity.* London: Pluto Press, 1998.

Nietzsche, Friedrich. *The Gay Science.* London: Vintage, 1974.

---. *Human All Too Human*. Translated by Marion Faber. Lincoln: University of Nebraska Press, 1984.

---. *On the Genealogy of Morals*. New York: Vintage, 1969.

---. *Thus Spoke Zarathustra*. In *The Portable Nietzsche*, edited and translated by Walter Kaufmann, 103–439. New York: Penguin Books, 1954.

Nomikoi. *Critical Legal Thinkers*. New York: Routledge, 2007.

Nozick, Robert. *Philosophical Explanations*. 15th ed. Cambridge, Mass.: Harvard University Press, 2003.

Odin, Stephen. *Process Metaphysics and Hua-Yen Buddhism: A Critical Study of Cumulative Penetration vs. Interpenetration*. Albany: State University of New York Press, 1988.

Olkowski, Dorothea. *Gilles Deleuze and the Ruin of Representation*. Berkeley: University of California Press, 1998.

Patton, Paul, ed. *Deleuze: A Critical Reader*. Oxford: Blackwell, 1996.

Patton, Paul, and John Protevi. *Between Deleuze and Derrida*. New York: Continuum, 2003.

Plato. *Timaeus*, 50b-c. In *Complete Works*, edited by John Cooper and D. S. Hutchinson, translated by Donald Zeyl, 1224–91. Indianapolis, Ind.: Hackett Publishing Company, 1997.

Putnam, Hilary. *Reason, Truth and History*. New York: Cambridge University Press, 1981.

Rajchman, John. *The Deleuze Connections*. Cambridge, Mass.: The MIT Press, 2000.

Rapp, Friedrich, and Reiner Wiehl, eds. *Whiteheads Metaphysik der Kreativität: Internationales Whitehead-Symposium Bad Homburg 1983*. Freiburg: Karl Alber, 1986.

Robinson, Keith, ed. *Deleuze, Whitehead and Bergson: Rhizomatic Connections*. New York: Palgrave Macmillan, 2008.

---. "The New Whitehead? An Ontology of the 'Virtual' in Whitehead's Metaphysics." *Symposium* 10 (Spring 2006): 69–80.

Rohmer, Stascha. *Whiteheads Synthese von Kreativität und Rationalität: Reflexionen und Transformationen in Alfred North Whiteheads Philosophie der Natur*. Alber Thesen, vol. 13. Freiburg: Karl Alber, 2000.

Sandford, S. "Contingent Ontologies: Sex, Gender and 'Woman' in Simone de Beauvoir and Judith Butler." *Radical Philosophy* (September/October 1999): 18–29.

Shaviro, Steven. "Deleuze's Encounter with Whitehead." At www.shaviro.com.

---. *Without Criteria: Kant, Whitehead, Deleuze, and Aesthetics*. Cambridge, Mass.: The MIT Press, forthcoming.

Simondon, Gilbert. *L'individuation à la lumière des notions de forme et de l'information*. Grenoble: Million, 2005.

Sokol, Alan, and Jean Bricmont. *Intellectual Impostures*. London: Profile Books, 1998.
Spengler, Oswald. *The Decline of the West*. New York: Vintage Press, 2006.
Stengers, Isabelle. *Cosmopolitique*. Paris: La Découverte, 2003.
———. *Penser avec Whitehead*. Paris: Editions du Seuil, 2002.
Suchocki, Marjorie. *God—Christ—Church: A Practical Guide to Process Theology*. New York: Crossroad, 1995.
Sudnow, David. *Ways of the Hand*. Cambridge, Mass.: Harvard University Press, 1978.
Surowiecki, James. *The Wisdom of Crowds: Why the Many Are Smarter Than the Few and How Collective Wisdom Shapes Business, Economics, Societies and Nations*. New York: Random House, 2004.
Thiem, Annika. *Unbecoming Subjects: Judith Butler, Moral Philosophy, and Critical Responsibility*. New York: Fordham University Press, 2008.
Weber, Michel. *Whitehead's Pancreativism: The Basics*. Frankfurt: Ontos, 2006.
Whitehead, Alfred North. *Adventures of Ideas*. New York: Free Press, 1967.
———. *The Concept of Nature: The Tarner Lectures Delivered in Trinity College November 1919*. Cambridge: Cambridge University Press, 1964.
———. *An Enquiry Concerning the Principles of Natural Knowledge*. New York: Dover, 1982.
———. *Essays in Science and Philosophy*. New York: Greenwood Press, 1968.
———. *The Function of Reason*. Boston: Beacon Press, 1958.
———. *Modes of Thought*. New York: Free Press, 1968.
———. *Process and Reality: An Essay in Cosmology*, corrected edition. Edited by David Ray Griffin and D. W. Sherburne. New York: Free Press, 1978.
———. *Religion in the Making*. New York: Fordham University Press, 1996.
———. *Science and the Modern World: Lowell Lecturers, 1925*. New York: Free Press, 1967.
———. *Symbolism: Its Meaning and Effect*. New York: Fordham University Press, 1985.
Wilber, Ken, *Integral Spirituality: A Startling New Role for Religion in the Modern and Postmodern World*. Boston: Shambala, 2006.
Williams, James. *The Transversal Thought of Gilles Deleuze: Encounters and Influences*. Manchester: Clinamen Press, 2005.
Wilson, E. A. "Introduction: Somatic Compliance—Feminism Biology and Science." *Australian Feminist Studies* 14, no. 29 (1999): 7–18.
Žižek, Slavoj. *For They Know Not What They Do*. London: Verso, 1991.
———. *Mapping Ideology*. London: Verso, 1994.
———. *The Sublime Object of Ideology*. London: Verso, 1989.
———. *Welcome to the Desert of the Real: Five Essays on September 11 and Related Dates*. London: Verso, 2002.

CONTRIBUTORS

JEFF BELL is professor of philosophy at Southeastern Louisiana University, where he teaches courses such as Introduction to Philosophy, Philosophy of Science, Theories of History, Ideas in Conflict, and American Political Theory. His books include *Deleuze's Hume: Philosophy, Culture and the Scottish Enlightenment* (forthcoming), *Philosophy at the Edge of Chaos: Gilles Deleuze and the Philosophy of Difference* (2006), and The *Problem of Difference: Phenomenology and Poststructuralism* (1998).

ROLAND FABER is Kilsby Family and John B. Cobb, Jr., Professor of Process Studies at the Claremont School of Theology and professor of religion and philosophy at the Claremont Graduate University, co-director of the Center for Process Studies, and executive director of the newly founded Whitehead Research Project (2007). His fields of research and publication are poststructuralism (Gilles Deleuze); process thought and process theology; comparative philosophy of religion; interreligious discourse, especially regarding Christianity/Buddhism; philosophy, systematic theology; cosmology, theology and spirituality of the Renaissance; and mysticism with an emphasis on multiplicity, infinite becoming, and theopoetics.

SIGRIDUR GUDMARSDOTTIR finished her PhD in 2007 at Drew University, New Jersey, and has since taught theology at Drew; the University of Winchester, United Kingdom; and the University of Iceland. She is currently working as an ordained minister and independent scholar in her native country, Iceland. Her research interests are in the field of constructive theology with special interests in ecofeminist, poststructuralist, and mystical theology. She is currently working on a book on Paul Tillich and the abyss of God.

MICHAEL HALEWOOD is a lecturer in social theory at the University of Essex, United Kingdom. His main area of research is the relationship of philosophy to social theory. His publications include "A. N. Whitehead, Information and Social Theory," in *Theory, Culture and Society* (2005), and

"On Whitehead and Deleuze—The Process of Materiality," in *Configurations* (2007). He has also edited a collection of papers on Whitehead for a special edition of *Theory, Culture and Society* (Vol. 25:4).

LUKE B. HIGGINS got his master's of divinity from the Pacific School of Religion in Berkeley, California, and is currently writing his dissertation for his doctorate at Drew University. Drawing on Whiteheadian process theology and the philosophy of Gilles Deleuze, his dissertation will propose an "eco-theology of intensive alliance" grounded in a postmodern reading of the cosmological *Logos*. He is also an adjunct professor of philosophy at Rockland Community College and works as a youth minister at a U.C.C. church in Cedar Grove, New Jersey.

CATHERINE KELLER, professor of constructive theology at Drew Theological School and the Graduate Division of Religion at Drew University, practices a theology of becoming, inspired by her work on process and poststructuralist thought. Catherine's books include *On the Mystery: Discerning God in Process* (2008) and *The Face of the Deep: A Theology of Becoming* (2003), among many others. Her newest project is *The Cloud of the Impossible: A Theology of Inseparability*, which explores the themes of non-knowingness and non-separability within Christian mysticism and recent physics.

ISABELLA PALIN obtained her master's degree in the history of philosophy from the Université Libre de Bruxelles in 1996, and is now a doctoral student in philosophy at the Hoger Instituut voor Wijsbegeerte of the Katholieke Universiteit te Leuven, Belgium. She is studying the theme of becoming in Alfred North Whitehead and Gilles Deleuze under the guidance of Professors André Cloots and Isabelle Stengers. Isabella Palin is also a translator and language teacher. Recent publications include "The Meaning and Use of Abstraction in Whitehead," in *Deleuze, Whitehead and the Transformation of Metaphysics* (2005).

KEITH ROBINSON is associate professor of philosophy at the University of South Dakota, with an interest in nineteenth- and twentieth-century continental philosophers. He has published books and articles on Foucault, Deleuze, and Whitehead including, most recently, *Deleuze, Whitehead, Bergson: Rhizomatic Connections* (2009).

STEVEN SHAVIRO is the DeRoy Professor of English at Wayne State University. He is the author of *The Cinematic Body* (1993), *Doom Patrols: A Theoretical Fiction About Postmodernism* (1997), *Connected, or, What It Means To Live in the Network Society* (2003), and *Without Criteria: Kant, Whitehead,*

Deleuze, and Aesthetics (2009), as well as numerous articles on film and video, science fiction, and cultural theory. He blogs at The Pinocchio Theory, http://www.shaviro.com/Blog.

ANDREA M. STEPHENSON recently achieved her PhD in the philosophy of religion and theology from Claremont Graduate University, Claremont, California. Her interests include poststructuralist philosophy, particularly the work of Gilles Deleuze and Judith Butler; social justice issues in theology; and the intersection between practical and academic theology. She is currently working as an independent scholar, guest lecturer, and freelance editor while revising her dissertation, "Post-Structuralism and Liberal Theology (Be)coming Together in Spirit."

ALAN R. VAN WYK is currently a PhD candidate at the School of Religion at the Claremont Graduate University, working in the Theology, Ethics, and Culture program. His research is in religious and cultural theory, in particular exploring the intersection of religious and political subjectivities. His dissertation is being written under the direction of Professor Faber and is entitled "Becoming Subjects: Conversion and the Production of Possibility." Currently he is adjunct professor of religion at Hamline University, in St. Paul, Minnesota. He recently co-edited *Creativity and Its Discontents: The Response to Whitehead's* Process and Reality.

Secrets of Becoming